TOPICS IN GEOPHYSICS

TOPICS IN GEOPHYSICS

Peter J. Smith
Senior Lecturer in Earth Sciences at The Open University

The MIT Press
Cambridge, Massachusetts

First MIT Press edition, 1973
ISBN 0 262 19115 6
Library of Congress catalog card number: 73–382

Filmset and printed in Great Britain

Contents

An asterisk (*) against a word in the text indicates the inclusion of that word in the Glossary (Appendix Four).

Preface

Topics in Geophysics has been specially written to form the core of a short course on geophysics at the Open University. At one level, this is a simple enough statement of fact; but its apparent straightforwardness conceals points which require further explanation. For one thing, the Open University, as its students know, does not take the material and organizational form the use of the word 'university' is likely to bring to the mind of the average reader. It has no undergraduate students on its small campus; it has (at least, at the time of writing) no students in the age range usually associated with the conventional residential university; and the basic mechanism for the transmission of knowledge is not the contact lecture. Instead, its students are working men and women over 21 years of age, who live at home and who study in their spare time using a combination of correspondence (textual) materials, radio and television programmes broadcast over a national network, face-to-face tutorial sessions at local study centres, and summer schools at some of Britain's residential universities.

What all this amounts to is that the average Open University student, in contrast to the average student at a conventional university, carries out the bulk of his or her study without the benefit of daily contact and interaction with fellow students and with little or no hand-holding by the academics who prepare the teaching material. Under these circumstances, the success of the system depends to a large extent on the nature of the textual material which carries the main burden of the teaching. In practice, this means that the prime requirement of the material is that it should *teach*—in other words, in the absence of any authority to whom the student can easily run for advice, the subject matter being taught should be capable of being followed step by step, should be free of unwarranted gaps or puzzling assumptions, and should require only that prerequisite knowledge which is clearly spelled out in advance. *Topics in Geophysics* has been written with these conditions in mind and so is, I believe, almost unique among books on geophysics, a subject with little (though a growing) tradition in undergraduate teaching but well served by advanced research monographs.

The second point arising from the opening sentence of this Preface concerns the question of length and thus of content. 'Short' in the context of the Open University geophysics course means that the average student is expected to spend about 70 hours on all components of the course together. *Topics in Geophysics* is not the whole course but only the nucleus of it—and, as such, is intended to represent about 40 hours study. This is a severe restriction on a subject as wide as geophysics and, though basically a mechanical one, is bound to dictate to some extent the nature of the subject coverage. In addition, however, there are two, more qualitative conditions. The first is simply that the course is terminal in the sense that Open University students will not find subsequent, higher level courses in geophysics within the University. This means that whatever the geophysical subjects covered, they must be taken to a level which transcends the trivial and which enables the student to proceed beyond the very basic mechanical operations into the realm of interpretation. The second consideration is based on my own view (which some would dispute) that, as far as undergraduates are concerned at least, the Open University is essentially a non-vocational institution. In other words, I take it as axiomatic that the purpose of the Open University geophysics course is not to train practical geophysicists but to impart a feeling for geophysics to people whose chief concern is to become better informed about this particular branch of science.

Taking these considerations together leads to the inevitable conclusion that a wide-ranging course on geophysics would not be appropriate, and thus that a severe restriction on the number of topics is necessary. But how to select from a large number of possibilities? In fact, I have chosen three topics which I take to be central to geophysics and which seem to me to represent, in practice if not in theory, three quite different types of geophysical activity or, at least, impart three quite different images of what geophysics is about. Obviously, in any situation demanding selection, the choice ultimately made is susceptible to criticism; but I believe that the approach taken here can be justified on reasonably objective grounds.

The first topic (Chapter Two) is the structure and physical properties of the Earth's crust and upper mantle as determined largely from seismology and gravity. The techniques and methods involved here are well-tried; and whilst it would certainly be untrue to suggest that the interpretation of data is necessarily always straightforward or routine, the basic procedures are clear and sufficient, in principle at least, to enable structure to be completely defined. Moreover, the data are relatively easily come by and thus plentiful; and so I take this subject to be reasonably typical of what may be called the hard-core observational aspect of geophysics. Furthermore, the structure of the Earth's upper layers is so central to the whole of the Earth sciences that it is difficult to envisage a representative geophysics course without some discussion of it; and in this sense the choice was inevitable.

By contrast, the second topic—the Earth's heat and thermal properties (Chapter Three)—suffers badly from a paucity of data, and not simply because enough measurements have not yet been made. It is certainly true that data on surface heat flow are far from adequate; but the real problem (or one of them) is the practical impossibility of making heat flow determinations at significant depths below the surface. This imposes upon the subject a high degree of intellectual reasoning in order to determine things about the Earth which are indeterminable on the basis of observational data alone. For example, determining the temperature distribution in the Earth on the basis of surface heat flow measurements alone can be regarded as analogous to defining a curve on the basis of a single point—a curve and a point, moreover, which are functions of time. This sort of problem imparts to the study of heat flow a nature quite distinct from that pertaining to studies of seismology and gravity; and I believe this distinction to be worth making in a course of this type. Another, not insignificant, consideration is that the Earth's heat processes are the most basic and fundamental geophysical topic of all in the sense that heat plays an essential part in every conceivable geophysical process. Inclusion of this topic in a short geophysics course could therefore be justified on this basis alone.

The third and final topic is the characteristics, prediction and modification of earthquakes (Chapter Four). In view of recent proposals for the modification and possible abolition of large earthquakes in some seismic zones, this subject could almost be justified on the grounds of excitement alone. The chief reason for its inclusion here, however, is its social implications, in which it contrasts with the more, though not entirely, academic matters of the two previous chapters.

The only significant geophysical prerequisite for the complete understanding of the material in Chapters Two, Three and Four is some knowledge of the Earth's gross features and the fundamental concepts of the new global tectonics. Open University students who study this book can be expected to come armed with this knowledge from previous courses; but to make the book complete in itself, and for the benefit of non-Open University readers, Chapter One is a brief summary of the global context of the material which follows. The book as a whole inevitably contains some mathematics but this has been largely limited to simple arithmetic and algebraic operations involving addition, subtraction, multiplication and division. The only exception to this is that differential equations are used in one of the appendices.

The question of units is a thorny one and raises the sort of feelings which a hundred years ago produced demands for meetings behind the cathedral at six. This is not the place to explore this issue in any great depth; but the facts are (i) that the Open University has adopted the SI unit system, and (ii) that, in general, the geophysical community has not. This is not entirely due to the inbred conservatism of geophysicists, for there can be little doubt that, in the purely numerical sense, cgs units are very often (usually?) more manageable in geophysical work. Clearly, however, this situation poses a dilemma, especially in a course where students are expected to read outside the confines of specially produced material.

For the present and the foreseeable future, students of geophysics are simply going to have to reconcile themselves to the need for familiarity with both SI and cgs units. In this book I have generally adopted the SI system. In two instances, however, I have compromised, I think legitimately, by having recourse to the device of "working units" (actually based on the cgs system)—in heat flow studies, where heat flow units (h.f.u.) are a common simplification, and in earthquake studies, where universal scales (for example, the Richter magnitude scale) are intimately associated with cgs units via relatively complicated functions. In these cases the relationships between the SI and working units are spelled out. I have also departed from the strict definition of SI units for one or two simple quantities. For example, there seems to me to be no merit whatever in abandoning km s^{-1} in favour of m s^{-1} as the unit of seismic velocity.

Finally, I would like to thank several people who were particularly closely associated with aspects of the preparation of this book. Professor I. G. Gass of the Open University, Professor M. H. P. Bott of the University of Durham, Dr. J. H. Sass of the United States Geological Survey and Dr. H. I. S. Thirlaway of the United Kingdom Atomic Energy Authority were kind enough to review Chapters One, Two, Three and Four, respectively. Their strict brief was to check factual accuracy; but in several cases, wider, helpful comments were made and proved useful. However, I make the usual reservation that the responsibility for organization and any lingering errors of content remains mine. I would also like to thank Andrew Clements and Richard Crabbe, both of the Open University, who have been cheerfully responsible for carrying out the many editorial tasks necessary to convert the typescript into a form suitable for students to read—and Janet Mills, who quietly but efficiently produced the typescript from my manuscript in the first place.

January 1973   *Peter J. Smith*

Acknowledgements

The publishers make grateful acknowledgement to the authors and organizations who have kindly granted permission for use of copyright material reproduced in this book. A full list of the items, together with details of the copyright holders appears in Appendix Five (page 237).

CHAPTER ONE

The Global Framework

1.1 Introduction

During the past decade or so there has taken place what J. Tuzo Wilson has identified explicitly as a revolution in the Earth sciences —a change in which certain cherished beliefs, first formulated in scientific terms by the great geologists of the eighteenth and nineteenth centuries and widely held as lately as the 1950s, have been overthrown and replaced by others, often directly opposed. Thus it is, for example, that the ocean floors, once thought to be the oldest and most mysterious parts of the Earth's surface, are now regarded as the youngest, being in a state of continuous production and destruction and having, in many respects, a much clearer and simpler geological evolution than the more accessible continents. Thus it is, too, that the continents themselves, once allowed only restricted movement in the vertical direction, are now required to have undergone horizontal motions of up to several thousand kilometres over the past 200 million years.

But the revolution in the Earth sciences has been more than the substitution of one set of facts and hypotheses for another and, in many respects, not even that. For the first time we now have a global view of the Earth and its behaviour—but a view which does less to invalidate much of the achievement of classical geology than to suggest that many of the geological discoveries of the past few hundred years need to be fitted into, and reinterpreted in terms of, the new global framework. In other words, much of the factual basis of the classical geologists' intellectual achievement remains as valid as it ever was; but it must now be seen against a wider background derived largely from recent insights into large-scale processes in the Earth's interior and upon its surface.

In this chapter we shall summarize very briefly, without detailed supporting evidence, and wherever possible diagrammatically, know-ledge of the large-scale features of the Earth's surface and interior in

1

their static and dynamic contexts. This is the global picture of the Earth as perceived by today's Earth scientist, although it carries with it no implication that it will necessarily stand for all time without change, or even without radical change. Not all of what follows derives directly from the recent revolutionary period. The division of the Earth into crust, mantle and core, for example, has been appreciated for many decades (since 1910, in fact); and the crustal surface (at least, the continental crustal surface) has been under investigation for many centuries. Taken as a whole, however, the following notes form a sketch of the framework within which more detailed geological and geophysical studies must be fitted. In particular, they form the background, or context, for the subject matter in the three subsequent chapters.

Table 1.2.1   Areas of the world's continents and oceans and mean ocean depths. *Source:* Wyllie (1971).

	Area (10^6 km^2)	Percent of land or ocean	Percent of world surface	Mean depth (km)
World surface	510	—	100	—
All continents	148	100	29.2	—
All oceans	362.0	100	70.8	3.729
Eurasia	54.8	36.8	10.8	—
Asia	44.8	29.8	8.7	—
Europe	10.4	7.0	2.1	—
Africa	30.6	20.5	6.0	—
North America	22.0	14.8	4.3	—
South America	17.9	12.0	3.5	—
Antarctica	15.6	10.5	3.1	—
Australia	7.8	5.2	1.5	—
Pacific Ocean	166.2	—	—	1.188
—with adjacent seas	181.3	50.1	35.4	3.940
Atlantic Ocean	86.6	—	—	3.736
—with adjacent seas	94.3	26.0	18.4	3.575
Indian Ocean	73.4	—	—	3.872
—with adjacent seas	74.1	20.5	14.5	3.840
Arctic Ocean	9.5	—	—	1.330
—with adjacent seas	12.3	3.4	2.4	1.117

1.2 Statistics of continents and oceans

The statistics for the horizontal (areal) distribution of continents and oceans are given in Table 1.2.1. Over seventy percent of the Earth's surface is covered by ocean. Each of the three main oceans (Atlantic, Pacific and Indian) is larger in area than Europe and Asia combined; and the Pacific Ocean, which with its adjacent seas accounts for over thirty-five percent of the Earth's surface, covers a larger area than all the continents combined. Over sixty-five percent of the continental area lies in the northern hemisphere. (*Note:* In Chapter 3 we shall refer to the Antarctic Ocean which may be defined arbitrarily as the oceanic region south of latitude 55 °S. Strictly speaking, however, there is no such ocean; and in Table 1.2.1 the region sometimes known as the Antarctic Ocean is divided appropriately between the Atlantic, Pacific and Indian Oceans.)

The statistics for the vertical distribution of the Earth's solid surface (continents and ocean floors) are summarized in Figure 1.2.1. The proportions and actual areas of the surface lying at the various depths and heights are shown in Figure 1.2.1 (a), from which it may be seen that the Earth's relief forms two dominant levels. The one at a height

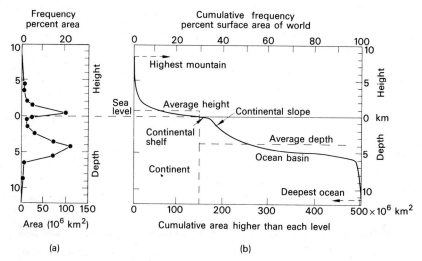

Figure 1.2.1 The distribution of levels of the Earth's solid surface: (a) the frequency distribution showing two dominant levels, and (b) the cumulative hypsographic curve. The curve in (b) gives directly the area of the Earth's surface above any given level. The left hand edge of the diagram, for example, corresponds to the highest mountain above which, of course, there is no surface (actual area = 0 on the bottom scale and percentage area = 0 on the top scale). The right hand edge corresponds to the deepest ocean above which all of the Earth's surface lies (actual area about 510×10^6 km^2 and percentage area = 100). *Source:* Wyllie (1971).

of a few hundred metres (0.875 km) above sea level represents the normal surface of the continents, whilst that between 4000 and 5000 metres (3.729 km) represents the deep ocean floor. Figure 1.2.1 (b), which is known as a *hypsographic curve*, shows the area (actual or proportional, but cumulative) of the Earth's solid surface which lies above any given height or depth. The meanings of the terms given on this diagram will become clear in the next section.

1.3 Provinces of the ocean floor

The ocean floor may be classified under three major divisions—continental margins, ocean basins and oceanic ridges—although further subdivisions may be made. This threefold classification is based on topography as determined by echo sounding; but as will become apparent later, the three major regions are also broadly indicative of three different processes occurring in the crust and mantle beneath the ocean floor. The three divisions are illustrated with respect to the Atlantic Ocean in Figure 1.3.1.

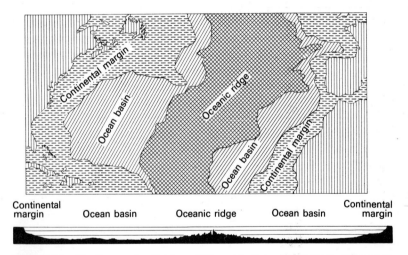

Figure 1.3.1   The three major divisions of the ocean floor, illustrated by reference to the Atlantic Ocean floor. The profile at the bottom runs from New England to the Spanish Sahara. *Source:* Heezen (1962).

Continental margins: These include the regions which are associated with the transition from continent to ocean floor. The Atlantic type

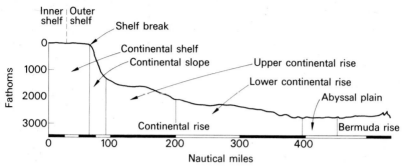

Figure 1.3.2 Continental margin regions as typified by a profile off the eastern United States. 1 fathom = 1.83 m; 1 nautical mile = 1.86 km. *Source:* Heezen (1962).

of continental margin comprises three parts which are illustrated in Figure 1.3.2. The *continental shelf* is merely that part of the continent which lies under water, obviously shallow water. At the shelf break, the slope increases rapidly (*continental slope*). The base of the continental slope then defines the beginning of the *continental rise* where

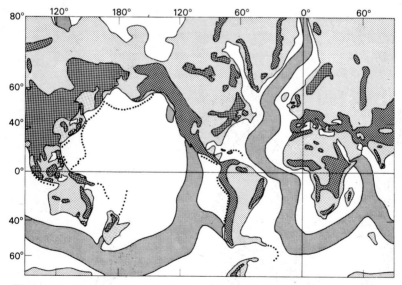

Figure 1.3.3 Major physiographic features of the world. White = abyssal ocean floor; medium shading = oceanic ridge system; light shading = continental platform; dark shading = mountains, intermontane basins, associated hills and elevated plateaus; dotted lines = oceanic trenches. *Source:* Wyllie (1971).

6

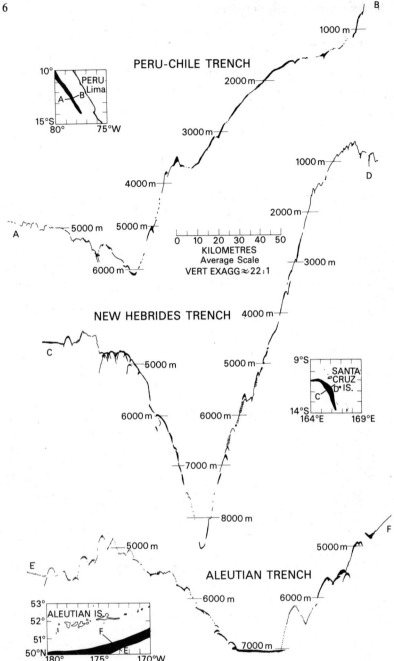

Figure 1.3.4 Topographic profiles of three Pacific trenches. *Source:* Menard (1964).

the gradient becomes much lower. In the Andean type of continental margin the continental shelf is very narrow; and at the base of the continental slope there is an *oceanic trench*. In a third type, the oceanic trench is associated with a band of volcanic islands (island arc) and

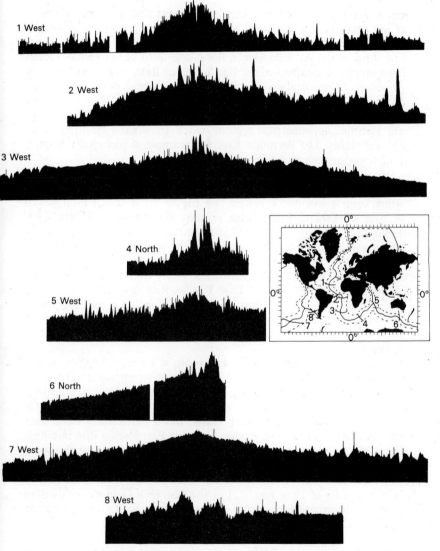

Figure 1.3.5 Eight topographic profiles across oceanic ridges. The upper six profiles all have a well-defined rift valley amid a very rugged relief; but this is not so with the remaining two (Pacific). *Source:* Heezen (1962).

both are separated from the continent by a small ocean basin (see below). The three types of continental margin are apparent on the physiographic map shown in Figure 1.3.3. The topographic profiles for three different oceanic trenches are shown in Figure 1.3.4.

Ocean basins: These have generally low relief and, with the exception of the small basins landward of island arc-trench systems, lie on the seaward side of continental rises or trenches. They account for about one third of the Atlantic Ocean floor, one third of the Indian Ocean floor and three quarters of the Pacific Ocean floor. There are two sub-provinces. *Abyssal plains* are smooth areas where bottom gradients do not exceed 1 in 1000 and which give way on their seaward side to *abyssal hills* up to about 400 m high and 10 km wide. *Oceanic rises* are aseismic, asymmetrical regions which are slightly elevated above abyssal plains. The Bermuda Rise, for example, is included in Figure 1.3.2 together with its adjacent abyssal plain.

Oceanic ridges: These are essentially underwater mountain ranges which form a worldwide system (see Figure 1.3.3) with a total length of over 60 000 km. Eight ridge profiles are shown in Figure 1.3.5. Topography is rugged with individual features rising several kilometres above the adjacent ocean basins; and the whole ridge zone may be over 1000 km wide. Some parts of the system (the mid-Atlantic Ridge in particular) have a well defined rift valley at the centre; but this seems to be absent in the East Pacific Rise (profiles 7 and 8 in Figure 1.3.5). (*Note:* The East Pacific Rise is called a 'rise' for purely historical reasons and should not be confused with the aseismic rises mentioned above. It is, in fact, part of the active oceanic ridge system)

   The crests of the ridge system are shown in Figure 1.3.6, from which it may be seen that the system is locally discontinuous. There are numerous displacements along fracture zones known as *transform faults.* Many transform faults are short compared with the lengths of the ridge crest offset by such faults; but a particularly interesting situation arises in the east Pacific. Here the East Pacific Rise impinges upon North America; and transform faults may be several thousand kilometres long. The San Andreas fault, which runs up the west coast of North America, is a transform fault along which relative movement is of the order of 1 cm year^{-1}. For the people of California this is an unfortunate circumstance—and one to which we shall return at greater length in Chapter Four.

Seamounts and guyots: Scattered about the ocean floor there are many hundreds of active and extinct volcanoes. If these are conical and higher than about 1000 m they are termed seamounts; but some have

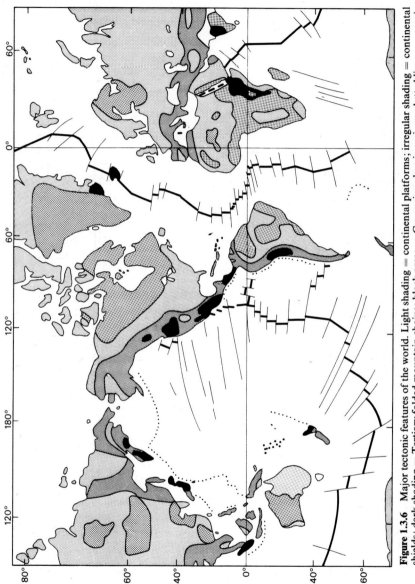

Figure 1.3.6 Major tectonic features of the world. Light shading = continental shields; dark shading = Tertiary folded mountain chains; black areas = Cenozoic volcanic regions; dotted lines = oceanic trenches; heavy lines = active rift systems of oceanic ridges; light lines = oceanic faults. *Source:* Wyllie (1971).

flat tops and are called guyots. Seamounts and guyots in the Pacific are shown in Figure 1.3.7. They are individual features but tend to form bands.

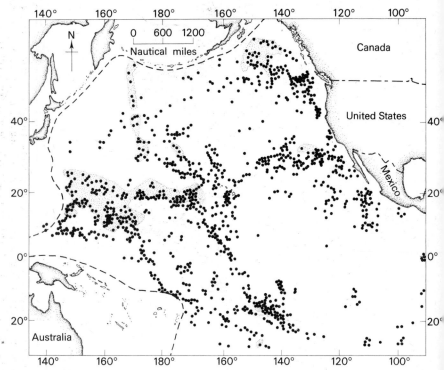

Figure 1.3.7   Volcanic mountains of the Pacific. Those within the shaded areas are predominantly guyots. *Source:* Menard (1959).

1.4 Continental provinces

Continents as defined structurally do not end at the water line but roughly at the base of the steep continental slope. Thus in numerical terms, about twenty-five percent of the world's continental area lies beneath water, a region equivalent to about eleven percent of the Earth's surface.

Continents are generally older than ocean floors by at least an order of magnitude and have thus had much more time to undergo geological alteration. The geology of continents is, in fact, infinitely varied, although several broad types of structural region may be usefully defined. These are shown in Figure 1.3.6. *Precambrian shields*

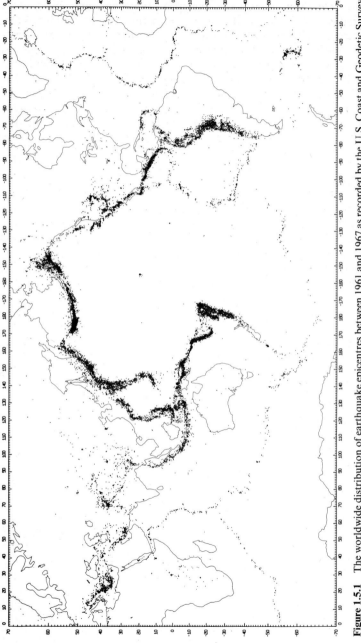

Figure 1.5.1 The worldwide distribution of earthquake epicentres between 1961 and 1967 as recorded by the U.S. Coast and Geodetic Survey. Earthquake foci lie at depths in the range 0–700 km. *Source:* Barazangi and Dorman (1969).

are large stable regions where Precambrian rocks are found at the surface. *Continental platforms* are also stable and are shield areas covered with thin, flat-lying younger sediments or continental borders adjacent to the continental shelves. Continental platforms are sometimes referred to as *post-Precambrian non-orogenic areas*—that is, areas which have generally avoided orogeny (mountain building) since Precambrian times. *Post-Precambrian orogenic areas* are regions which have undergone mountain building mainly during either the Tertiary or Cenozoic. The two principal post-Precambrian orogenic areas are the circum-Pacific belt which forms a ring around the Pacific Ocean, and the Himalayas.

1.5 Earthquakes

The distribution of the world's earthquake epicentres between 1961 and 1967 is shown in Figure 1.5.1. Clearly, present-day earthquakes mostly lie in belts which coincide with the oceanic ridges and post-Precambrian orogenic areas. The oceanic ridges may thus be seen as seismically active regions, a fact which is of extreme significance in interpreting the Earth's global behaviour.

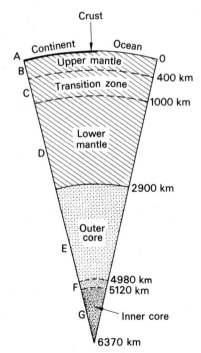

Figure 1.5.2 The gross layering within the Earth. *Source:* Bott (1971).

The behaviour of the elastic waves produced in the Earth by earthquakes has been used to determine the Earth's gross layering structure. This structure is shown both pictorially (Figure 1.5.2) and in tabular form (Table 1.5.1). The crust (A) is a thin surface layer whose base is

Table 1.5.1 The Earth's gross layering. The regional notation (A, B, C, etc.) is due to Bullen (1963). *Source:* Bott (1971).

Region	Name	Depth range (km)
A	crust	0–33 (average)
B	upper mantle	33–400
C	transition zone	400–1000
D	lower mantle	1000–2900
E	outer core	2900–4980
F	transition zone	4980–5120
G	inner core	5120–6370

defined around the world by a distinct boundary known as the *Mohorovičić discontinuity*, or Moho. The thickness of the oceanic crust (depth to the Moho) averages about 5 km; but the thickness of the continental crust varies more widely between 20 km and 80 km with an average in the range 30–35 km. The *core*, whose upper surface is also marked by a distinct discontinuity (the core-mantle boundary), actually comprises two parts. The inner core (G) is probably solid and the outer core (E) is fluid. There also appears to be a narrow transition zone (F) between the two within which, anomalously, the velocity of seismic waves decreases with depth. The *mantle* is the solid region between the core and crust which accounts for over eighty percent of the Earth's volume. Within the mantle there is also apparently a transition zone (C) between about 400 km and 1000 km within which the increase in the velocity of seismic waves with depth is rather greater than in either the upper mantle (B) or lower mantle (D).

Not shown in Figure 1.5.2 is a *low velocity layer* in the region of approximately 100–150 km—that is, a layer in which seismic wave velocity is lower than in the regions immediately above and below. The existence of this layer is now well established although there is less agreement on its precise limits or whether or not these limits vary around the Earth. The low velocity layer is extremely significant in the context of the global view of the Earth because, though solid, it is thought to be sufficiently plastic to be able to flow over long periods of time and thus cause horizontal motion in the material above it. For this reason it is sometimes convenient to regard the crust-mantle as the *asthenosphere*, which is the low velocity plastic zone itself, the *lithosphere*, which comprises the crust together with that part of the upper mantle lying above the asthenosphere, and the *mesosphere*, which is that part of the mantle lying below the asthenosphere.

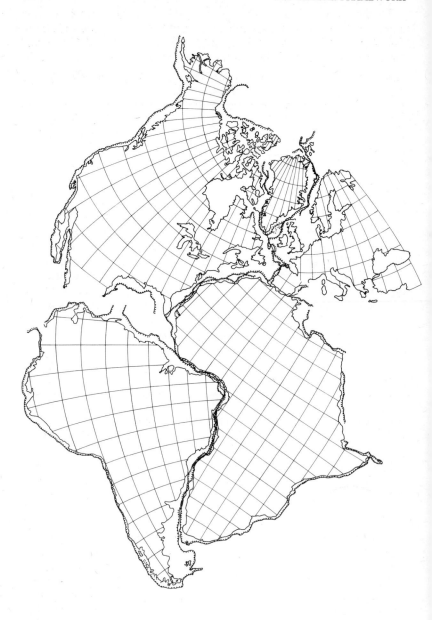

Figure 1.6.1 The fit of continents around the Atlantic at the 500-fathom contour. *Source:* Bullard, Everett and Smith (A.G.) (1965).

1.6 Continental drift

Figures 1.3.3 and 1.3.6 show the continents in their present positions, although this is apparently a temporary, instantaneous configuration of land masses which are on the move. About 200 million years ago the continents were all together in one (or perhaps two) supercontinent which then broke up and dispersed. The evidence for this is now so abundant that continental drift is now regarded in some quarters as a fact rather than as a hypothesis or even a theory. The most convincing evidence, and the evidence which finally clinched the case for continental drift after many decades of argument, comes from paleomagnetism. Most rocks contain magnetic grains which enabled them to acquire, at the time of their formation, a magnetization which was in the direction of the contemporary geomagnetic field. In many rocks this magnetization has remained stable to this day, thereby allowing the ancient geomagnetic field direction to be measured. It turns out that the magnetic directions thus obtained only make sense as a whole if the continents have moved relative to each other over the past 200 million years; and these directions may be used to 'reconstruct' the continents in their original relationships.

Two examples of reconstructed continents are shown in Figures 1.6.1 and 1.6.2. These particular reconstructions are not based on paleomagnetic data but on direct matching of continental margins.

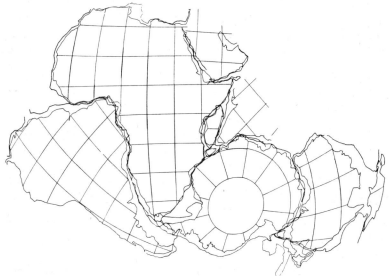

Figure 1.6.2 The fit of the southern continents. *Source:* Smith (A.G.) and Hallam (1970).

1.7 Ocean floor spreading

One of the main reasons why the idea of continental drift failed to gain acceptance for many decades was that there appeared to be no reasonable mechanism whereby continents could move relative to each other through a solid mantle and against solid oceanic crust. The existence of the low velocity plastic layer (asthenosphere) offers a solution to this problem, for it is conceivable that within the asthenosphere there are large-scale convection currents which can produce large-scale horizontal motions in the overlying lithosphere. Implicit in this scheme is that the oceanic crust undergoes large horizontal displacement along with the continents; and so the idea that moving continents must always do battle against the oceanic crust is no longer required.

Accepting, for the moment, that convection currents exist in the asthenosphere, it is then possible to visualize the oceanic ridges as active zones (supported by the earthquake distribution) beneath which convection currents in the asthenosphere are rising. Magma upwells at ridge crests to form new oceanic lithosphere which, under the action of the long, upper horizontal limbs of the convection cells, is forced to move laterally away from the ridges, thereby leaving space for more upwelling magma. Ultimately the oceanic lithosphere sinks in trench regions. The processes involved here are shown schematically in Figure 1.7.1.

However, although the broad features of this system are thought to be correct, ideas on the precise roles played by convection currents and the asthenosphere are still fluid. Historically, the concept of convection cells was first thought of in the context of mantle-wide convection. Later, it seemed more reasonable to limit convection to the asthenosphere, the properties of which seemed more conducive to plastic or semi-fluid flow, although complete convection cells were still envisaged. In each case, however, the cells (possibly the result of thermal convection) were regarded as the prime movers in the sense that the convection currents were thought to push the overlying lithosphere along. More recently, it has been proposed that the lithosphere is the prime mover (for example, that the oceanic lithosphere is spreading towards the trenches under the action of gravity) so that the asthenosphere merely acts as a channel for the flow of material in the direction opposite to that in which the lithosphere itself is moving. In this case, magma still upwells at ridge crests and oceanic lithosphere still sinks along trenches—the difference is that the flow in the asthenosphere (now one way only) becomes the consequence of spreading lithosphere, not the cause of it.

The most convincing evidence for ocean floor spreading comes from a study of the magnetic anomalies above the ocean floor and particularly across oceanic ridges. Throughout its history, the Earth's

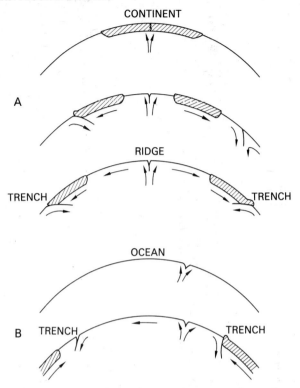

Figure 1.7.1 Schematic diagram illustrating the consequences of ocean floor spreading. A shows the effect of a rising convection current beneath a continent, the end result being an Atlantic-type situation with no trenches around the central ocean. B shows the effect of a similar current originally in an oceanic region, the end result being a Pacific-type situation in which lithospheric material is subsumed along ocean-margin trenches. *Source:* Vine (1969).

magnetic field has reversed itself many times; and the reversal pattern for the past 4.5 million years is now known in some detail, having been determined by measuring the magnetic polarities of continental rocks within this time range and by dating them accurately by radiometric methods. This polarity–time scale is shown in Figure 1.7.2. The pattern of reversals is reflected in the magnetic anomalies measured across oceanic ridges, just one example of which is illustrated in Figure 1.7.3. The similarity in the patterns is taken to mean that as magma upwells at oceanic ridges and cools to form new lithosphere it becomes magnetized in the prevailing geomagnetic field direction. As the lithosphere moves away laterally to allow more new lithosphere to form and become magnetized, a record of the Earth's magnetic field reversal pattern is gradually built up as a function of distance from the ridge

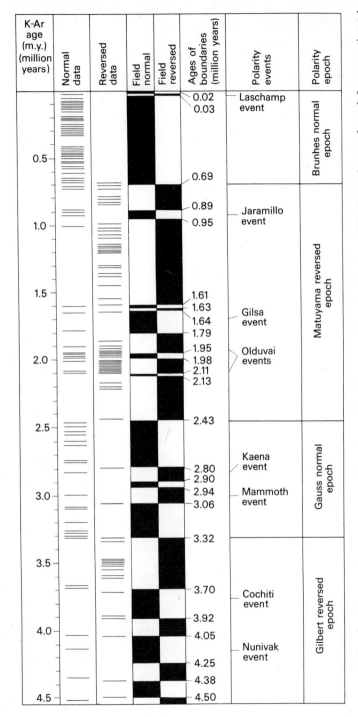

Figure 1.7.2 The geomagnetic polarity–time scale for the past 4.5 million years. Each short horizontal line shows the age of a rock from a continental volcanic unit as determined by potassium–argon dating and its magnetic polarity, normal or reversed. The scale is divided into longer epochs and shorter events. *Source:* Cox (1969).

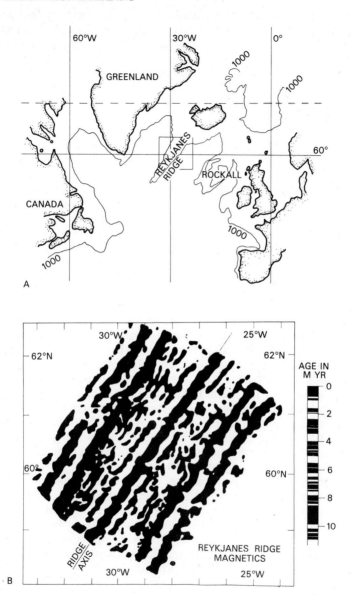

Figure 1.7.3   Magnetic anomalies across an oceanic ridge as illustrated by the Reykjanes Ridge. A shows the location of the ridge together with the 1000-fathom contour. B shows the magnetic anomaly pattern with positive (normal) anomalies in black and negative (reversed) anomalies in white. The central anomaly corresponds with the ridge axis. *Source:* Vine (1969).

with the present field being recorded at the ridge crest. By comparing the well-dated scale obtained from continental rocks with the undated pattern over the oceanic ridge, it is possible to assign ages to the oceanic anomaly pattern and thus calculate the rate at which the lithosphere is spreading away from the ridge.

1.8 Plate tectonics

In recent years, the motional aspects of continental drift and ocean floor spreading have been conceptually subsumed within plate tectonics —a framework which considers the Earth's lithosphere to be made up of a number of rigid crustal plates, or blocks, moving relative to each other. As shown in Figure 1.8.1, six large plates (named) are recognized although several smaller ones are required.

The large plates may be almost completely continental (for example, the Eurasian plate), completely oceanic (Pacific), or a combination (American, African). The need for such types follows directly from the acceptance of continental drift and ocean floor spreading; and is well illustrated by a comparison of the behaviour of the Atlantic and Pacific Oceans. There are no major trenches along the continental margins bordering the Atlantic; and so the material upwelling along the mid-Atlantic Ridge and moving, for example, westwards towards the Americas clearly cannot be subsumed. What seems to be happening in this case is that the spreading Atlantic floor is 'pushing' the Americas westwards. In short, there is no tectonic break or deformation between the Americas and the western Atlantic floor—the two regions must be part of the same tectonic unit. In the Pacific, on the other hand, the material spreading, for example, northwestwards from the East Pacific Rise is not pushing Eurasia but is being subsumed along the trenches of the northwest Pacific. In short, the Pacific west of the East Pacific Rise is a self-contained tectonic unit, or plate.

From this it may be gathered that the crustal or lithospheric plates, though generally tectonically inactive within themselves, are bounded by active margins which define them. In fact, three types of margin are recognized: (i) oceanic ridges, where lithosphere is being created, (ii) oceanic trenches, where lithosphere is being consumed, and (iii) transform faults, where there is relative motion but neither the production nor destruction of lithosphere. All three types involve tectonic activity and are thus generally earthquake zones, as Figure 1.8.1 demonstrates.

Plate tectonics as such is concerned less with mechanisms than with geometrical relationships. Its success stems largely from the simplification allowed by Euler's theorem which states that a layer on a sphere can be moved to any other position by a single rotation about a suitable

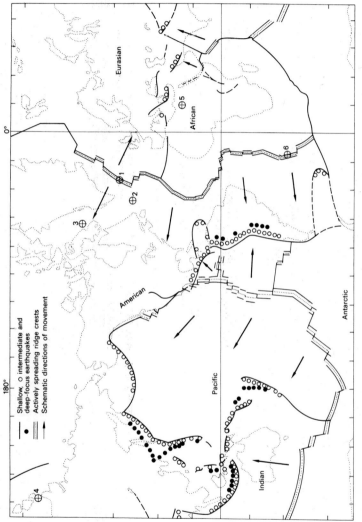

Figure 1.8.1 The Earth's lithospheric plates. The poles of rotation for plate pairs are numbered 1–6 as follows: 1, South Atlantic (America–Africa); 2, North Pacific (America–Pacific); 3, South Pacific (Antarctica–Pacific); 4, Arctic Ocean (America–Eurasia); 5, N.W. Indian Ocean (Africa–India); 6, S.W. Indian Ocean (Antarctica–Africa). The spreading rates at ridge crests are indicated schematically and vary from 1 cm year^{-1} near Iceland to 6 cm year^{-1} in the equatorial Pacific. *Source:* Wyllie (1971).

axis passing through the centre of the sphere. The point at which such an axis cuts the surface of the sphere is known as the *pole of rotation*. The relative movement of two plates expressed as a rotation about an axis or pole is shown in Figure 1.8.2. The poles of rotation for the six major Earth plates are indicated in Figure 1.8.1.

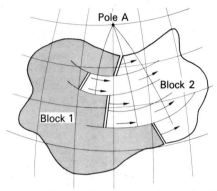

Figure 1.8.2   The rotation of blocks (plates) on a spherical surface. Whatever the relative motion, it may be regarded as a simple rotation about a pole such as A. All the transform faults on the boundary between blocks 1 and 2 must be small circles concentric with the pole A. *Source:* Morgan (1968).

1.9 General remarks

The global-dynamic view of the Earth presented above is now accepted, in general terms, by the majority of Earth scientists. But accepted as what? Clearly it may be regarded as a working hypothesis and perhaps even as what P. J. Wyllie has recently termed a 'ruling theory'. However, some scientists have, rather arrogantly, announced to the world that the new global tectonics may now be regarded as fact. History and philosophy suggest otherwise, or at least doubt. Wyllie has also recently noted† that

> this is not the first time in geological history that a theory has been acclaimed as virtually proven. It has been said that Abraham Werner's promulgation of the Neptunian theory elevated geology to the rank of a real science. For years his theory appeared to be unassailable. He maintained that all geological formations, and rocks of all types except for those actually observed to emerge from volcanoes as lavas, had originated as successive deposits or precipitates from a primeval ocean. Werner's thesis was challenged by the school of Plutonists and subsequently abandoned; this was one of the most celebrated and bitter controversies in science. James Hutton

† P. J. Wyllie (1971), *The Dynamic Earth: Textbook in Geosciences*. New York, John Wiley.

and the Plutonists presented evidence satisfying most geologists that many rocks were formed by the cooling and crystallization of hot material that had risen in a fused condition from subterranean regions. Neptunism, which dominated geological thought for many years, simply disappeared.

A sense of caution is always required in science, for as Einstein is reported as observing:

> By reflecting on any scientific problem one was bound to make some progress, for every scientific proposition, without exception is incorrect. This comes of the inadequacy of human thought and the impossibility of comprehending nature, so that any logical formulation of nature is bound not to fit somewhere.

Further reading

E. R. Oxburgh (1971), Plate tectonics, in I. G. Gass, P. J. Smith and R. C. L. Wilson (Eds.), *Understanding the Earth*. Sussex, Artemis Press and Cambridge, Mass., M.I.T. Press.

A. G. Smith (1971), Continental drift, in I. G. Gass, P. J. Smith and R. C. L. Wilson (Eds.), *Understanding the Earth*. Sussex, Artemis Press and Cambridge, Mass., M.I.T. Press.

F. J. Vine (1971), Sea-floor spreading, in I. G. Gass, P. J. Smith and R. C. L. Wilson (Eds.), *Understanding the Earth*. Sussex, Artemis Press and Cambridge, Mass., M.I.T. Press.

P. J. Wyllie (1971), *The Dynamic Earth: Textbook in Geosciences*. New York, John Wiley.

CHAPTER TWO

The Earth's Crust and Uppermost Mantle

2.1 Introduction

The broad division of the Earth into crust, mantle and core was defined by observing the behaviour of the elastic waves produced by earthquakes. When an earthquake occurs in the Earth, a part of the energy released is propagated away from the source (focus) in the form of elastic waves which travel at a definite velocity depending upon the physical properties of the transmitting medium. Two types of earthquake wave travel through the body of the Earth: (i) P (or longitudinal) waves, which correspond to the transmission of compressions and rarefactions and in which the motion of the particles of the medium is in the same direction as that of the wave propagation, and (ii) S (or transverse) waves, which correspond to shear displacement and in which the particles of the medium move at right angles to the direction in which the wave travels.

The velocities of P and S waves are given by:

$$u = \sqrt{\frac{k + \frac{4\mu}{3}}{\rho}} \quad \text{and} \quad w = \sqrt{\frac{\mu}{\rho}} \tag{2.1.1}$$

where u = velocity of P waves,
$\quad\quad w$ = velocity of S waves,
$\quad\quad \rho$ = density of the medium,
$\quad\quad \mu$ = rigidity modulus* of the medium,
and $\quad k$ = bulk modulus* of the medium.

(*Note:* The expression for the velocity of P waves may also be written:

$$u = \sqrt{\frac{\psi}{\rho}} \tag{2.1.1a}$$

where $\psi = k + 4\mu/3$ = axial modulus* of the medium.)

Because k is positive, $(k + 4\mu/3)$ must be greater than μ; and so u must be greater than w—that is, in any given material the velocity of P waves is higher than the velocity of S waves. Also, for a fluid, $\mu = 0$ and so $w = 0$—that is, S waves cannot pass through a fluid. Finally, the elastic moduli increase with density faster than the density itself increases and so, in general, rocks with higher densities have higher wave velocities.

These properties are reflected in Figure 2.1.1, which shows the broad variation of seismic velocity with depth throughout the Earth according to two slightly different interpretations. In the P wave curves there

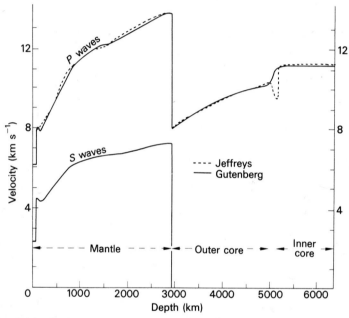

Figure 2.1.1 The broad seismic velocity–depth distributions in the Earth according to Gutenberg (P and S waves) and Jeffreys (P waves only shown). *Source:* Gutenberg (1959).

are three marked discontinuities. At a depth of a few tens of kilometres a sudden increase in P wave velocity defines the boundary between crust and mantle; and a large decrease at about 2900 km marks the core–mantle boundary. Within the core, at a depth of just over 5000 km, there is a small P wave velocity jump (Gutenberg), or a fall followed by an increase (Jeffreys), which defines the boundary between the fluid outer core and an inner core which is probably solid. The main evidence for a fluid outer core is that S waves terminate abruptly at the core surface. The S wave curve also reflects the crust–mantle boundary.

Historically, the discontinuity which is now recognized as marking the boundary between the crust and mantle was discovered beneath continent by Mohorovičić early this century and, as a result, is frequently referred to as the Mohorovičić discontinuity, or Moho. Whilst studying the Croatia (Yugoslavia) earthquake of 8 October 1909, Mohorovičić found that observatories within a few hundred kilometres of the earthquake epicentre received not one but *two* sets of P and S waves at different times. The second set to arrive (designated P_g and S_g)—that is, the set with the lower velocity—Mohorovičić interpreted as having travelled directly to the observatory through a comparatively low velocity layer near the Earth's surface, namely, the continental crust. The faster set of P and S waves (designated P_n and S_n), the set arriving at the observatory first, he interpreted as having travelled for most of the path through an underlying, higher velocity medium, namely, the mantle. From these data Mohorovičić calculated that:

velocity of P waves in overlying crust, $u_g = 5.6 \, \text{km s}^{-1}$,
velocity of P waves in underlying mantle, $u_n = 7.9 \, \text{km s}^{-1}$,
and distance to crust–mantle boundary, $h = 54 \, \text{km}$.

Since Mohorovičić's discovery, the crust–mantle boundary has been found beneath many regions of the Earth's surface; and is now regarded as an almost worldwide discontinuity beneath both continents and oceans, although its depth varies from place to place.

A more contentious question is that of the possible existence of a second major discontinuity which may divide the crust itself. Whilst studying the Tauern (Austria) earthquake of 28 November 1923, Conrad discovered another set of P and S waves (designated P^* and S^*) with velocities $u^* = 6.29 \, \text{km s}^{-1}$ and $w^* = 3.57 \, \text{km s}^{-1}$, on the basis of which he suggested that the crust forms two layers divided by a boundary which has since become known as the Conrad discontinuity (velocities P_g and S_g above the discontinuity and velocities P^* and S^* below). Jeffreys later applied the names 'granitic layer' to the upper crust and 'intermediate layer' to the lower crust, although some seismologists have replaced the latter term by 'basaltic layer'. It is now evident, however, that the Conrad discontinuity is not found everywhere and cannot therefore be regarded as a worldwide boundary.

During the four decades following the discovery of the Moho, most investigations of crustal thickness and structure were based on earthquake wave observations. Since about 1950, however, most of the seismic work on the crust has utilized man-made explosions. The chief advantages of explosions are (i) that the time and position of the seismic source are accurately known, (ii) that seismologists may produce explosions at will rather than having to await an unpredictable natural event, and thus (iii) that experiments may be planned in relation to geological structure and in regions where no earthquakes occur.

The main disadvantage is that, with the exception of underground nuclear explosions over which seismologists generally do not have control anyway, explosion magnitudes cannot approach earthquake magnitudes and so investigations are limited to comparatively shallow depths in the crust and upper mantle. On the other hand, explosions are ideal for determining small-scale, fine structure.

In this chapter we shall examine the contribution that explosion seismology and other, related techniques have made to our knowledge of the physical (as opposed to chemical) properties of the Earth's upper layers. In general, however, details of experimental equipment will not be considered. Thus as far as seismology is concerned, for example, an explosion (or earthquake) will be regarded simply as a source of elastic waves; and a detector (or recorder) will be considered simply as a device for measuring the time it takes for an elastic wave to reach it from the source.

2.2 The seismic refraction method

There is no difference in principle between the elastic waves produced by explosions and those produced by earthquakes. Thus a P wave produced by an explosion will travel through a given medium with the same velocity as that of an earthquake-produced P wave and that velocity will depend upon the physical properties of the medium according to equation (2.1.1). In explosion seismology S waves are not usually important, however. There is no reason why, in principle, S waves should not be used to investigate crustal structure; but the problem is to obtain S waves of sufficient energy. Explosions themselves produce predominantly P waves and so in what follows we shall generally restrict the discussion to P waves.

The principle of the seismic refraction method is to initiate seismic waves at one point and then determine how long it takes for the waves to reach a series of observation points. In travelling from the source to the detectors the waves may be refracted (or reflected) by any discontinuities which happen to lie in their path; and the information the seismic method is designed to obtain is (i) the positions of these discontinuities, and (ii) the velocities of the waves in the layers formed by the discontinuities or boundaries. The use of the terms 'refracted' and 'reflected' here is deliberate, for elastic waves impinging upon physical boundaries in the Earth behave in the same way as light waves impinging upon, for example, mirrors and lenses (the surfaces of which form boundaries between air and glass). The simple laws of optics may thus be applied equally to elastic waves in the Earth.

Consider, for example, a seismic source (S) emitting elastic waves at the surface of a two-layer system in which the velocity of the waves is V_1 in the upper layer and V_2 in the lower layer, where $V_1 < V_2$ (Figure 2.2.1). The source will give off waves in all directions; but consider just one of the wave paths which passes down through the

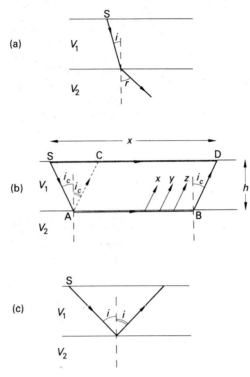

Figure 2.2.1 The behaviour of elastic waves from a seismic source S situated at the surface of a two-layer system. The velocities of the waves in the upper and lower layers are V_1 and V_2, respectively, where $V_2 > V_1$. In (a) the wave path strikes the boundary at an angle i which is smaller than the critical angle and is refracted into the lower layer at an angle r which is less than 90°. In (c) the angle of incidence is greater than the critical angle and so no refraction takes place at all—the wave is totally reflected back to the surface. In (b) the angle of incidence is equal to the critical angle and so the refracted wave travels along the path AB in the lower layer. Secondary waves emitted along AB are refracted back into the upper layer and may be detected at a point such as D. A direct wave which has travelled entirely in the upper layer is also received at D. No refracted wave may emerge at the surface between S and C.

upper layer and strikes the boundary between the two layers at an *angle of incidence, i.* As long as i is not greater than a certain critical angle, the wave will pass through the boundary and emerge at an *angle of refraction, r,* as shown in Figure 2.2.1 (a). Because $V_2 > V_1$, the angle r will be larger than angle i, the exact relationship between i and r being given by Snell's Law:

$$\frac{\sin i}{\sin r} = \frac{V_1}{V_2} \qquad (2.2.1)$$

At one particular value of i, however, r will be $90°$, in which case the refracted wave travels just inside the lower layer and parallel to the boundary as shown in Figure 2.2.1 (b). For this situation, equation (2.1.1) becomes, putting $r = 90°$:

$$\frac{V_1}{V_2} = \frac{\sin i}{\sin 90°} = \sin i_c, \text{ because } \sin 90° = 1 \qquad (2.2.2)$$

This particular value of i is known as the *critical angle*, i_c. If i is larger than i_c, the wave will not be refracted through the boundary at all but will be reflected back up through the upper layer as shown in Figure 2.2.1 (c). If i is smaller than i_c, the wave will pass through the boundary and emerge into the lower layer at angle r as shown in Figure 2.2.1 (a). But if $i = i_c$, then $r = 90°$ and we have the situation shown in Figure 2.2.1 (b) where the refracted wave travels in the lower layer parallel to the boundary. It is this last case which is of particular importance in seismology. Because the source (S) emits waves in all directions there is bound to be one wave path which strikes the boundary at the critical angle; and so in the two-layer system we are considering here there is bound to be a wave travelling along the path AB in Figure 2.2.1(b). And as it travels it will, of course, be continuously emitting secondary waves, some of which will be refracted back upwards into the upper layer (x, y, z, etc.). Each of these newly refracted waves will obey Snell's Law at the refraction; but because the wave is now passing from a layer with higher velocity to a layer with lower velocity, and because the new angle of incidence is now $90°$, equation (2.2.1) becomes:

$$\frac{V_2}{V_1} = \frac{\sin i}{\sin r} = \frac{\sin 90°}{\sin r} = \frac{1}{\sin r} \qquad (2.2.3)$$

or

$$\frac{V_1}{V_2} = \sin r \qquad (2.2.4)$$

But from equation (2.2.2):

$$\frac{V_1}{V_2} = \sin i_c \qquad (2.2.5)$$

and so:

$$\sin r = \sin i_c \text{ and therefore, } r = i_c \qquad (2.2.6)$$

In other words, the waves will re-emerge into the upper layer at the critical angle. The first wave to behave in this way will be the wave from point A and this wave will strike the upper surface of the upper

layer at C. Thus there can be no *refracted* waves striking the upper
surface between S and C. The distance SC is known as the *critical
distance*. Refracted waves will, however, be received at the surface at
every point beyond C and a detector (D) placed at any one of these
points will pick up a refracted wave. (There does, of course, come a
point at which the wave becomes too weak to detect, and so in practice
there is a limit to the distance CD.)

A refracted wave such as SABD is known as a *head wave*. However,
D will also receive a *direct wave* from S which has travelled along the
path SD entirely in the upper layer. There is, of course, no critical
distance for the receipt of the direct wave, and so whereas a detector
placed between S and C will not pick up a refracted wave, it will pick
up a direct wave. A detector placed beyond C (that is, outside the range
SC) will pick up both direct and head waves. But which wave will
arrive at D first, the direct wave or the head wave?

Time taken for direct wave to reach D

Because velocity = distance/time, the time (t_1) for the direct wave to
travel from S to D is simply:

$$t_1 = \frac{\text{distance}}{\text{velocity}} = \frac{x}{V_1} \qquad (2.2.7)$$

Time taken for head wave to reach D

In this case the problem is slightly more complicated because the
head wave path has three separate segments (SA, AB, BD) in one of
which (AB) the velocity is V_2 and in two of which (SA, BD) the velocity
is V_1. In other words:

travel time from S to D (t_2) = time over SA + time over AB +
time over BD.

Working out t_2 is just a matter of routine trigonometry, the answer
being:

$$t_2 = \frac{x}{V_2} + \frac{2h\sqrt{V_2^2 - V_1^2}}{V_1 V_2} \qquad (2.2.8)$$

where h is the thickness of the upper layer.

The answer to the question of whether the direct wave or head
wave reaches D first thus depends upon which is the smaller, the
expression for t_1 or the expression for t_2, in other words, on the
quantities V_1, V_2, h and x. In qualitative terms, however, it is quite
easy to see what will happen. If D is close to C, the direct wave reaches
D first because the head wave, which in this case travels mostly in the
upper layer, has a greater distance to cover. But as D is moved further

away from C there comes a point where D receives the head wave
first. This is because as D moves further from C, the higher velocity
part of the head wave's path, AB (remember that $V_2 > V_1$), becomes
longer. There thus comes a point where the time saved by the head
wave's higher velocity in the lower layer outweighs the disadvantage
of having to travel a longer distance; and the head wave 'overtakes'
the direct wave. The position of D at which this happens is, of course,
the point at which the head wave and the direct wave arrive at the same
time. This is the point at which:

$$t_1 = t_2$$

and so from equations (2.2.7) and (2.2.8):

$$\frac{x}{V_1} = \frac{x}{V_2} + \frac{2h\sqrt{V_2^2 - V_1^2}}{V_1 V_2} \qquad (2.2.9)$$

whence:

$$x = 2h\sqrt{\frac{V_2 + V_1}{V_2 - V_1}} = x_d \qquad (2.2.10)$$

It is thus clear that the point ($x = x_d$) at which the first wave to arrive
at D changes from being the direct wave to the head wave depends
on the values of V_1, V_2, and h. Moreover, equation (2.2.10) shows
that if we can determine x_d, V_1, and V_2 we can then determine h,
the thickness of the upper layer.

Determination of V_1

Equation (2.2.7) represents a straight line of the form $y = mx$. Thus
if t_1 is plotted against x, the result will be a straight line which passes
through the origin and which has a gradient of $1/V_1$. This is the line
OP in Figure 2.2.2. This line expresses the variation of t_1 with x—
in other words, it shows how the time taken for the direct wave to
reach D varies with the distance SD(x). V_1 may be obtained simply
by measuring the gradient of OP.

Determination of V_2

Equation (2.2.8) represents a straight line of the form $y = mx + c$.
Thus if t_2 is plotted against x, the result will be a straight line which
has gradient $1/V_2$ but which does not pass through the origin. This
is the line QR in Figure 2.2.2. This line expresses the variation of t_2
with x—it shows how the time taken for the head wave to reach D
varies with the distance SD. Note that this line does not reach back
to the time axis because there is a critical distance (x_c) over which
D cannot receive the head wave. This is the distance SC in Figure
2.2.1 (b). V_2 may be obtained by measuring the gradient of QR.

Determination of h

V_1 and V_2 are now known. x_d may be obtained from the point at which the lines OP and QR cross. h may then be calculated from equation (2.2.10) which when re-written becomes:

$$h = \frac{x_d}{2}\sqrt{\frac{V_2 - V_1}{V_2 + V_1}} \tag{2.2.11}$$

Alternatively, h may be calculated from the intercept of the head wave curve on the t axis (that is, at $x = 0$). The value of t ($= t_0$) when $x = 0$ may be obtained by putting $x = 0$ into equation (2.2.8), whence:

$$t_0 = \frac{2h\sqrt{V_2^2 - V_1^2}}{V_1 V_2} \quad \text{or} \quad h = \frac{t_0 V_1 V_2}{2\sqrt{V_2^2 - V_1^2}} \tag{2.2.12}$$

The time–distance graph

Figure 2.2.2 is known as a *time–distance graph* and may be constructed by measuring the time it takes for the waves from S to reach D as D is moved farther away from S (that is, as x is increased). The heavy part of the line (OXR) represents the *first arrival* at D—that is, the

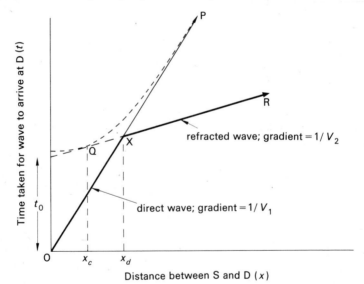

Figure 2.2.2 The time–distance graph for the situation shown in Figure 2.2.1 (b). OP represents the direct wave arriving at D and QR represents the head wave. The first wave to arrive at D is represented by the heavy line OXR. For $x < x_d$ this is the direct wave; but at $x > x_d$ the head wave becomes the first arrival. No refracted wave arrives at all at D when $x < x_c$. The dotted line is the time–distance curve for waves reflected at the boundary between upper and lower layers.

time it takes for the first wave to arrive at D whether it be the head wave or the direct wave. Up to a distance x_d the first arrival is, of course, the direct wave but beyond x_d the first arrival is the head wave. Conversely, up to distance x_d the head wave appears at D as the *second arrival* (except that there is no head wave at all in the range $x = 0$ to $x = x_c$); and beyond x_d the second arrival is the direct wave.

More complex situations

Naturally, the two-layer model we have discussed so far is a great over-simplification of what actually happens in the Earth for the following reasons:

(a) In practice, there may be more than two layers present; and in this case further refractions may take place at the lower boundaries. For example, if there is a third layer in which the wave velocity is V_3, one of the waves from S (such as that in Figure 2.2.1 (a) which strikes the first boundary at an angle less than i_c and is thus refracted into the second layer at $r < 90°$) will strike the second boundary at the critical angle for that boundary and thus be refracted there at $90°$. This wave will ultimately return to the surface to give another arrival at D and at a certain value of x will become the first arrival as long as $V_3 > V_2 > V_1$. The time–distance graph for the first arrivals will then look something like Figure 2.2.3. V_3 may then be calculated from the gradient of the

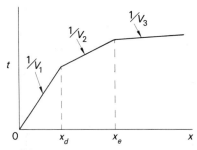

Figure 2.2.3 The time–distance graph *for first arrivals only* for a three-layer system in which $V_3 > V_2 > V_1$. In the range $0-x_d$ the first arrival is the direct wave in the upper layer. In the range x_d-x_e the first arrival is the head wave refracted at the first boundary. Beyond x_e the first arrival is the head wave refracted at the second boundary.

third segment. The equation for the calculation of d, the thickness of the second layer, may be obtained by the same methods as before but will be much more complicated. Thus:

$$d = \frac{x_e (V_3 - V_2) - \dfrac{2h}{V_1}\left[V_2\sqrt{V_3^2 - V_1^2} - V_3\sqrt{V_2^2 - V_1^2} \right]}{2\sqrt{V_3^2 - V_2^2}} \qquad (2.2.13)$$

where x_e has the significance shown in Figure 2.2.3. The analysis may be extended for even more layers, each of which leads to even more complicated mathematics and each of which adds a segment to the time–distance graph.

(b) The velocity of the wave within any given layer may not be constant. For example, if, as sometimes happens, the velocity within a layer increases significantly with depth, the corresponding segment of the time–distance graph will not be straight but will be concave towards the x axis.

(c) If a layer has a lower velocity for wave travel than the layer above, a 90° refraction at its surface will be impossible and the corresponding segment at the time–distance graph will be missing. A segment may also be missing, at least from the *first* arrivals, if a layer is very thin or if it does not have sufficient velocity contrast with adjacent layers. This will introduce errors into the depths determined for lower boundaries. Figure 2.2.4 shows what may happen in a three-layer system when the middle layer is thin and has a velocity which, though greater than, is close to that of the upper layer.

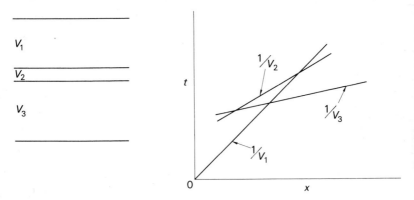

Figure 2.2.4   The time–distance graph for a three-layer system $(V_3 > V_2 > V_1)$ in which the second layer is thin and has a velocity close to that of the upper layer. The wave refracted at the surface of the middle layer never appears as a first arrival.

(d) Another complication which may arise is that the detector may pick up not only refracted waves and the direct wave but waves which have been *reflected* at the various boundaries. In the simple two-layer system of Figure 2.2.1 (b) the wave reflected from the first boundary is relatively weak in the range SC and is known as the *subcritical reflection*; but its strength (amplitude) increases rapidly beyond C, where it may actually be the strongest wave to arrive at the detector. In this range the reflected wave is known as the *supercritical reflection*. The reflected time–distance curve is shown by the dotted line in Figure 2.2.2. If the boundary concerned is the Moho, the wave reflected there is designated $P_m P$. The reflection at the Conrad discontinuity (where it exists) is designated $P_1 P$.

(e) The simple model discussed above, whatever the number of boundaries, has assumed that the layers are horizontal and the boundaries parallel. Unfortunately, nature does not normally conform to horizontal, parallel surfaces. If the first boundary, for example, dips with respect to the surface, a set-up involving a seismic source and one set of detectors will certainly give a value for h but it will be false. A way out of this difficulty is to array a second set of detectors on the opposite side of S as shown in Figure 2.2.5.

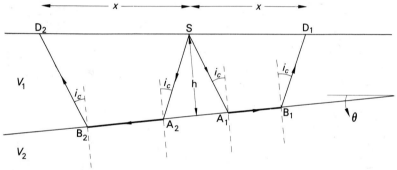

Figure 2.2.5 The refraction behaviour of elastic waves from a seismic source S situated at the surface of a two-layer system in which the boundary dips at an angle θ.

For an up-dip wave such as $SA_1 B_1 D_1$:

$$\text{time of travel, } t_u = \frac{2h \cos i_c}{V_1} + \frac{x \sin (i_c - \theta)}{V_2 \sin i_c} \qquad (2.2.14)$$

And for a down-dip wave such as $SA_2 B_2 D_2$:

$$\text{time of travel, } t_d = \frac{2h \cos i_c}{V_1} + \frac{x \sin (i_c + \theta)}{V_2 \sin i_c} \qquad (2.2.15)$$

where θ is the angle of dip below the horizontal.

Because we now have two sets of detectors, two refracted waves and two direct waves, there will also be two time–distance curves as shown in Figure 2.2.6. On each one the curve segment for the direct wave to D_1 or D_2 will, as before, have gradient $1/V_1$. For

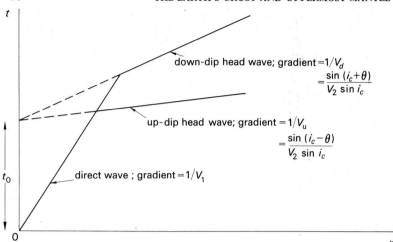

Figure 2.2.6 The time–distance graph for the situation shown in Figure 2.2.5. The up-dip and down-dip refracted wave curves are different, although the direct wave curve is common.

the up-dip time–distance curve, the head wave segment will have gradient (from equation (2.2.14)):

$$\frac{\sin(i_c - \theta)}{V_2 \sin i_c} = \frac{1}{V_u} \tag{2.2.16}$$

where V_u is the *apparent* velocity in the up-dip direction. The significance of the quantity V_u can be explained this way. The gradient of the up-dip head wave time–distance curve is $1/V_u$. If the layers are parallel, as in the case we originally considered, the gradient of the head wave time–distance curve is $1/V_2$. In other words, $V_u = V_2$ and V_u represents the *true* velocity in the lower layer. But if the boundary between the layers dips, the velocity V_u we determine from the gradient of the time–distance curve is not the true velocity V_2 but the velocity V_2 modified by the expression $\sin(i_c - \theta)/\sin i_c$ as given in equation (2.2.16). In short, the apparent velocity V_u is determined from the gradient but in order to determine the true velocity V_2 we need to know, in addition, the values of θ and i_c. A similar situation arises in the case of the down-dip wave, the gradient of the head wave time–distance curve being (from equation (2.2.15)):

$$\frac{\sin(i_c + \theta)}{V_2 \sin i_c} = \frac{1}{V_d} \tag{2.2.17}$$

where V_d is the apparent velocity in the down-dip direction and will be different from V_u.

From equations (2.2.16) and (2.2.17) it is possible to obtain expressions for the dip angle, θ, and the critical angle, i_c, as follows:

$$\theta = \tfrac{1}{2}\left(\sin^{-1}\frac{V_1}{V_d} - \sin^{-1}\frac{V_1}{V_u}\right) \qquad (2.2.18)$$

$$i_c = \tfrac{1}{2}\left(\sin^{-1}\frac{V_1}{V_d} + \sin^{-1}\frac{V_1}{V_u}\right) \qquad (2.2.19)$$

(*Note:* $\sin^{-1}\alpha$ is mathematical shorthand for 'the angle whose sine is α'.)

θ and i_c may thus be calculated once V_1, V_u and V_d have been obtained from the gradients of the time–distance curves. The value of i_c may then be used in equations (2.2.14) or (2.2.15) to calculate h, where h is the thickness of the upper layer at the position of S (that is, at $x = 0$). Thus from equations (2.2.14) or (2.2.15), putting $x = 0$:

$$t_0 = t_u = t_d = \frac{2h\cos i_c}{V_1} = \text{intercept on } t \text{ axis.}$$

whence:

$$h = \frac{t_0 V_1}{2\cos i_c} \qquad (2.2.20)$$

V_2 may be calculated from either equation (2.2.16) or (2.2.17) using previously calculated values of θ, i_c, V_u and V_d, or more simply from the calculated values of V_1 and i_c using Snell's Law directly:

$$V_2 = \frac{V_1}{\sin i_c}$$

Practical points

In the theoretical treatment developed so far we have assumed the set-up to be a single seismic source, S, with a set of detectors arrayed in a line either on one side or both sides of S. These arrangements are illustrated schematically in Figures 2.2.7 (a) and 2.2.7 (b). How-ever, in practice it is usually more convenient to use a single detector, D, and a series of shots as shown in Figures 2.2.7 (c) and 2.2.7 (d). The arrangement (c) is known as a *single profile*; and, as we have seen, suffers from the disadvantage that variations in the thickness of the upper layer cannot be detected. If the boundary dips a single profile will lead to a false determination of velocity and hence a false value for layer thickness.

This problem may be overcome by using the *split profile* in Figure 2.2.7 (d). However, although the split profile allows the dip to be determined, an improvement in the measurement of the dip is obtained if the two parts of the split profile are effectively overlapped as in Figure 2.2.7 (e) (i). In practice, this arrangement may be simplified to that shown in 2.2.7 (e) (ii) which is simply a series of shots with a

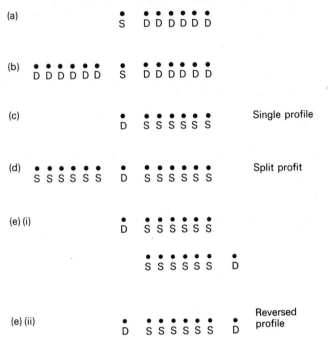

Figure 2.2.7 Possible arrangements (profiles) for seismic sources and detectors. Note, however, that sources and detectors are interchangeable. Thus, for example, (e) (ii) would still be a reversed profile if D and S were interchanged.

detector at each end of the line. This is known as a *reversed profile*. The length of such a profile is usually several times the depth of penetration required, which, for the investigation of continental structure, means 200–300 km.

An example of the time–distance graph for a reversed profile is shown in Figure 2.2.8. The theory is the same as for the case considered in Figures 2.2.5 and 2.2.6 except that h, the thickness of the upper layer under the source S, now varies because the position of S varies (we are no longer dealing with a single source). If the layer thickness beneath source S_1 is h_1 and the layer thickness under source S_2 is h_2:

equation (2.2.14) (up-dip) becomes

$$t_u = \frac{2h_1 \cos i_c}{V_1} + \frac{x \sin (i_c - \theta)}{V_2 \sin i_c} \qquad (2.2.21)$$

and equation (2.2.15) (down-dip) becomes

$$t_d = \frac{2h_2 \cos i_c}{V_1} + \frac{x \sin (i_c + \theta)}{V_2 \sin i_c} \tag{2.2.22}$$

The gradients of the up-dip head wave curves remain as they were before; but the effect of modifying the theory is to make the intercepts

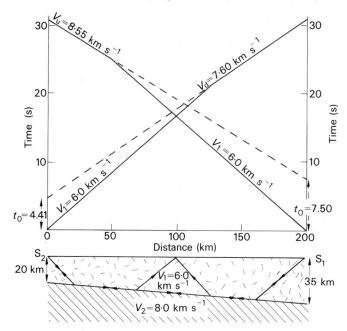

Figure 2.2.8   The time–distance graph for a reversed profile over a two-layer system in which the boundary dips at an angle θ. The down-dip curve has been plotted as before, using the left hand bottom corner of the graph as the origin corresponding to source S_2. The up-dip curve has been plotted in the 'reverse' direction using the right hand bottom corner of the graph as the origin corresponding to source S_1; but there is no reason of principle why it should not have been plotted using the same origin as the down-dip curve as shown in Figure 2.2.6. The numerical values shown in the diagram are consistent with each other and with the equations in the text. *Source:* Bott (1971).

of these curves on the time axis unequal, as Figure 2.2.8 demonstrates. From these intercepts, the layer thickness (h_1 or h_2) is given by:

$$h_1 \text{ or } h_2 = \frac{t_0 V_1 V_2}{2 \cos \theta \sqrt{V_2^2 - V_1^2}} \tag{2.2.23}$$

where t_0 is the intercept relevant to the particular layer thickness required.

The final practical point is that time–distance graphs are often displayed as *reduced time–distance graphs* in which instead of plotting time (t) against distance (x), the quantity plotted against x is:

$$t - \frac{x}{V_1} \qquad (2.2.24)$$

The reason for this simply concerns the presentation (in reports, for example) of graphs with manageable scales. One consequence of plotting the reduced time–distance graph concerns the curve for the direct wave. From equation (2.2.7), for the direct wave:

$$t = \frac{x}{V_1}$$

and so:

$$t - \frac{x}{V_1} = 0$$

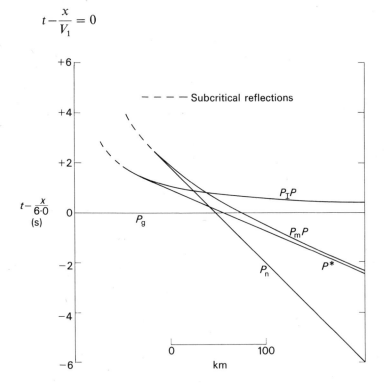

Figure 2.2.9 The reduced time–distance graph for a region where the Earth's crust is two-layered with the upper layer having velocity 6.0 km s^{-1}. The direct wave through the upper layer (P_g) appears as a straight line passing through the zero point. P_n is the wave refracted at the surface of the mantle; P^* is the wave refracted at the surface of the lower crustal layer (Conrad discontinuity); P_IP is the wave reflected at the Conrad discontinuity; and P_mP is the wave reflected at the Moho. *Source:* Eaton (1963).

In other words, for the direct wave, the expression (2.2.24) is equal to zero. What this means is that in the Earth the P_g wave (direct wave through the upper crust) should appear on the reduced time–distance graph as a straight line passing through the zero point as shown in Figure 2.2.9.

2.3 Seismic refraction study: an example

In 1966, Bott, Holder, Long and Lucas carried out a seismic refraction investigation in southwest England. Beneath the region which includes the line AA′ in Figure 2.3.1 (a) lies a composite granite batholith* which is known from evidence other than seismic to extend to a depth of 10–11 km. But given this information, what is the overall structure and thickness of the continental crust beneath this area?

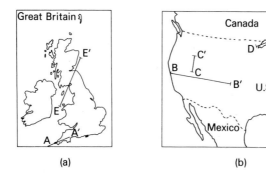

(a)   (b)

Figure 2.3.1   Maps of (a) Britain, and (b) North America, showing the locations of seismic profiles discussed in the text.

To answer this question, Bott and his colleagues set up several seismic recording stations along the line AA′ and also on the Scilly Isles. Twenty 300 pound depth charges were then exploded from a ship at about 10 km intervals along a line running roughly southwestwards from Land's End. The seismic recordings from one of the stations for shots numbered 6–20 are shown in Figure 2.3.2 where they are stacked together in such a way as to produce a reduced time–distance graph directly. This graph clearly shows that the first arrivals (that is, the first seismic signals to appear from the left hand edge of the diagram) lie along two straight line segments. At short source-detector distances (top edge of diagram) the first wave to arrive at the station is P_g, the direct upper crustal wave; but at about 120 km the first arrival becomes

P_n, the head wave refracted at the Moho. Gradient calculations show the velocity of P_g to be $5.77 \, \text{km s}^{-1}$ and that of P_n to be $7.93 \, \text{km s}^{-1}$. Assuming a two-layer model (crust and mantle) with uniform velocity in the upper layer, the crustal thickness then works out as 23 km with a horizontal Moho.

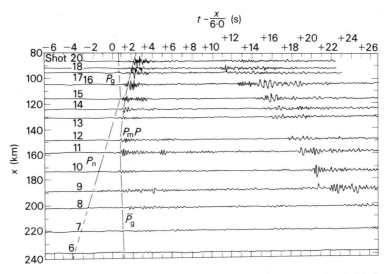

Figure 2.3.2 The reduced time–distance graph produced by arranging in suitable form the seismic recordings from a station on Bodmin Moor. P_g is the direct wave travelling through the upper crust; P_n is the refracted head wave from the Moho; P_mP is the super-critical reflection from the Moho; and $\bar{P}_g$ is a channel wave trapped in the upper crust by the velocity increase below (see section 2.4). The high amplitude waves arriving much later than the P waves are S waves. *Source:* Bott, Holder, Long and Lucas (1970).

But is it reasonable to regard the crust in this region as a simple, uniform-velocity layer in practice? In other words, is it valid to interpret the seismic data from first arrivals in the simplest way possible and leave it at that? The evidence suggests not, for the granite is known to be 10–11 km thick whereas the whole crust is over 20 km thick. Presumably, then, the lower crust is of different material from the (granitic) upper crust and will, barring coincidence, have a different seismic velocity. This does not necessarily mean that the lower crust forms a distinct layer with an upper boundary such as the Conrad discontinuity; indeed, there is no evidence from the first-arrival time–distance curve for any such discontinuity. But on the other hand, there could be variations in velocity in the crust and so the question arises as to whether the seismic data may be used to infer such variations.

It is at this point that waves other than the first arrivals become important. The second arrival up to source-detector distances of 160 km (see Figure 2.3.2) is interpreted as the supercritical reflection from the Moho (P_mP). This reflection may also be used to calculate the crustal velocity. A way in which this may be done is described in Appendix One. Here, however, it is pertinent to note that whereas P_g travels through the upper crust, P_mP travels down to the Moho and back; that is, it travels through the whole crust. The velocity of P_mP, if it can be determined, is thus more representative of the overall crust than is the velocity of P_g. In this case, the average crustal velocity calculated from the behaviour of P_mP turns out to be 6.15 km s^{-1}, which is significantly higher than the velocity of P_g. This suggests that the velocity in the crust beneath southwest England must increase with depth. Moreover, a more accurate knowledge of the average crustal velocity enables a more accurate crustal thickness to be calculated—in this case, 27 km. The interpretation by Bott and his colleagues of crustal structure in southwest England is shown in Figure 2.3.3.

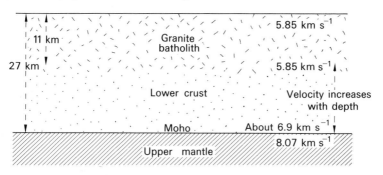

Figure 2.3.3 Interpretation of the crustal structure and thickness beneath the granite batholith of southwest England, based on seismic data (except for the depth of the granite). *Source:* Bott, Holder, Long and Lucas (1970).

2.4 The thickness and structure of the continental crust

Crustal thickness

The Moho, which marks the base of the crust, is usually a fairly well defined velocity discontinuity which is now thought to be present beneath most parts of the continents and oceans, although the fact is that there are large areas where this supposition has not been rigorously tested. Beneath the continents the depth to the Moho is usually in the range 20–50 km although beneath mountain ranges crustal thicknesses may reach 70–80 km. The average thickness of the continental crust is about 35 km, which compares to 5–7 km for ocean basins.

Very often, crustal thickness beneath continents correlates well with structural regions. One of the areas where such correlations have been investigated particularly closely is the western United States. Figure 2.4.1 shows, for example, how the depth to the Moho varies along the line BB′ in Figure 2.3.1 (b). In numerical terms, the average crustal thickness for the various geological provinces are:

Californian Coast Range	25 km
Californian Central Valley	20 km
Sierra Nevada	>40 km
Basin and Range	25–30 km
Colorado Plateau	40 km
Rocky Mountains	>60 km
Great Plains	45–50 km

In other words, each geological province in the western United States appears to have its own characteristic crustal thickness with local

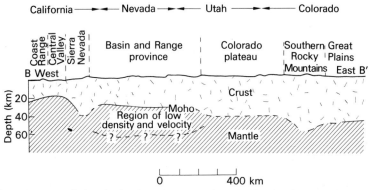

Figure 2.4.1 Variations in depth to the Moho along the line BB′ in Figure 2.3.1 (b), which runs from San Francisco, California to Lamar, Colorado. Crustal thickness correlates quite well with different structure (geological provinces). *Source:* Pakiser (1963).

increases in the depth to the Moho beneath the mountain ranges. We shall see later in this chapter that these correlations are far from arbitrary.

Crustal velocities

Seismic refraction studies usually indicate the velocity (u_g) of direct (P_g) waves in the upper crust to be in the range of 5.9–6.2 km s^{-1}, values which are significantly higher than the 5.6 km s^{-1} obtained from earthquake studies (see, for example, Mohorovičić's determination in section 2.1). But why should this be so? After all, as we have already noted, within a given medium P waves have a definite velocity irrespective of how they were produced in the first place. However, there are several possible explanations for this discrepancy:

(i)   When earthquake waves are used to determine crustal structure, the time and focus of the relevant earthquake must be determined and will thus be subject to some error. Explosions, by contrast, may be initiated at exactly known times and locations. The effect of these differences is well illustrated by an experiment carried out in the 1930s using quarry blasts in California. When blasts at known times were used, the values of u_g obtained were found to lie in the range 5.9–6.2 km s^{-1}; but experiments involving blasts for which the times had to be estimated yielded a u_g value of only 5.5 km s^{-1}.

(ii) An investigator who wishes to make use of earthquakes is limited to areas where earthquakes occur, chiefly the active seismic belts shown in Figure 1.5.1. But in such regions crustal structure may be quite untypical of the Earth in general.

(iii) There may be a comparatively low velocity layer in the Earth's crust which 'traps' earthquake waves by multiple reflection as shown in Figure 2.4.2, especially if the earthquake takes place

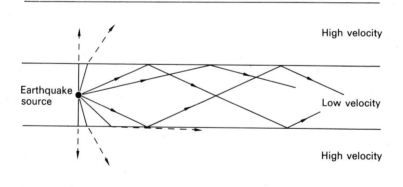

Figure 2.4.2   The trapping of seismic waves within a low velocity layer by multiple reflection. Waves which strike the inner boundaries at angles greater than the critical angle are not refracted out of, but reflected back into, the low velocity layer.

within the low velocity layer itself. Explosions, on the other hand, are generally initiated near the Earth's surface where their waves are free to travel entirely in the higher velocity region above the supposed lower velocity layer.

The most favoured explanations for the discrepancy between the velocities of earthquake-induced and explosion-induced P_g waves are (i) and (ii) although some seismologists are of the view that a low velocity in the crust does exist, at least in some regions, between depths of about 6 km and 10 km. However, the idea of such a low velocity layer is not yet widely accepted. Nor is the idea of the Conrad discontinuity—a distinct boundary marking the division between an upper and lower crust—widely accepted. The possible existence of such a discontinuity has been an issue ever since Conrad first recognized the arrival of P^* and S^* waves in addition to P_g and S_g and P_n and S_n waves (see section 2.1). The problem is that P^* rarely ever occurs as a first arrival but, as a later arrival, tends to be obscured by supercritical reflections which have much larger amplitudes and which arrive at similar times. Indeed, it seems likely that in some studies, waves interpreted as P^* were in reality P_mP—supercritical reflections from the Moho.

An example of such a possible misinterpretation is a study of crustal structure carried out in the Transvaal during the 1950s using earth tremors in the Johannesburg area. Some of the records obtained in this investigation are shown in Figure 2.4.3. In each case, the first

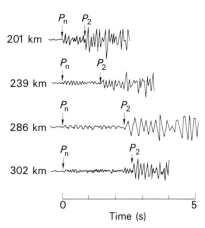

Figure 2.4.3 Seismic records of Earth tremors near Johannesburg. The lengths recorded on the left represent the distances from Johannesburg at which the seismic traces were observed. In each case the first arrival is P_n. The second arrivals, P_2, originally thought to be P^*, are probably P_mP. The traces have been re-aligned in the diagram so that the P_n arrivals lie along the same vertical line at $t = 0$; but this does not imply that the first arrivals reached each station at the same time. *Source:* Hales and Sacks (1959).

arrival shown is P_n. The second arrivals, P_2, which gave seismic velocities in the range 6.7–7.2 km s^{-1}, were originally interpreted as P^* waves refracted at the Conrad discontinuity at a depth of 25 km (compared to a depth to the Moho of 37 km). But the fact that the amplitudes of the second arrivals are large suggests that they are not P^* but P_mP. If this be the case, the evidence for the Conrad discontinuity in this region disappears. Following Conrad's discovery, many seismologists claimed to recognize P^*—so much so that as recently as the 1950s the Conrad discontinuity was widely regarded as being universally present throughout the crust. Nowadays, however, with a better understanding of the role of supercritical reflections, much of the evidence for the Conrad discontinuity is discounted. There appears to be a general increase in seismic velocity with depth within the crust; but evidence for discrete layering is not universal.

Examples of crustal structure

Some of the most detailed seismic work has been carried out in the United States where it is now clear that crustal layering is present in some areas but not in others. Figure 2.4.4 shows, for example, the

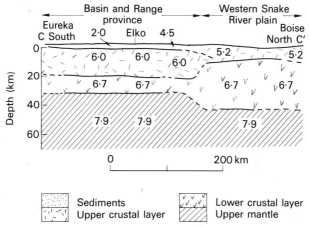

Figure 2.4.4   Crustal structure along the line CC′ in Figure 2.3.1 (b). Seismic velocities are in km s⁻¹. *Source:* Hill and Pakiser (1966).

structure determined from seismic refraction along the line CC′ in Figure 2.3.1 (b). Here, apart from a thin surface layer, there are two well defined crustal layers, the lower of which has the higher velocity. Beneath the Snake River Plain of eastern Colorado and New Mexico (the C′ end) the lower crustal layer is about 20 km thick; and its upper boundary gives rise to refracted head waves which appear as first arrivals. This is often the case where the lower layer is relatively thick and where the velocity contrast with the upper layer is relatively large. In the Basin and Range province, however, the upper boundary of the thin layer gives no first arrivals. This lower layer was actually detected by the wave *reflected* at its upper boundary (P_1P). Note also that in the upper layer the velocity varies laterally, the change taking place at the structural boundary.

   Figure 2.4.5 shows the crustal structure beneath line DD′ of Figure 2.3.1 (b), which lies across the Lake Superior region. Here an upper

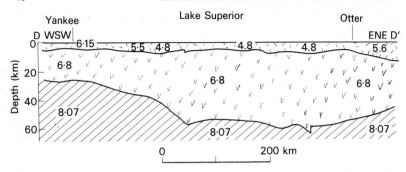

Figure 2.4.5 Crustal structure along the line DD′ in Figure 2.3.1 (b) with seismic velocities in km s^{-1}. The shading key is the same as for Figure 2.4.4. *Source:* Smith, Steinhart and Aldrich (1966).

layer of sediment and volcanic rocks about 5–10 km thick overlies a very thick lower layer, the thickness of which varies considerably between 25 and 60 km from place to place. An example of British crustal structure is shown in Figure 2.4.6 which corresponds to the line EE′

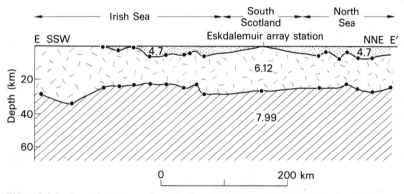

Figure 2.4.6 Crustal structure along the line EE′ in Figure 2.3.1 (a). Seismic velocities are in km s^{-1}; and the shading key is the same as for Figure 2.4.4. *Source:* Agger and Carpenter (1964).

in Figure 2.3.1 (a). Here apart from a thin veneer of sediment, the crust comprises a single layer about 20–30 km thick.

These are but a few examples of continental structure based on seismic refraction studies. We shall return to other cases later; but in the meantime it is necessary to consider another geophysical tool which may be used in conjunction with seismic surveys to aid structural determination—gravity observations.

2.5 The Earth's gravity

The basis of all gravitational studies is Newton's Law of gravitation which states that the force (F) between two point masses (m_1 and m_2) separated by a distance (r) is given by:

$$F = \frac{Gm_1m_2}{r^2} \quad \text{newtons} \tag{2.5.1}$$

G is a universal gravitational constant equal to 6.67×10^{-11} N m^2 kg^{-2}. The attraction which is exerted by the Earth (mass, M) on an outside mass (m) is a special case of Newton's Law. In this situation the outside mass will, as long as it is not constrained, fall vertically downwards with an acceleration (denoted by g) which is roughly equal to 9.8 m s^{-2}. However, the acceleration due to gravity is not precisely the same at all points on the Earth's surface; there are small variations resulting from variations in the Earth's shape and from inhomogeneities in the Earth's density. Geophysical interest in gravity centres particularly on the measurement and interpretation of these small variations of g in terms of the Earth's shape and structure.

The force on a mass (m) falling towards the Earth under the influence only of gravity may also be written:

$$F = \text{mass} \times \text{acceleration} = mg \tag{2.5.2}$$

and so combining this with equation (2.5.1) for the Earth:

$$F = mg = \frac{GmM}{r^2} \tag{2.5.3}$$

where r is the distance to the Earth's centre. So from (2.5.2) and (2.5.3):

$$g = \frac{GM}{r^2} \tag{2.5.4}$$

and so at points on the Earth's surface:

$$g = \frac{GM}{R^2} \tag{2.5.5}$$

where R is the Earth's radius.

The general relationship between gravity and the Earth's average density (ρ) is easily deduced. For the Earth (assumed here to be spherical):

$$\rho = \frac{\text{mass}}{\text{volume}} = \frac{M}{\frac{4}{3}\pi R^3} = \frac{3M}{4\pi R^3} \tag{2.5.6}$$

and from equation (2.5.5):

$$M = \frac{gR^2}{G}$$

Thus: $\quad \rho = \dfrac{3gR^2}{G4\pi R^3} = \dfrac{3g}{4\pi RG}$ \hfill (2.5.7)

What this equation shows is that if g, R and G are known or measured, the Earth's average density (ρ) may be calculated. Using modern measurements, ρ turns out to be 5.52×10^3 kg m^{-3}. The fact that this value is much greater than the densities of surface rocks (2.5–3.0×10^3 kg m^{-3}) indicates that the Earth's density must increase towards the centre.

The geophysicist who is interested in using the Earth's gravity to say something about the Earth's shape and/or structure, on the other hand, makes use of equation (2.5.7) but in re-arranged form. Thus from equation (2.5.7):

$$g = \frac{4\pi\rho RG}{3} \hspace{3cm} (2.5.8)$$

What this equation says is that g depends on two variables, R and ρ. If the Earth were perfectly spherical (R = constant) and perfectly uniform (ρ = constant), g would have the same value everywhere on the Earth's surface. (In fact, it is not strictly necessary for ρ to be constant throughout the Earth. All that is required for g to be constant over the surface of an Earth of constant radius is that if ρ varies within the Earth it should vary in the same way along every radius.) However, if at some point the Earth departs from sphericity slightly, the value of g at that point will depart from the mean value. And again, if there is a local anomaly in density at a point, g will vary. In principle, therefore, it should be possible to use measured variations in g at the Earth's surface to deduce variations of R and ρ; that is, to deduce variations in the distance from the point of measurement to the Earth's centre, and lateral variations in density beneath the Earth's surface.

The effect of shape

In reality, the Earth is not spherical at all; its shape is very close to that of an ellipsoid of revolution. In simple terms, this means that there is a 'flattening' at the poles. This flattening may be described in terms of the quantity f which is defined as:

$$f = \frac{\text{equatorial radius} - \text{polar radius}}{\text{equatorial radius}} = \frac{1}{297} \hspace{1.5cm} (2.5.9)$$

Because of this flattening—that is, because the Earth's radius is not everywhere constant—g will vary with latitude. According to the

International Gravity Formula (IGF) adopted by the International Union of Geodesy and Geophysics, the value of g *at sea level* varies with latitude (λ) as follows:

$$g = 9.780\,49\,(1 + 0.005\,288\,4\,\sin^2\lambda - 0.000\,005\,9\,\sin^2 2\lambda)\ \text{m s}^{-2}$$

$$(2.5.10)$$

In this formula λ is measured in radians (rad), where π radians $= 180°$. The sea-level surface over which the IGF applies corresponds to mean sea level over the oceans and the equivalent level beneath the continents.

In the IGF, the value of $9.780\,49$ m s^{-2} is the value of g at the equator ($\lambda = 0$). As λ increases towards the poles, g will increase because the distance from a point on the Earth's sea-level surface to the Earth's centre decreases. Thus at the poles, $\lambda = \pi/2$ radians ($90°$), $\sin^2\lambda = 1$ and $\sin^2 2\lambda = 0$, so that:

$$g = 9.780\,49 \times 1.005\,288\,4\ \text{m s}^{-2}$$

$$(2.5.11)$$

(*Note:* Although the IGF was accepted as correct until quite recently, it has now become clear that it really requires revision. The formula was constructed using a standard value of $g = 9.812\,74$ measured at Potsdam in 1906 and a value of $f = 1/297$. A more accurate value of g at Potsdam is now available and satellite measurements have shown that $f = 1/298.25$. For the time being, however, equation (2.5.10) is still regarded as the international standard formula.)

The effect of inhomogeneities

If there were no lateral variations of density in the Earth, g would vary smoothly from equator to poles in accordance with the IGF (bearing in mind that the IGF applies over the sea-level surface). In practice, however, large-scale inhomogeneities in the Earth produce departures of the measured values of g at sea level from the values predicted from the IGF. Indeed, the fact that the value of g certainly does not vary smoothly from the equator to the poles may be regarded as evidence for lateral inhomogeneities within the Earth.

There is another way of looking at this effect. If there were no lateral variations of density in the Earth, the sea-level surface over which gravity is given by the IGF would be the smooth surface of the 'flattened' sphere described in the previous subsection. In practice, however, because of inhomogeneities, the actual surface over which gravity is given by the IGF is irregular—it undulates. This surface is known as the *geoid*. The geoid may be constructed either from surface measurements of g or from satellite observations. A version of the geoid based on the latter is shown in Figure 2.5.1, from which it may be seen that the undulations are up to tens of metres high (deep).

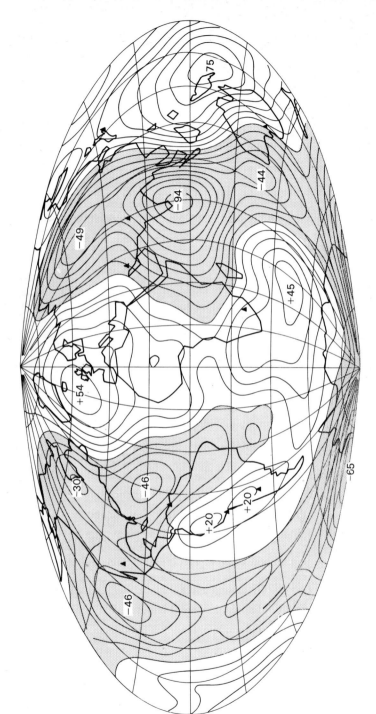

Figure 2.5.1 The geoid constructed from satellite observations of gravity. The units used on the contours are metres. Contours are at 10 m intervals. *Source*: Gaposchkin (1966).

2.6 Gravity anomalies

The geophysicist who wishes to use gravity as a tool in structural determination is less interested in absolute values of g than in relative values. What he wants to be able to do is to define inhomogeneities and density contrasts in that part of the Earth he is investigating; that is, to describe features which in some way depart from uniformity. The important thing is thus the *difference* between the effect on the gravity of the particular feature and the effect if no such feature were present. In short, he is interested only in *gravity anomalies*. In principle, he thus *measures g* at an appropriate point in the area of investigation and again at a point of reference away from the area but *calculates and interprets* the Δg value—the difference between the gravity at the site and the gravity at the reference point. Because such gravity anomalies are usually very small the unit $m\,s^{-2}$ is inconveniently large. Gravity anomalies are thus measured in *gravity units* (g.u.) where:

$$1 \text{ gravity unit (g.u.)} = 10^{-6}\,m\,s^{-2}$$

Since $g \sim 10\,m\,s^{-2}$, the gravity unit is about one ten-millionth of the absolute value of gravity at the Earth's surface.

Unfortunately, the gravity difference between two points (such as a site and a reference point) depends on many factors other than the presence of density variations. Once the geophysicist has obtained his value of Δg he thus needs to 'correct' it to eliminate these other effects before he can use it to say something about the physical state of the crust in his particular area of investigation. The principal corrections required, and the reasons for them, are as follows:

(a) *Latitude*: We have already mentioned that gravity varies with latitude (increases with higher latitude) because of the Earth's shape. It follows, therefore, that even if the Earth were perfectly uniform structurally (that is, even if there were no lateral variations in density), there would be a finite value of Δg between the site (S) and the reference point (P) if site and reference point were to differ in latitude. This latitude effect must therefore be removed from the measured value of gravity difference (Δg) before any interpretation may be made in terms of density variations.

Accepting that the variation of g with latitude is given by the IGF, it follows from equation (2.5.10) (actually by differentiation) that if S and P differ in latitude by $\Delta\lambda$, the difference in gravity, $\Delta_1 g$, introduced into the measured difference in gravity, Δg, by the latitude effect is:

$$\Delta_1 g = (517\,23 \sin 2\lambda)\Delta\lambda \quad \text{g.u. per radian} \qquad (2.6.1)$$

If $\Delta\lambda$ is small, $\Delta_1 g$ may be written in terms of the north–south distance between S and P as:

$$\Delta_1 g = 0.81 \sin 2\lambda \quad \text{g.u. per 100 m} \tag{2.6.2}$$

If S is at a higher latitude than P (that is, where, because of the latitude effect, g is greater), $\Delta_1 g$ must be subtracted from Δg. Conversely, if S is at a lower latitude than P, $\Delta_1 g$ must be added. If the north–south distance between S and P is known to within 10 m, the error in $\Delta_1 g$ will be less than 0.1 g.u.

(b) *Elevation:* Equation (2.5.4) shows that g varies with distance (r) from the Earth's centre according to $1/r^2$. It thus follows that g will decrease with increasing height above the Earth's surface and thus if S and P are not at the same elevation this will have an effect on Δg.

Let us suppose that S is at a height h above P. Then if P is at distance r from the Earth's centre, S will be distance $(r+h)$ from the Earth's centre.

If g_p is the value of gravity at P, then, from equation (2.5.4):

$$g_p = \frac{GM}{r^2} \tag{2.6.3}$$

If g_s is the value of gravity at S, then, from the same equation:

$$g_s = \frac{GM}{(r+h)^2} \tag{2.6.4}$$

Then dividing equation (2.6.4) by equation (2.6.3):

$$\frac{g_s}{g_p} = \frac{r^2}{(r+h)^2} \tag{2.6.5}$$

If h is small, it is mathematically permissible to write this as:

$$g_s = g_p\left(1 - \frac{2h}{r}\right) = g_p - \frac{2hg_p}{r} \tag{2.6.6}$$

Then the difference in gravity, $\Delta_2 g$, between S and P due to the elevation effect is:

$$\Delta_2 g = g_p - g_s = \frac{2hg_p}{r} \tag{2.6.7}$$

In most practical cases, r may be taken as the mean radius of the Earth ($R = 6367$ km), in which case equation (2.6.7) becomes:

$$\Delta_2 g = 3.086\, h \quad \text{g.u.} \tag{2.6.8}$$

where h is measured in metres. If S lies above P, h is positive, $\Delta_2 g$ is positive and must therefore be added to Δg. Conversely, if S lies below P (h negative), $\Delta_2 g$ must be subtracted. If $\Delta_2 g$ is to be known to within 0.1 g.u., the elevation difference (h) between S and P must be known to within 4 cm.

(c) *Material between S and P:* The correction for elevation, $\Delta_2 g$, is known as the *free air correction* because in calculating it, it was assumed that the only material between S and P was air. In practice, of course, the main reason for there being an elevation difference between S and P in the first place is usually one of topography. Measurements of g are usually made on the Earth's surface and if, in the region under investigation, the Earth's surface were flat, h would be zero, and there would be no benefit in making it otherwise. If, on the other hand, the topography were not flat, an elevation difference between S and P might be inevitable. By the same token, there would be crustal material between the levels of S and P which would effect the measured value of Δg.

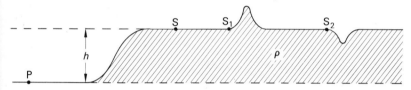

Figure 2.6.1 Diagram to illustrate the 'corrections' which must be made to the observed gravity anomaly when the site (S) differs in elevation from the 'reference point' (P). Additional correction is required if the site lies near a hill (S_1) or a valley (S_2).

Such a situation is shown in Figure 2.6.1. Here, both S and P lie on the Earth's surface but because of topography, S lies at height h above P. The gravity at S will be less than that at P by an amount $\Delta_2 g$ (free air correction) because S is further from the Earth's centre than P. At the same time, however, the gravity at S will be greater than that at P by an amount $\Delta_3 g$ because of the additional attraction exerted by the material of density ρ (shaded in the diagram) which lies between the levels of S and P. It may be shown that:

$$\Delta_3 g = 2\pi G \rho h$$
$$= 41.91 \times 10^{-5}\, \rho h \text{ g.u.} \qquad (2.6.9)$$

where h is in metres and ρ is in kg m^{-3}. $\Delta_3 g$ must be subtracted from Δg if S is above P and added if S is below P.

$\Delta_3 g$ is known as the *Bouguer correction*; and it is clear that unlike for the free air correction, the density ρ must either be known or assumed. For a typical crustal rock for which ρ is, say, 2.67×10^3 kg m^{-3} and if S lies 1 metre above P, we have:

from equation (2.6.9) $\qquad \Delta_3 g = 1.118$ g.u.

and from equation (2.6.8) $\qquad \Delta_2 g = 3.086$ g.u.

In other words, the Bouguer correction is typically smaller than the free air correction. Thus even though the Bouguer and free air corrections are opposite in sign, gravity measured on the Earth's surface will generally still decrease with height—in the case given above, by 1.968 g.u.

(d) *Topography:* Gravity at a site such as S_1 in Figure 2.6.1 will be lower than at S because the hill adjacent to S_1 will exert an attraction whose net effect will be upwards. Similarly, gravity at S_2 will also be lower than at S because the valley has removed an attracting mass from below the level of S_2. The principles involved here are further illustrated in Figure 2.6.2.

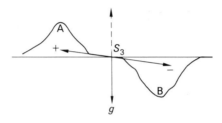

Figure 2.6.2 The effect of topography on the gravity at a point (S_3). The hill (A) exerts an additional attraction in the direction of the + arrow. The net attraction is thus upwards at S_3 and the value of g at S_3 is thus reduced. The valley (B) has removed an attracting mass and thus exerts a 'negative' attraction in the direction of the—arrow or a positive attraction in the opposite direction. The net effect at the valley is thus also an upward attraction at S_3 and the value of g is again reduced. To eliminate the effects of topography the necessary correction must therefore always be additive, to increase g to what it would have been had the topography been flat. *Source:* Garland (1965).

What all this means is that a gravity measurement must be corrected for the effects of hills and valleys in the vicinity of the site; that is, for the effects of topography. This correction is calculated by dividing the area around the site into segments as shown in Figure 2.6.3. The mean elevation within each segment is then estimated, neglecting the sign of the elevation because the correction is always additive. (In other words, any variation in topography lowers the gravity and so the correction for topography must always be added to Δg.) The effect on the gravity from each segment's topography is then read from specially constructed standard tables. The topographic correction, $\Delta_4 g$, which must be added to Δg is then obtained by summing the corrections from the individual segments.

Once the latitude, free air, Bouguer and topography corrections have been determined, it is possible to calculate a 'corrected' value for the gravity difference between S and P—a value which, hopefully, has eliminated all effects except that of density variations below the surface of the region under investigation. In general, this will be given by:

$$\text{corrected value} = \Delta g \pm \Delta_1 g \pm \Delta_2 g \pm \Delta_3 g + \Delta_4 g \qquad (2.6.10)$$

Where in each case the $+$ or $-$ sign is chosen according to the relevant criterion under (a), (b) or (c) above.

At the beginning of this section we said that, *in principle*, the geophysicist measures g at P and S but then calculates and interprets Δg (or the corrected value of Δg as we have defined it) and this may be so in practice, especially in local studies. In geophysical investigations of larger-scale Earth structure, however, it is often convenient to interpret

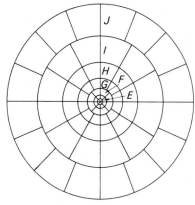

Figure 2.6.3 Application of the topography correction. *Source:* Hammer (1939).

the reference point, P, as a theoretical point, Q, corresponding to S, at which the value of g is that given by the IGF. This sounds complicated; but all it means is that Q is a point at the same latitude as S, at mean sea level, and on an Earth in which there are no lateral variations in density. Clearly there is no such point on the real Earth at which g could be measured; but this does not matter because the value of g such a point would have is easily calculated from the IGF.

To put this in another way, we may define a gravity anomaly as *the difference between the measured value of gravity at some point and the theoretical value of gravity at the same point predicted by the IGF, after corrections have been applied for factors other than density variation in the Earth.* The steps involved in the determination of such a gravity anomaly are thus:

(i) g is measured at the site in question (call this value g_S);
(ii) the theoretical value of g given by the IGF for a site at the same latitude (and at sea level, because the IGF applies to sea level) is calculated (call this g_0);

(iii) the gravity difference is then calculated (this is $\Delta g = g_S - g_0$);
(iv) the free air, Bouguer and topography corrections are then applied to Δg to give a 'corrected' value which we shall here call $\Delta_B g$ (note that the latitude correction is not necessary because g_0 applies to the same latitude as g_S).

The final value to emerge, $\Delta_B g$, may then be regarded as the gravity difference (anomaly) attributable solely to density variations below the sea-level surface at the site. Thus from equation (2.6.10):

$$\Delta_B g = \Delta g \pm \Delta_1 g \pm \Delta_2 g \pm \Delta_3 g + \Delta_4 g$$

except that $\Delta_1 g = 0$ for the reason given under (iv) above. Thus:

$$\Delta_B g = \Delta g + 3.086h - 41.91 \times 10^{-5} \rho h + \Delta_4 g \qquad (2.6.11)$$

where h is the height of the site in metres above or below sea level (positive if above, negative if below), ρ is the density of the material within the height h in kg m^{-3}, and $\Delta_B g$ is measured in g.u.

$\Delta_B g$ is known as the *Bouguer anomaly* and should not be confused with the Bouguer correction which is just one of the several corrections to Δg required to give the Bouguer anomaly. On the other hand, it is sometimes useful to consider the *free air anomaly* which is, as in this case its name implies, the value of Δg corrected only by the free air correction. The free air anomaly, $\Delta_F g$, is thus given by:

$$\Delta_F g = \Delta g + 3.086h \qquad (2.6.12)$$

Choice of anomaly

Gravity anomalies are used for several different geophysical purposes; and which type of anomaly to use in any given situation depends on the particular purpose. Moreover, the choice of anomaly often depends on other, more complex factors than those we have considered so far. In general, however, if we wish to investigate density variations below the sea-level surface beneath *continents*, the Bouguer anomaly is the best one to use because, by definition, this anomaly reflects only density variations below the sea-level surface.

For measurements made at the ocean surface, the free air anomaly represents the density variations below sea level. Unfortunately, this is not the information we require. What we wish to know is not what the density variations below sea level are but what the density variations below the surface of the sea bed are; in other words, we wish to investigate the oceanic crust. The free air anomaly over the oceans must therefore be corrected additionally to eliminate the effects of sea water and the topographic features on the ocean floor. Once this is done we are again able to interpret the resultant anomaly in terms of density variations in the (oceanic) crust.

As an example, the profile of the Bouguer anomaly across the Alps is shown in Figure 2.6.4. There is no doubt that the anomaly profile generally correlates with the mountain topography—the higher the topography the more negative is the Bouguer anomaly. However, it is important to remember here that *the large negative Bouguer anomaly has nothing directly to do with the mountains rising above sea level.*

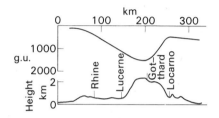

Figure 2.6.4 Profile of the Bouguer anomaly across the Alps. *Source:* Garland (1965).

This is because the Bouguer anomaly is, by definition, the anomaly remaining after all effects above the sea-level surface have been eliminated. Thus the Bouguer anomaly in Figure 2.6.4, notwithstanding its apparent correlation with topography, can only indicate something about the structure *below* sea level.

2.7 Isostasy

As we saw in section 2.5, the principle involved in the interpretation of gravity anomalies is embodied in equation (2.5.8):

$$g = \frac{4\pi R G \rho}{3} \tag{2.5.8}$$

Thus if g is measured at a point on the Earth's surface below which ρ is anomalously low, g will be anomalously low; and if g is measured at a point below which ρ is anomalously high, g will be anomalously high. This correlation may also be described in terms of mass rather than density. Volume for volume, a region of lower density will possess less mass; and conversely, a region of higher density will possess more mass. Thus an anomalously low value of g at a point implies that below that point there is a *mass deficiency*; and an anomalously high value of g implies a *mass excess*. This conclusion could also have been reached more directly from equation (2.5.5):

$$g = \frac{GM}{R^2} \tag{2.5.5}$$

where M is the mass of the Earth. If there is a local mass deficiency below the point at which g is measured, M will be effectively reduced as viewed from that point, and g will be reduced. Conversely, for a mass excess, g will be locally increased.

The basic factor in the interpretation of gravity anomalies is thus that *a negative anomaly indicates a region of mass deficiency/lower density and a positive anomaly indicates a region of mass excess/high density*. We may now apply this conclusion to the Bouguer anomaly shown in Figure 2.6.4, remembering that the explanation for this anomaly must lie in the material below sea level. Thus the large negative Bouguer anomaly across the Alps (and across mountains in general) must indicate a mass deficiency/lower density region beneath the Alps and below sea level.

This is actually an example of the *principle of isostasy*. The first observations which led to the discovery of this principle were not gravity measurements as such but determinations of the vertical. Between 1735 and 1745 Bouguer led an expedition to Peru, one of the aims of which was to measure an arc of meridian. Bouguer and his colleagues realized that the Andes would produce a horizontal attraction on their plumbline and thus cause a local deviation from the true vertical; but later analysis of their data showed that the observed deviation was much smaller than that to be expected on the basis of the Andes' topography and density. Much later, when it had become clear that other mountain ranges (for example, the Himalayas) behaved similarly, it became necessary to postulate a mass deficiency beneath these ranges roughly equal to the mass above sea level represented by the mountains themselves. In other words, when it had become clear that mountain ranges were not exerting the attraction they were obviously capable of, the only conclusion that could be drawn was that the mass of the ranges above sea level must be compensated by an almost equal mass deficiency below sea level, thus producing a *net* attraction which is very small.

In 1889 Dutton coined the term 'isostasy' to describe this compensation phenomenon. The principle is that there exists in the Earth a certain *level of compensation* above which all columns of material having unit cross-sectional area must have the same mass. Thus if there is apparently an excess mass at the Earth's surface (a mountain range, for example) this must be compensated by a mass deficiency below the surface feature but above the level of compensation. However, this assumes that equilibrium has been reached. There may be (and are) cases where isostasy does not strictly apply because once a system has been disturbed it may take some considerable time before isostatic equilibrium is restored; but this does not contradict the basic principle. Thus when, during the last Ice Age, Scandinavia was loaded with ice, the 'excess' mass of ice caused the region to sink. When the ice retreated, Scandinavia began to rise again and is still rising today —that is, it has not yet returned to isostatic equilibrium.

This is a useful example to consider further. When the mass of ice appeared on Scandinavia it broke the isostatic equilibrium because the total mass above the level of compensation increased with respect to non-glaciated areas. In order to restore the equilibrium, Scandinavia sank, the implication here being that material must somehow have flowed out laterally beneath the region in order to ensure that the mass above the level of compensation did not stay in excess. By the same token, of course, as Scandinavia is now rising, material must be flowing in beneath it. This lateral movement of material implies that at some depth within the Earth there must be fluid or plastic flow, presumably at, or just below, the level of compensation. Nowadays, this necessary fluid or plastic layer is often identified with the asthenosphere—the same asthenosphere which has proved so useful in accounting for the mechanism of continental drift and sea floor spreading. In fact, the term asthenosphere was actually introduced over fifty years ago to explain isostatic adjustment and was later taken over by the new global tectonics.

Having postulated the principle of isostasy, it remains to determine just *how* the Earth's surface features are compensated at depth. In other words, what is the mass distribution at depth which is consistent with isostatic equilibrium? There are, in fact, two rival theories involved here, both of which date from over 120 years ago:

Pratt's Hypothesis: Pratt suggested that the level of compensation lies at a constant depth around the Earth (see Figure 2.7.1) and that the material above the level of compensation adjusts to isostatic equilibrium by lateral variations in density. In other words, the density varies laterally depending on the elevation of the overlying topography— thus mountains are underlain by material of anomalously low density which extends down to the level of compensation and ocean basins, by contrast, are underlain by relatively high density material. The principle of isostasy then requires that the mass of a column of material of unit cross-sectional area above the level of compensation must be the same irrespective of the column's position (continents or oceans). Thus for all columns, neglecting the Earth's curvature:

$$\text{mass} = \text{constant}$$
$$\therefore \text{ density} \times \text{volume} = \text{constant}$$
$$\therefore \text{ density} \times \text{area of base } (= 1) \times \text{height} = \text{constant}$$
$$\therefore \rho_c h + \rho_w d = \text{constant} \qquad (2.7.1)$$

where ρ_c = density of crust (which varies laterally) (see caption to
      Figure 2.7.1),
    h = thickness of crust (which varies only by the top),
   ρ_w = density of sea water (if any),
and d = depth of sea water (if any).

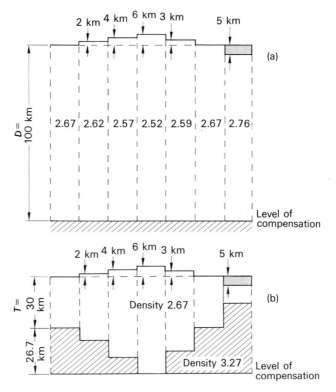

Figure 2.7.1 Isostatic compensation according to the hypotheses of (a) Pratt and (b) Airy. In (a) compensation takes place by a lateral adjustment in density, in (b) by adjustment of the crustal base. In modern terms, the level of compensation can probably be taken as the base of the lithosphere. Thus in (a) crust and lithosphere are identical whereas in (b) the lithosphere comprises both crust and part of the upper mantle. The numerical values in (a) have been chosen to be consistent with equation (2.7.1) and in (b) to be consistent with equation (2.7.2). Densities are in units of 10^3 kg m^{-3}. The 'normal crustal thickness' is defined as the thickness of the crust whose surface lies at sea level. This is denoted by D in (a) and T in (b). *Source:* Heiskanen and Vening Meinesz (1958).

Airy's Hypothesis: Airy suggested that although the level of compensation lies at a constant depth around the Earth (see Figure 2.7.1), the material above forms a lower density crust overlying a higher density substratum. The crust and substratum each have uniform (but different) density, although the boundary between them reflects the surface topography. In other words, isostatic equilibrium is reached by variations in the depth of the crust–substratum boundary rather than, as in Pratt's hypothesis, by lateral variations in crustal density. Thus mountains, for example, are underlain by thicker than normal crust forming a 'root' and oceans are underlain by thinner than normal crust. In this hypothesis, isostasy requires that for columns of unit cross-sectional area above the level of compensation:

$$\rho_c h + \rho_s \iota + \rho_w d = \text{constant} \tag{2.7.2}$$

where ρ_c = density of crust (which is constant),
　　　h = thickness of crust (which varies by the top and the bottom),
　　　ρ_s = density of substratum (which is constant),
　　　ι = thickness of substratum (which varies only by the top),
　　　ρ_w = density of sea water (if any),
and　　d = depth of sea water (if any).

It is clear from equations (2.7.1) and (2.7.2) that both the Airy and Pratt hypotheses are consistent with the principle of isostasy—but which, if either, applies to the real Earth? Moreover, how does one assess whether or not any given area is in isostatic equilibrium in the first place? In 'testing for isostasy' there are thus two different problems: (i) to test whether or not, and to what extent, isostatic equilibrium exists, and (ii) to test which hypothesis of isostatic compensation applies. Over the long term, of course, it may be taken that isostatic equilibrium is reached in most situations of fairly wide areal extent; but as we have seen from the Scandinavian example, the achievement of equilibrium may require considerable time.

In early investigations of isostasy, the experimental approach was to measure deflections from the vertical (as Bouguer and his colleagues did in Peru) and compare the observations with values predicted from one hypothesis or another. At least during the present century, however, gravity observations have replaced plumbline measurements, largely because they can be made much more quickly. In testing for isostasy by gravity, it is convenient to define an *isostatic anomaly* from the gravity data, where:

isostatic anomaly =
Bouguer anomaly − predicted anomaly of root.   (2.7.3)

It is clear from this definition that isostatic anomalies are different in nature from the Bouguer and free air anomalies. The latter two are measured (though corrected) phenomena making no prior assumptions about structural variations in the Earth whereas isostatic anomalies contain an element of prediction. Thus the predicted anomaly of the root, and the corresponding isostatic anomaly, will be different depending upon whose hypothesis is used to make the calculation. In principle, therefore, it should be possible to use isostatic anomalies as defined above to decide between the Pratt and Airy hypotheses. In practice, although gravity measurements have been very successful in estimating the degree of isostatic equilibrium they have been much less successful in differentiating between conflicting hypotheses of compensation. This is partly because gravity anomalies lack sensitivity to the precise geometry of the bodies producing the anomalies.

Figure 2.7.2. illustrates the general principles involved in the use of gravity anomalies to investigate isostasy. Suppose we have a (schematic) mountain range with a surface topography as shown in the lower part of the Figure, and measured free air and Bouguer anomalies which appear as in the upper part of the Figure. The fact that the Bouguer

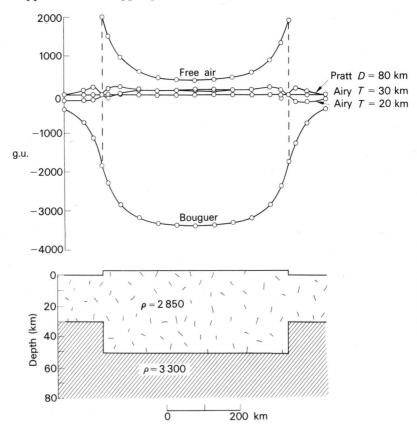

Figure 2.7.2 The Bouguer, free air and isostatic anomalies over a schematic mountain range. Isostatic equilibrium is perfect according to the Airy hypothesis with $T = 30$ km. *Source:* Bott (1971).

anomaly is large and negative shows that beneath the mountain range there is a large mass deficiency. This in itself implies that at least some isostatic compensation has taken place. But how much and according to whose hypothesis?

The next step is to calculate the gravitational effects of possible sub-surface structures according to both the Airy and Pratt hypotheses and corresponding to various values of normal crustal thickness (D and T, respectively, in Figure 2.7.1). The related isostatic anomalies may then be calculated by subtracting the predicted root anomalies from the Bouguer anomaly in accordance with equation (2.7.3). Three such anomalies are shown in the upper part of Figure 2.7.2—Airy's isostatic anomalies corresponding to $T = 20$ km and $T = 30$ km, and Pratt's isostatic anomaly corresponding to $D = 80$ km. These are 'reasonable' values of T and D. We shall discuss what 'reasonable' means in a moment; but for the time being it is clear that the three isostatic anomalies are quite small.

Now, a zero isostatic anomaly means perfect isostatic equilibrium. This follows from equation (2.7.3) as long as the predicted root anomaly has been calculated correctly. The Bouguer anomaly is, of course, the measured anomaly of the root; and so if the predicted anomaly of the root has been calculated correctly it should equal the Bouguer anomaly and thus give a zero isostatic anomaly if there is isostatic equilibrium. In Figure 2.7.2 all three isostatic anomalies calculated using 'reasonable' values of T and D are small; and so it is likely that the system is in near equilibrium. In fact, by taking $T = 30$ km for the Airy hypothesis, the isostatic anomaly is precisely zero, indicating perfect equilibrium. There is thus a strong presumption that (a) perfect isostatic equilibrium obtains, and (b) that Airy's hypothesis for $T = 30$ km is the most appropriate for describing the subsurface structure. The depth to the base of the crust which corresponds to $T = 30$ km is 50 km according to equation (2.7.2)—this was the depth used to predict the anomaly of the root in the first place and so the best subsurface structure is that drawn into Figure 2.7.2.

But it should not have escaped attention that in making this inter-pretation we have pulled what, on the face of it, is a fast one. We may be agreed that a zero isostatic anomaly indicates perfect isostatic equilibrium; but have we not fiddled the books by choosing the value of T which will give just the zero isostatic anomaly required? In short, quite apart from the fact that we have assumed the two values of density shown in Figure 2.7.2, we have chosen an arbitrary value of T which gives us perfect isostatic equilibrium. So in what sense have we tested that isostatic equilibrium actually obtains? Could we not, in any situation whatsoever, always get the appearance of perfect isostatic equilibrium by suitably 'choosing' an appropriate value of T (or perhaps D)?

This brings us back to the question of what is 'reasonable'. The values of T and D chosen to compute the isostatic anomalies were 'reasonable' in this case in the sense that they were roughly what would be expected from previous experience. This experience, in turn, is based on information other than that from gravity surveys—perhaps from seismic data, for example. For instance, in the case in Figure 2.7.2, had it been necessary to adopt a T value of, say, 300 km to produce a zero isostatic anomaly, it would have been quite clear that the system could not be in isostatic equilibrium. This is because we know from seismic data that the thickness of the Earth's crust is far less than 300 km; and so $T = 300$ km is 'unreasonable'.

This highlights a very important fact about gravity surveys *that structure cannot be determined uniquely from gravity alone*. For example, in spite of the strong presumption in favour of the 'root' structure shown in the case in Figure 2.7.2, there is no definite proof that the deduced structure is correct. All we can really say is that the deduced structure is *consistent* with the observed Bouguer anomaly. But for any observed gravity anomaly there is, in fact, an infinite number of different structures which are consistent with it. The particular interpretation of structure we choose must therefore be based on information other than that obtained from gravity itself.

The situation is thus this: Gravity observations have shown that most of the Earth's major surface features are in rough isostatic equilibrium but they cannot be used to deduce unambiguously what form the subsurface compensating structures take. Seismic refraction studies, on the other hand, enable structure and thickness, and thus the geometry of anomalous bodies, to be determined. Thus together, gravity and seismic refraction studies are a powerful tool for the investigation of the Earth.

2.8 The interpretation of gravity anomalies

In spite of the acknowledged fact that gravity anomalies cannot by themselves be interpreted uniquely in terms of structure, some progress in interpretation may be made by trial and error. The principle of the method involved here is that the measured anomaly is compared with anomalies calculated from simple forms; and the parameters of the simple structures are adjusted to give as close a correspondence as possible with the measured anomaly. However, even if the agreement is perfect the result must remain ambiguous in the absence of specific knowledge of density and at least a part of the shape.

The gravity anomalies produced by some simple bodies are shown in Figure 2.8.1. As an example, the anomaly produced by the sphere in (a) may be deduced as follows:

Consider a unit mass at any point such as A on the Earth's surface, where A is distance r from the centre of the sphere of radius R and density ρ. The sphere is embedded in crust of density ρ_0, and $\rho > \rho_0$.

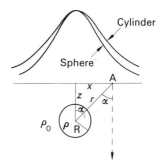

Figure 2.8.1(a) Computed gravity anomalies from a sphere and a horizontal cylinder.

Then the force of attraction on the unit mass by the sphere is given by equation (2.5.1), putting $m_1 = 1$ (because we are dealing with a unit mass) and putting $m_2 = V\rho$ for the sphere (mass = volume, V, multiplied by density, ρ). Thus:

$$F_1 = \frac{GV\rho}{r^2} \qquad (2.8.1)$$

However, if the sphere of density ρ were not there, crustal material of density ρ_0 would be present in its place; and, using the same method as before, the force of attraction at A due to this material would be:

$$F_2 = \frac{GV\rho_0}{r^2} \qquad (2.8.2)$$

Thus the *extra* force (the anomalous force) of attraction at A due to the presence of the sphere of anomalously high density will be:

$$F = F_1 - F_2 = \frac{GV\rho}{r^2} - \frac{GV\rho_0}{r^2} = \frac{GV}{r^2}(\rho - \rho_0) \qquad (2.8.3)$$

This force is directed along the line joining A to the centre of the sphere; but the gravity, or gravitational force, at A is the *vertical* (downwards) force exerted on unit mass at A. Thus the *extra* vertical force (the extra gravitational force, or gravity anomaly) caused by the presence of the anomalous sphere will be:

$$\Delta g = F \cos \alpha$$

where α is the angle shown in Figure 2.8.1 (a), and where, by trigonometry:

$$\cos \alpha = \frac{z}{r}$$

$$\therefore \Delta g = F \cos \alpha = \frac{GV}{r^2} (\rho - \rho_0) \frac{z}{r} = GV(\rho - \rho_0) \frac{z}{r^3} \qquad (2.8.4)$$

Also, by Pythagoras' theorem, $r^2 = x^2 + z^2$ (see Figure 2.8.1 (a)) and the volume of a sphere is given by $V = 4\pi R^3/3$. Thus:

$$\Delta g = \tfrac{4}{3}\pi R^3 G(\rho - \rho_0) \frac{z}{r^3} = 4\pi R^3 G(\rho - \rho_0) \frac{z}{(x^2 + z^2)^{\frac{3}{2}}} \qquad (2.8.5)$$

The shape of this anomaly is shown in Figure 2.8.1 (a). Its maximum value occurs at $x = 0$, this maximum value being:

$$\Delta_0 g = \tfrac{4}{3}\pi R^3 G(\rho - \rho_0) \frac{1}{z^2} \qquad (2.8.6)$$

If, on the other hand, the body in (a) is regarded not as a sphere but as an infinitely long horizontal cylinder directed into the plane of the paper, it may be shown that:

$$\Delta g = 2\pi GR^2(\rho - \rho_0) \frac{z}{x^2 + z^2} \qquad (2.8.7)$$

and the maximum at $x = 0$ is given by:

$$\Delta_0 g = 2\pi GR^2(\rho - \rho_0) \frac{1}{z} \qquad (2.8.8)$$

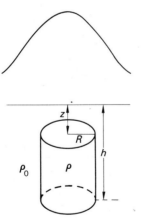

Figure 2.8.1(b) Computed gravity anomaly from a vertical cylinder.

For the vertical cylinder in (b) along its axis only (the formula for a point off the axis is extremely complicated):

$$\Delta_0 g = 2\pi G(\rho - \rho_0)\left[h - z + \sqrt{R^2 + z^2} - \sqrt{R^2 + h^2}\right] \qquad (2.8.9)$$

If the cylinder extends to an infinite depth ($h \to \infty$), then:

$$\Delta_0 g = 2\pi G(\rho - \rho_0)\left[\sqrt{R^2 + z^2} - z\right] \qquad (2.8.10)$$

In (c) is shown the anomaly produced by a step-like structure, although no equation is given for it here.

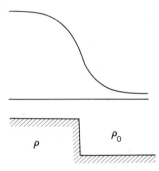

Figure 2.8.1(c) Computed gravity anomaly from a step structure.

These are just a few of the more simple cases, although many others could be derived. In practice, of course, subsurface geological structures are usually irregular bodies rather than simple shapes; but a surprisingly large number of geological structures may be approximated by regular shapes either alone or in combination. As an example, Figure 2.8.2 shows the Bouguer anomaly across part of the Malvern Hills in Worcestershire. To the west lie hard, dense rocks close to the surface; but to the east these are overlain by up to 3 km of softer, less dense sandstones. The anomaly produced by this arrangement bears a remarkable resemblance to that in Figure 2.8.1 (c). In general, however, even if a measured anomaly may be successfully simulated by a known shape, it still does not follow that the real structure in the

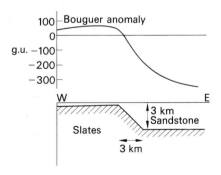

Figure 2.8.2 The Bouguer anomaly across the Malvern Hills. *Source:* Cook (1969).

Earth is that shape. The fundamental ambiguity in the gravity interpretation remains because there is no guarantee that an equally good simulation will not be produced by a quite different model.

A real gravity interpretation is shown in Figures 2.8.3 and 2.8.4. You may recall that in section 2.3 we discussed the results of a seismic refraction study carried out in southwest England and leading to the structural interpretation shown in Figure 2.3.3. We pointed out at the

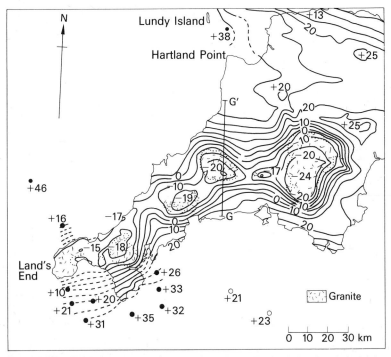

Figure 2.8.3 The Bouguer anomaly map of southwest England showing the negative anomalies associated with the chain of granites. Units are 10 g.u.—that is, for example, the figure 24 on the contours represents 240 g.u. *Source:* Bott and Scott (1964).

time that prior to the seismic work the depth of the granite batholith had already been deduced. This was actually a conclusion based on gravity data. The Bouguer anomaly map for this area is shown in Figure 2.8.3, from which it may be seen that negative gravity anomalies are associated with the chain of granite outcrops. The Bouguer anomaly across one of the outcrops is shown in Figure 2.8.4 together with its interpretation. The anomaly is negative and reaches a minimum of about -600 g.u. To explain it, it is necessary to assume that the granite has a density at least 100 kg m^{-3} lower than the density of the surrounding basement rock, and probably about 160 kg m^{-3} lower.

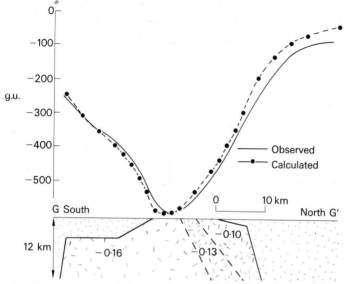

Figure 2.8.4 Interpretation of the Bouguer anomaly profile along the line GG' in Figure 2.8.3 Density is in units of 10^3 kg m^{-3}. *Source:* Bott and Scott (1964).

The granite itself has a measured density of 2600 kg m^{-3} and so the basement rocks must have an average density of about 2750 kg m^{-3}. The interpretation in terms of shape shows the granite batholith with outward sloping edges and as extending to a depth of at least 10 km. The anomaly computed from the model structure then agrees well with the observed Bouguer anomaly.

2.9 Crustal and upper mantle structure

In previous sections we have discussed the principles involved in the determination of Earth structure by the seismic refraction and gravity methods and in section 2.4 we looked at a few examples of structure based largely on seismic work. Here we will look more closely at the physical properties of the Earth's crust and upper mantle making use of both gravity and seismic (explosion and earthquake) data.

General views

Up to the 1960s, the Moho was regarded as a fairly sharp boundary at which the velocity of *P* waves increases abruptly, usually from the range 6.8–7.2 km s^{-1} in the lower crust to the range 8.0–8.2 km s^{-1} in the almost homogeneous upper mantle. Figure 2.9.1 shows the view

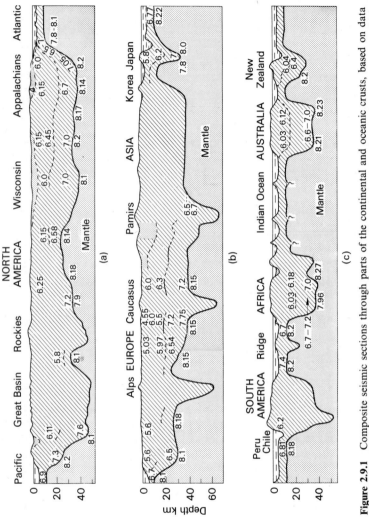

Figure 2.9.1 Composite seismic sections through parts of the continental and oceanic crusts, based on data available through 1962. The figures refer to *P* wave velocities in km s^{-1}. Dotted regions in the upper crust are thick layers of sediment. *Source:* Holmes (1965).

of the crust and upper mantle based on data available up to 1962. The Moho is seen here as a more or less continuous discontinuity around the world. Beneath stable continental regions the depth to the Moho is about 35 km, but in ocean basins the depth from the crustal surface (that is, not including the sea water) to the Moho is about 5–7 km, made up of 5–6 km of basement material and about 1 km of sediment. The oceanic crust was believed to thicken beneath some oceanic ridges but not beneath others. Thus below the mid-Atlantic ridge the Moho was reported at a depth of about 25 km, but no such thickening was thought to take place beneath the East Pacific Rise. Beneath the mountain ranges the Moho is shown as extending to depths of over 60 km. In general, higher topography corresponds to thicker crust, which would seem to be in general agreement with Airy's view of isostasy, although there are some exceptions to this rule.

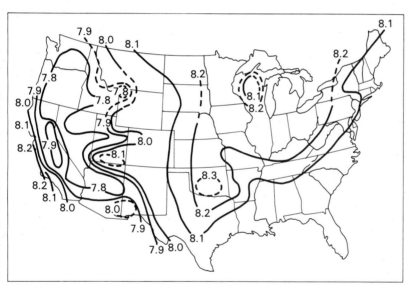

Figure 2.9.2 Estimated P_n velocity (km s^{-1}) in the upper mantle beneath the United States. *Source:* Herrin (1969).

More recently this simple picture has been modified somewhat, partly because the upper mantle now appears to be less homogeneous than was previously supposed. Figure 2.9.2 shows how, for example, the P_n wave velocity varies in the upper mantle beneath the United States. In parts of the central United States the P_n velocity exceeds 8.3 km s^{-1} whereas beneath the mountain regions of the west it falls to below 7.7 km s^{-1}. Low values of P_n velocity have also been measured in other parts of the world, especially beneath tectonically active regions such as island arcs and oceanic ridges. Moreover, in many tectonically active regions there appear to be layers of rock with P wave velocities in the range 7.2–7.7 km s^{-1}; that is, with velocities intermediate between the typical lower crustal range and the typical upper mantle range. Some estimates of P_n velocity for world regions are shown in Table 2.9.1.

Table 2.9.1. Examples of P_n wave (upper mantle) velocity throughout the world. *Source:* Bott (1971).

Area	P_n velocity (km s^{-1})
Western United States	7.8–8.0
Eastern United States	8.0–8.3
Britain	8.0
Western Alps	8.1–8.2
Finland	8.2
Japan	7.5–7.9
Ocean basins	8.0–8.5
Ocean ridges	7.3–8.2
Iceland	7.4

Nowadays, the crust is usually defined as the outer shell of the Earth above the level at which P wave velocity rises to over 7.7 km s^{-1}. (However, there are exceptions. Beneath Iceland, for example, the material with velocity 7.4 km s^{-1} (see Table 2.9.1) is clearly upper mantle.) The Moho is then defined as the *layer* within which the P wave velocity rises discontinuously or rapidly from crustal values to values above 7.7 km s^{-1}. In other words, although still a sharp boundary on the Earth's scale and still one of the major boundaries in the Earth, the Moho is not quite as sharp as was previously believed—the transition from lower crustal velocities to higher mantle velocities may take place over a finite depth. Estimates of the thickness of this transition layer range from 0.1 km beneath parts of the Pacific Ocean through 0.5 km in some stable continental regions to several kilometres elsewhere.

At first, the layers of rock having P wave velocities in the range 7.2–7.7 km s^{-1} were regarded as unusual and anomalous but they are now known to be characteristic features of tectonically active regions. The existence of this layering draws attention to the fact that layering is a common feature of the crust and upper mantle, although much of the layering is a regional rather than a global phenomenon. Figure 2.9.3 shows, for example, a series of models for different parts of the Earth's crust in the U.S.S.R. On the basis of this and other work it is

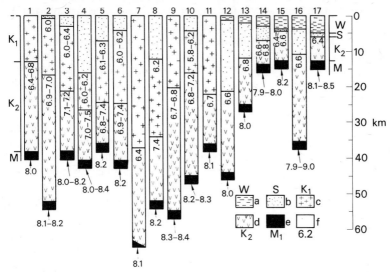

Figure 2.9.3 Seismic models of the Earth's crust in the U.S.S.R. The key is: (a) water; (b) sedimentary rocks; (c) upper crust; (d) lower crust; (e) mantle; (f) velocity in km s^{-1}. *Source:* Kosminskaya (1969).

possible to classify the U.S.S.R. crust and upper mantle into four characteristic types—continental, oceanic, subcontinental regions of the continental margins, and suboceanic regions of the continental margins. The *average P* wave characteristics for the four types are shown in Figure 2.9.4. The Moho is clearly seen in all types except for the subcontinental which contains a considerable thickness of material with P wave velocity between 7.6 and 7.8 km s^{-1}.

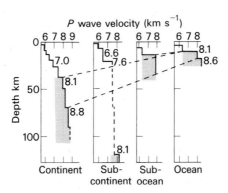

Figure 2.9.4 Average velocity sections for four different types of crust–upper mantle in the U.S.S.R. Note that in the subcontinental section the Moho is not clearly defined. *Source:* Kosminskaya and Zverev (1968).

Similar data, but with a far greater world coverage, are plotted in different ways in Figures 2.9.5 and 2.9.6. In Figure 2.9.5, P wave velocities for ocean basins, continental margins, and shield areas with elevations less than 500 m, throughout the world are plotted with depth. The P wave velocities for ocean basins fall into four discrete boxes each of which represents a distinct layer of the oceanic crust–mantle with no velocity overlap. (The oceanic crust is described in more detail in the next-but-one subsection.) P wave velocities for the low-lying shield areas lie in three discrete boxes representing, respectively, the upper crust, the lower crust and the mantle. In this case, however, there is a velocity overlap between the upper and lower crust. P wave velocities beneath continental margins are much more scattered, covering all values between oceanic sediments and mantle, although there is a general tendency for velocity to increase with depth. Figure 2.9.5 clearly shows that material with P wave velocities

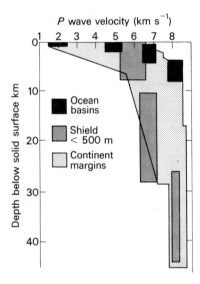

Figure 2.9.5 Worldwide seismic velocities for three types of crust–upper mantle. Ocean basin velocities fall in four discrete areas representing four distinct layers in which there is no velocity overlap. Shield velocities fall into three discrete areas representing three distinct layers, although the two upper layers overlap in velocity. Continental margin velocities are scattered, although there is a general tendency for velocity to increase with depth. *Source:* Drake and Nafe (1968).

in the range 7.2–7.7 km s^{-1} is absent beneath stable shields and ocean basins but present beneath some continental margins.

The data in Figure 2.9.6 cover an even wider range of environments. For each environment there are four columns each of which represents a definite range of P wave velocities and the vertical range of these columns shows the depth range within which the velocities are encountered. Again, it is clear that the layers with the intermediate (7.2–7.7 km s^{-1}) velocities are limited to continental margins, orogenic belts and anomalous oceanic and continental regions.

From what has been said so far, it is evident from seismic evidence that there is a very wide range of crust–mantle models in the Earth, that crustal thickness is equally variable, and that in general terms the thicker crust is associated with higher topography not only because

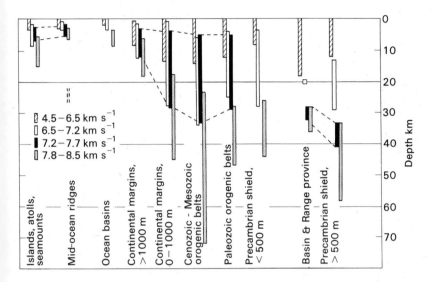

Figure 2.9.6 Depth intervals for P wave velocities expressed in four ranges for various different structural provinces, based on worldwide data. The four velocity ranges represent: (i) the upper crust, (ii) the lower crust, (iii) intermediate crust/mantle in tectonically active regions, and (iv) upper mantle. *Source:* Drake and Nafe (1968).

the topography is higher as such but also because the Moho beneath it lies at greater depth. In Figure 2.9.7, crustal thicknesses in different continental and oceanic regions are compared with the Bouguer and isostatic anomalies. The fact that isostatic anomalies—whether calculated according to the Pratt or Airy hypotheses, or some variation on them—are systematically close to zero shows that some mechanism of isostatic compensation is operating. Equally striking is the fact that the Bouguer anomalies over the oceans tend to high positive values (indicating mass excess, higher density subsurface) and that over the mountains they tend to high negative values (indicating mass deficient, lower density subsurface). We may thus conclude that on a worldwide scale the crust is close to isostatic equilibrium and that this compensation is consistent generally with Airy's view. On the other hand, it is not possible to rule out the Pratt hypothesis entirely.

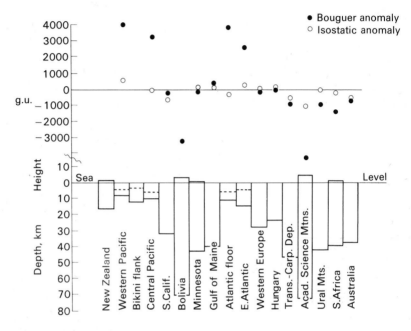

Figure 2.9.7 Relations between the Bouguer anomalies, isostatic anomalies and seismically determined crustal thicknesses for different continental and oceanic regions. *Source:* Garland (1971).

Structure of the United States

The general worldwide relationship between topographic height and crustal thickness is not confirmed in detail when crustal sections from a single continent are studied. Figure 2.9.8, for example, shows crustal thickness, layering, Bouguer anomalies and isostatic anomalies for a number of regions in the western United States. It is immediately obvious that elevated areas such as Arizona and Nevada do not have as great a crustal thickness as other areas of lower elevation. The Great Plains (see Figure 2.4.1), to take another example, are elevated 1 km above sea level and are underlain by a crust which is 45–50 km thick, whereas the Basin and Range province, which stands, on average,

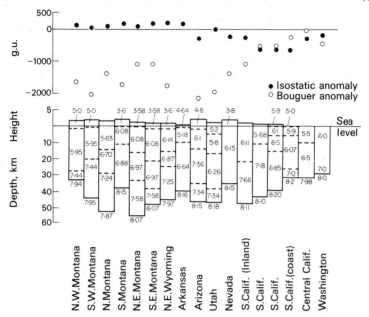

Figure 2.9.8 Seismic velocity sections, Bouguer anomalies and isostatic anomalies in the western United States. *Source:* Garland (1971).

about 2 km above sea level, possesses a crust of only 25–30 km. In short, it is clear that on this sort of scale Airy's hypothesis does not strictly apply.

There are three general mechanisms whereby isostatic compensation may take place:

(i) by variation in crustal thickness—this is Airy's hypothesis;
(ii) by lateral variation in crustal density—this is Pratt's hypothesis; and
(iii) by lateral variation in upper mantle density—this is a modified form of Pratt's hypothesis.

The situation in the western United States appears to be that where Airy's hypothesis does not apply exactly, the additional compensation largely takes place in the upper mantle by density variation. If there are lateral density variations in the upper mantle this implies, of course, that there will be seismic wave velocity variations; and this is confirmed by Figure 2.9.2. On the other hand, in regions such as the Basin and Range, where P_n velocities remain roughly constant, changes in topography do appear to be related quite well to changes in crustal thickness. The moral here is that no single theory is adequate to explain the near isostasy of all the Earth's surface features. The conflict between the Airy and Pratt hypotheses is thus more apparent than real because either or both may be applicable in any given situation. Heiskanen has estimated, in fact, that about sixty-three percent of the crust's isostatic equilibrium is achieved by the Airy mechanism and about thirty-seven percent by the Pratt mechanism.

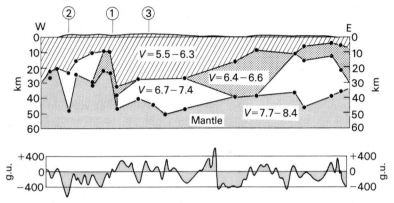

Figure 2.9.9   A composite seismic section through the crust and upper mantle beneath the United States together with the corresponding isostatic anomaly profile. Units of P wave velocity are km s^{-1}. *Source:* Woollard (1968).

Figure 2.9.9 is a modern composite seismic crust–mantle profile across the whole of the United States from Chesapeake Bay, Maryland, to central California, showing units of the crust having similar P wave velocity ranges and (below) the isostatic anomaly profile. The most spectacular features are (a) the abrupt structural transition at the base of the Wasatch Mountains (location 1), and (b) the root (and corresponding negative isostatic anomaly) beneath the Sierra Nevada (location 2). The structural change at location 1 affects both the crust and upper mantle and is in good agreement with the boundary between the west region where the P_n velocity is low (Figure 2.9.2) and the region to the east where the P_n velocity is high. In short, this boundary appears to divide the United States into two superprovinces involving both the crust and upper mantle. The Sierra Nevada is clearly not in isostatic equilibrium; and in this sense contrasts strongly with the Rocky Mountains (location 3) where there is no single strong isostatic anomaly.

The oceanic crust

The structure of the oceanic crust is quite different from that of the continents—a reflection of the fact that whereas the continental crust may be up to over 3000 million years old, the oceanic crust has been formed almost entirely during the past 200 million years. The structural difference was illustrated by the boxes of Figure 2.9.5 for stable oceanic and continental regions. The oceanic crust comprises three quite distinct layers (the upper mantle makes a fourth) with no P wave velocity overlap between layers. Figure 2.9.10 shows a typical reversed refraction arrangement at sea together with the time–distance graph for direct, refracted and reflected waves. For investigations of the oceanic crust, refraction lines need only be 50–70 km long because the Moho is less deep than under the continents.

In most stable oceanic regions (ocean basins) the structure is remarkably uniform throughout (see Table 2.9.2). The top of layer 1 is difficult

Table 2.9.2   The oceanic crustal layers.

Layer	P wave velocity† (km s^{-1})	Average thickness (km)
sea water	1.5	4.5
layer 1	1.6–2.5	0.4
layer 2	4.0–6.0	1.5
layer 3	6.4–7.0	5.0
upper mantle	7.4–8.6	

† These are the ranges within which most seismic velocities lie. In some instances, velocities outside these ranges have been determined.

to detect by refraction (G_1 in Figure 2.9.10) because the layer's velocity contrast with the overlying water is usually very low and so G_1 seldom appears as a first arrival. However, the layer 1 surface may easily be determined by the reflection R_1 or by the ship's precision depth recorder. The velocity in layer 1 is more difficult to determine but may be estimated using a procedure which utilizes the amplitude of R_1. The head wave G_2 refracted at the layer 1–layer 2 boundary occurs as a first arrival only over a short distance or, if layer 2 is thin, not at all; and so it may be necessary to use the reflection R_1' to measure the depth to the layer 1–layer 2 boundary and then assume a velocity for layer 2 in order to interpret the underlying layers. Head waves G_3 and G_4 are received as first arrivals, however; and the direct wave D travels through the sea water.

Layer 1 is easily identified as the unconsolidated sediment forming the sea bed; and its thickness is very variable (up to 3 km in places), being zero on, for example, ridge flanks and other areas of steep topography. Also, there is a marked difference in the average thickness of layer 1 between the Atlantic Ocean (>1 km) and the Pacific Ocean (<0.5 km), largely because the Atlantic is smaller and has more sediment-bearing rivers flowing into it. The range of P wave velocities in layer 1 is quite wide.

Layer 1 also possesses a fine structure which does not show up in seismic refraction studies but becomes apparent from *seismic reflection profiling*. This is a method whereby waves from a source (usually an air gun) are sent vertically downwards from the ship, the intention being to get them to reflect from boundaries at normal incidence (zero angle of incidence). The reflection method is thus basically the same as echo sounding for measuring the depth to the sea bed except that the source is more powerful and that the waves have a lower frequency than echo sounding waves to enable them to penetrate the water–sediment interface. The return waves are then detected at the surface; and if their velocity is known, or can reasonably be assumed, the distance of travel may be calculated.

Reflection techniques have revealed two internal horizons within layer 1. In addition, they show that the layer 1–layer 2 boundary is rougher than the water–layer 1 interface, having topographic features up to 1 km in height. The various *P* wave velocities and horizons in layer 1 are given in Table 2.9.3. Within the American basin of the

Table 2.9.3   The structure of oceanic layer 1. *Source:* Bott (1971).

Horizon	Sublayer	*P* wave velocity (km s^{-1})
sea bed		
		1.5–2.2 (unconsolidated sediments)
Horizon A		
	layer A	1.7–2.9 (semi-consolidated sediments)
Horizon β		
	layer β	2.7–3.7 (consolidated sediments)
Horizon B or layer 1–layer 2 boundary		

north Atlantic, Horizon A appears as a persistent and prominent boundary 300–500 m below the sea bed but is much smoother than the sea bed. It has also been detected in the south Atlantic and the Pacific. Horizon β is less common. Horizon B is a smooth boundary in the Atlantic where it locally appears to replace the layer 1–layer 2 interface but, more probably, conceals it rather than replaces it. It only occurs far from the mid-Atlantic Ridge. Finally, the velocity just below the surface of layer 1 is known to be 1.47–1.55 km s^{-1}, which suggests that velocity probably increases with depth down to Horizon A.

Layer 2 is the most variable of the three oceanic crustal layers both as regards thickness and seismic velocity although, as we have seen,

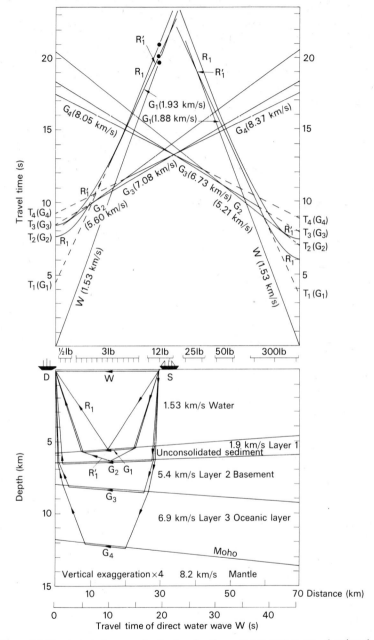

Figure 2.9.10 A typical reversed seismic refraction arrangement at sea, showing the time–distance graph for refractions, reflections and the direct water wave. The distance between source (S) and detector (D) is 30 km. *Source:* Talwani (1964).

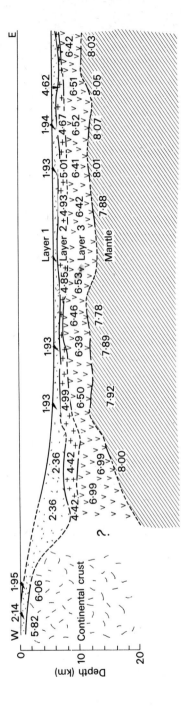

Figure 2.9.11 Oceanic crustal structure determined by seismic refraction in the Atlantic Ocean east of Argentine. The line runs from 46 °S, 60 °W on the continental shelf to 43 °S, 50 °W in the ocean. Figures refer to seismic velocities in km s^{-1}. *Source*: Ewing (1965).

accurate velocities are difficult to obtain. However, the observed range of P wave velocities in this layer could be produced by either consolidated sediments or basaltic lavas. On balance, the evidence supports the view that layer 2 is basalt. Mohole penetrated 14 m of basalt below layer 1 before the drilling was terminated, although this evidence is not conclusive because nearby Guadalupe Island is volcanic and the basalt could therefore be local. On the other hand, seismic profiling data show that layer 2 reaches the sea bed on the flanks of the mid-Atlantic ridge from which basalt has been dredged. The most convincing evidence, however, comes from the familiar linear magnetic anomalies over the ocean floor. These anomalies cannot be caused by the sediments of layer 1 which are essentially non-magnetic. Moreover, it turns out that excessively strong and highly irregular patterns of magnetization are needed in layer 3 if the source of the anomalies lies there. The linear magnetic anomalies must therefore be caused by alternating normal and reversed magnetizations in layer 2 which must therefore be formed of highly magnetic rocks (that is, basalt as opposed to sediment).

Layer 3 is the thickest of the three layers, the most uniform in thickness, and the most uniform in velocity. Its nature is basically unknown. At one time it was thought to be consolidated basic igneous rock such as gabbro; but more recent suggestions have included partially serpentinized peridotite and amphibolite resulting from the metamorphism of basaltic crust.

A particularly clear cut oceanic seismic refraction profile, showing the three crustal layers, forms Figure 2.9.11.

Oceanic ridges

Oceanic ridges are particularly significant features from the point of view of sea floor spreading because they are the tectonically active regions along which new oceanic crust is being produced. Figure 2.9.12 is a purely schematic view of the Atlantic Ocean floor, based on P wave velocities. Here, the mantle beneath the ridge is shown as penetrating layer 3 in accordance with the view that mantle material upwells along ridge axes; but the upwelling material has lower P wave velocities than 'normal' mantle. In short, the mid-Atlantic Ridge is underlain by intermediate material previously identified as being characteristic of tectonically active regions. An experimental example of seismically-determined structure beneath the mid-Atlantic Ridge is shown in Figure 2.9.13.

The Bouguer anomaly across the mid-Atlantic Ridge is shown in Figure 2.9.14. The form of the anomaly (it reaches a minimum over the feature in question) shows that the ridge is in overall isostatic equilibrium. (However, local topographic features are not always in

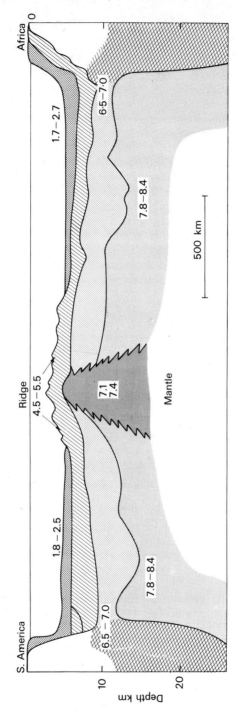

Figure 2.9.12 Schematic cross-section across the Atlantic close to the equator, showing *P* wave velocities in km s⁻¹. *Source*: Wyllie (1971).

equilibrium—this is why the Bouguer anomaly is irregular.) The seismic evidence in Figure 2.9.13 rules out any suggestion that the equilibrium is reached by crustal thickening. The required mass deficiency must therefore be due to anomalously low density material in the upper mantle. Three possible density models which satisfy

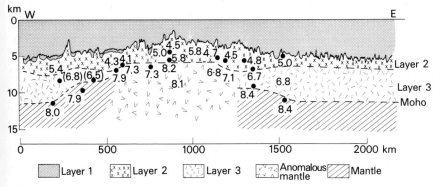

Figure 2.9.13 Seismically determined crustal and upper mantle structure across the mid-Atlantic Ridge from about 37 °N, 48 °W to 26 °N, 30 °W. Seismic velocities are in km s^{-1}. The intermediate (anomalous) mantle material penetrates layer 3. *Source:* Talwani, Le Pichon and Ewing (1965).

both the gravitational and seismic requirements are also shown in Figure 2.9.14. It is necessary in each case to have lower density material beneath higher density material below the ridge flanks in order to explain the gravity; but the thin extensions ('arms') of the lower density material would not be detected seismically because of the shielding effect of the higher density region above.

The East Pacific Rise (Figure 2.9.15) is similar to the mid-Atlantic Ridge in that it is in isostatic equilibrium and in that anomalous material underlies it; but differs in that layer 3 is continuous above the mantle.

Continental margins

There are two general types of continental margin—the inactive, aseismic margin characteristic of the edges of oceans such as the Atlantic (see Figures 2.9.11 and 2.9.12) and which do not form plate boundaries, and the seismically active margins (for example, around the Pacific) where oceanic crust is being consumed. Surprisingly little is known about the former, partly because most effort has been devoted to those margins which play a significant role in theories of plate tectonics. However, one example of an inactive margin is shown in some detail in Figure 2.9.16.

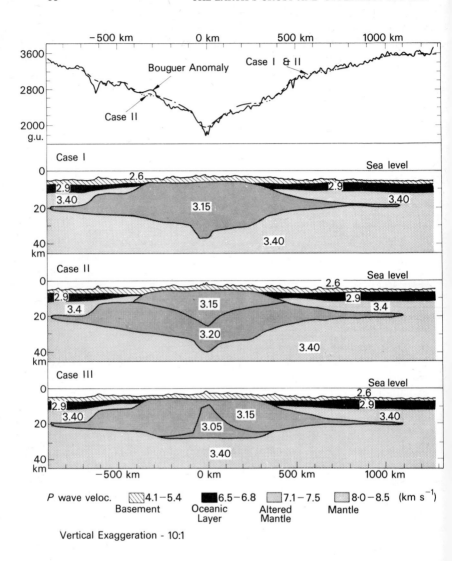

Figure 2.9.14 The Bouguer anomaly across the mid-Atlantic Ridge and three possible structural/density models which satisfy both gravitational and seismic data. The anomalies computed from the models are compared with the observed Bouguer anomaly. In Case I the intermediate (anomalous) mantle material is assumed to have uniform density; in Case II its density is assumed to increase downwards; and in Case III the material is assumed to have lower density near the ridge axis. Density units are 10^3 kg m^{-3}. *Source:* Talwani, Le Pichon and Ewing (1965).

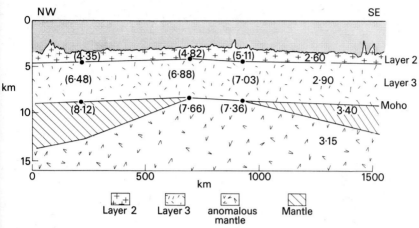

Figure 2.9.15 Seismically determined crustal and upper mantle structure across the East Pacific Rise west of Peru at about latitude 16 °S. Seismic velocities in parentheses are in km s^{-1}; and densities not in parentheses are in 10^3 kg m^{-3}. Layer 3 is not penetrated by the intermediate (anomalous) mantle material; but the boundaries of the intermediate material need to slope outwards as shown to satisfy the gravity data. *Source:* Talwani, Le Pichon and Ewing (1965).

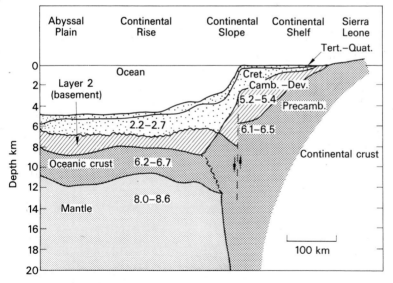

Figure 2.9.16 Seismic cross-section across the inactive Sierra Leone continental margin with velocities in km s^{-1}. Vertical exaggeration is 20 : 1. *Source:* Sheridan, Houtz, Drake and Ewing (1969).

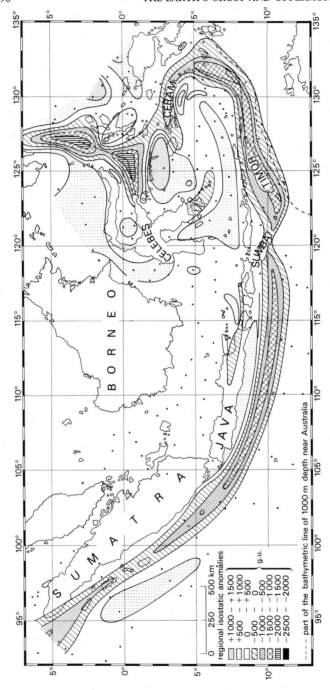

Figure 2.9.17 The isostatic anomaly map of the East Indies. The small circles are gravity stations. *Source*: Vening Meinesz (1955).

The typical active margin has a trench along its oceanic side and either a mountain range or an island arc along its landward side. The striking, narrow strips of negative isostatic gravity anomaly associated with trenches and island arcs—an example of which is given in Figure 2.9.17—were actually discovered long before sea floor spreading had been thought of. Because such anomalies must indicate narrow strips of mass deficiency they were, in the early 1950s, interpreted as regions where the light crust downbuckles into the denser mantle. Superficially at least, this interpretation is surprisingly like the present view which would have oceanic crust downwelling into the denser mantle.

As Figure 2.9.17 shows, the negative isostatic anomaly is also associated with a positive one. This association is clearly brought out by the gravity–seismic profile across the Puerto Rico trench system shown in Figure 2.9.18. Over the trench itself the gravity anomaly is

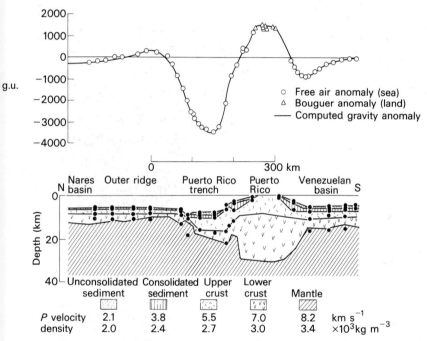

Figure 2.9.18 Crustal structure across the Puerto Rico trench together with the associated gravity anomaly. The interpretation, which approximately satisfies both gravity and seismic data, is actually based on an empirical relationship between P wave velocity and density (see section 2.10). *Source:* Talwani, Sutton and Worzel (1959).

negative, indicating a mass deficiency; and, although the isostatic anomaly is not shown, the trench is known to be strongly out of isostatic equilibrium. (Hence also, the strong isostatic anomalies in

Figure 2.9.17). The crust beneath the trench is oceanic and very little thicker than that of the adjacent ocean. However, the crust is depressed, so that dense underlying mantle material is effectively replaced by low density water in the surface depression, thereby giving the mass deficiency leading to the negative anomaly. Similar considerations apply to the Peru–Chile trench shown in Figure 2.9.19. In both cases

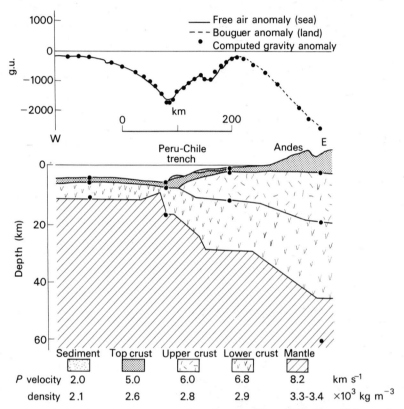

Figure 2.9.19 The crustal structure and gravity anomaly across the Peru–Chile trench near 13 °S, derived on the same basis as in Figure 2.9.18. *Source:* Hayes (1966).

the sediment in the trench is thin; and this is typical, although sediment thickness can be large in places. For example, the principal part of the Peru–Chile trench contains less than 500 m of sediment although at the southern end the thickness rises to 2 km. In general, however, the thinness of sediment indicates that the sediment is not the cause of the subsidence. The positive anomalies over Puerto Rico and the maximum in the anomaly to the landward side of the Peru–Chile trench are not yet fully understood (but may be 'explained' by the models in Figures 2.9.18 and 2.9.19), although they must clearly represent mass excess. One suggestion is that the mass excess is produced by the descending lithosphere which, being cold compared to the mantle into which it is dragged, possibly has a higher density.

2.10 The variation of physical parameters with depth

In this chapter we have been concerned with such parameters as density, elastic moduli, seismic wave velocity, gravity, and so on, largely because they are the essential quantities involved in studies of the Earth's crustal and upper mantle structure. In this penultimate section we will look briefly at how these physical parameters vary in a general, average way throughout the Earth, but especially in the crust and upper mantle.

Seismic velocity

Seismic wave velocity is the most accurately known physical parameter in the deep Earth, the accuracy throughout most of the mantle, for example, being probably within two percent. The broad velocity-depth distributions for both P and S waves according to the interpretations of Gutenberg and Jeffreys were shown in Figure 2.1.1. The general features of these curves are still thought to be correct today, even though there are some obvious differences between Gutenberg and Jeffreys.

The most striking difference between the Jeffreys and Gutenberg P wave curves for the mantle occurs in the region immediately below the Moho. Here Jeffreys shows a continuous increase in P wave velocity from the Moho downwards whereas Gutenberg shows a decrease in velocity, reaching a minimum at a depth of about 100 km, followed by an increase starting at about 200 km. This dip in P wave velocity, if real, represents a *low velocity layer*; that is, a layer in which the velocity is somewhat lower than in the regions above and below. The low velocity layer is also evident in Gutenberg's S wave velocity curve. But is it real? More modern evidence suggests that there *is* a low velocity layer in the upper mantle; but it is still not clear (i) whether it is continuous around the Earth, or (ii) what its precise depth limits are. The essential problems are (a) that earthquakes occur in zones which are, by definition, not typical of the Earth's crust-mantle and so there is a danger in extrapolating information from seismic zones to the Earth as a whole, and (b) that, as Figure 2.9.2 shows, there is a certain degree of inhomogeneity in the mantle, which suggests that even if the low velocity layer exists around most of the Earth its depth could easily vary. In this connection, an important piece of non-earthquake information came from the nuclear explosion GNOME, detonated in New Mexico during the early 1960s. Data from this explosion have been interpreted in terms of a low velocity layer beneath the United States at a depth between 150 and 215 km.

In addition to the upper mantle discontinuities represented by the boundaries of the supposed low velocity layer, discoveries of other discontinuities in the region 400–1000 km (the transition zone in Table 1.5.1) have been claimed. This aspect of geophysics is not yet very developed; and so it is not yet very clear how many discontinuities there are in this part of the upper mantle, how local they are, how deep they are, or, in some cases, whether or not they are real. Nevertheless,

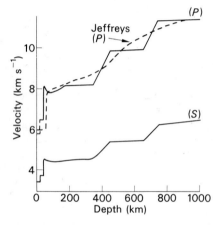

Figure 2.10.1 Seismic velocity discontinuities in the upper mantle. The Jeffreys P wave velocity distribution is shown for comparison. *Source:* Julian and Anderson (1968).

there is quite convincing evidence for at least two discontinuities— one in the region 300–400 km and one in the region 600–700 km. According to the interpretation shown in Figure 2.10.1, each of these discontinuities is essentially a 'slope'. Finally, there is some evidence from nuclear explosions for two more discontinuities rather deeper

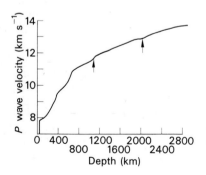

Figure 2.10.2 P wave velocity model of the mantle, showing additional discontinuities (indicated by arrows) below 1000 km. *Source:* Toksöz, Chinnery and Anderson (1967).

in the mantle, around 1200 km and 1900 km. These are illustrated in Figure 2.10.2.

As far as the crust is concerned, seismic velocities in relation to layering are much better known and there are more data. Thus it is possible to construct average P and S wave velocity–depth curves solely from experimental results. Average curves for continents and oceans are shown in Figure 2.10.3.

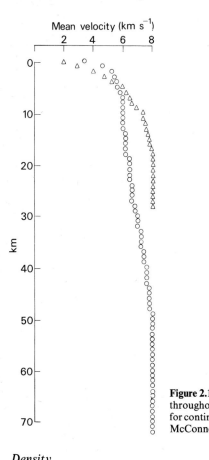

Figure 2.10.3 P wave velocity as a function of depth throughout the crust based on experimental values for continents (circles) and oceans (triangles). *Source:* McConnell and McTaggart-Cowan (1963).

Density

According to equations (2.1.1), P and S wave velocities are related to density by, respectively:

$$u = \sqrt{\frac{k + \frac{4}{3}\mu}{\rho}} \quad \text{and} \quad w = \sqrt{\frac{\mu}{\rho}} \qquad (2.1.1)$$

Even if u and w are known, we are still left with three unknowns ρ, k and μ) but only two equations and ρ cannot therefore be calculated without other information. In other words, the seismic velocity–depth curves are insufficient in themselves to enable a density–depth curve to be constructed.

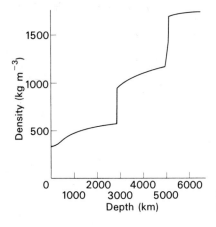

Figure 2.10.4 Variation of density in the Earth. *Source:* Bullen (1963).

Determination of the density distribution is an involved process; and further details are given in Appendix Two. Numerous people have produced versions of the density distribution but the best known is that by Bullen shown in Figure 2.10.4.

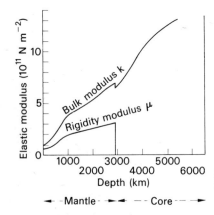

Figure 2.10.5 Variation of bulk and rigidity moduli with depth in the Earth. *Source:* Bott (1971).

Elastic moduli, gravity and pressure

Once the density and seismic velocity distributions are known, the elastic moduli (k and μ) distributions may be determined from equations

(2.1.1). The variations of k and μ with depth are shown in Figure 2.10.5. At a point in the Earth distance r from the centre, the gravity results only from the attraction of the mass (m) contained within the sphere of radius r. Thus at such a point, equation (2.5.4) may be rewritten as:

$$g = \frac{Gm}{r^2} \qquad (2.10.1)$$

The mass within such a sphere of radius r may be calculated from the density distribution because density = mass/volume. Once this mass is known for different values of r, g may be calculated as a function of r from equation (2.10.1). The gravity–depth distribution is shown in Figure 2.10.6. Finally, the pressure–depth distribution may be calculated from ρ and the bulk modulus k because k is defined by:

$$k = \text{density} \times \text{rate of change of pressure with density}$$

(see Appendix Two). The variation of pressure with depth is also shown in Figure 2.10.6.

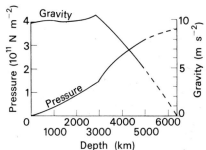

Figure 2.10.6 Variation of gravity and pressure with depth in the Earth. *Source:* Bott (1971).

Relationship between crustal P wave velocity and density

According to equations (2.1.1), if the elastic moduli were constant throughout the crust, seismic wave velocity would vary as the square root of $1/\rho$. In other words, because density generally increases with depth, seismic wave velocity would decrease with depth. But this clearly does not happen; on the contrary, seismic velocity also increases with depth. This must mean that the elastic moduli increase with increasing density at a faster rate than the density itself increases.

The experimental relationship between density and P wave velocity in the crustal range has been investigated by Nafe and Drake on the basis of both laboratory and field measurements. As Figure 2.10.7 shows, there appears to be a systematic trend between the two quantities with both increasing together. Accepting this empirical relationship as valid makes it possible to estimate the density of shallow rocks

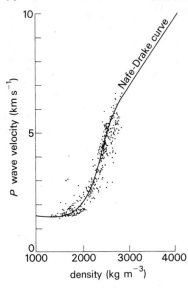

Figure 2.10.7 The variation of P wave velocity with density. The experimental points are based on water-saturated sediments and sedimentary rocks. The upper extension for hard rocks is continuous but differs in gradient. *Source:* Nafe and Drake (1963).

from the P wave velocity to the nearest $100 \, \text{kg m}^{-3}$. The Nafe–Drake curve has been quite widely used in interpreting gravity–seismic surveys, including those shown in Figures 2.9.18 and 2.9.19.

2.11 General remarks

In this chapter we have concentrated on purely geophysical methods and examples—methods which lead to, and examples which illustrate, the *physical* structure of the Earth's crust and upper mantle. However, for the Earth scientist, as opposed to the geophysicist, this is not sufficient. The Earth scientist wants to know not just the physical structure but also the chemical and mineralogical composition—in other words, he wants to know what the materials concerned are as well as what form they take.

Such considerations in detail are beyond the scope of this work. In very general terms, however, the approach to interpretation is to compare the geophysically determined parameters with the corresponding parameters of known minerals in the light of theories of the chemical evolution and structure of the Earth and, in the case of the more accessible upper crust, in the light of direct investigations of the rocks concerned. The comparative parameters of known minerals are usually derived from laboratory experiments carried out over the appropriate ranges of temperature and pressure. As examples, recent compilations of the densities and P wave velocities in some Earth minerals are given in Tables 2.11.1 and 2.11.2. What is immediately apparent from these tables is that unique interpretations are likely to be difficult, if not impossible, because the ranges of the physical properties of various minerals overlap. For example, a material with a geophysically determined density of 2690 kg m^{-3} could, by simple comparison with Table 2.11.1, be granite, granodiorite, syenite, quartz diorite or even something quite different—and a geophysically determined P wave velocity of 6.4 km s^{-1} would add very little restriction.

Table 2.11.1 Average densities and density ranges of coarse-grained igneous rocks and eclogites. *Source:* Clark (1966).

Rock	Mean density (kg m^{-3})	Density range (kg m^{-3})
granite	2670	2520–2810
granodiorite	2720	2670–2790
syenite	2760	2630–2900
quartz diorite	2810	2680–2960
diorite	2840	2720–2960
gabbro and norite	2980	2720–3120
peridotite	3230	3150–3280
dunite	3280	3200–3310
eclogite	3390	3340–3450

Table 2.11.2 P wave velocities in rocks. *Source:* Clark (1966).

Rock	Mean velocity (km s^{-1}) at 10^8 N m^{-2} pressure	at 10^9 N m^{-2} pressure
granite	6.13	6.45
granodiorite	6.27	6.56
quartz diorite	6.44	6.71
gabbro and norite	7.02	7.24
dunite	7.87	8.15
eclogite	7.52	7.87
greywacke	5.84	6.20
slate	5.79	6.22
amphibolite	7.17	7.35

And finally, a word of warning which applies equally to physical structure and geochemical interpretation. Figure 2.11.1 shows the result of a typical gravity–seismic interpretation—in this case, across the Pacific margin of North America, though the precise location is not particularly relevant to the present context. It is immediately

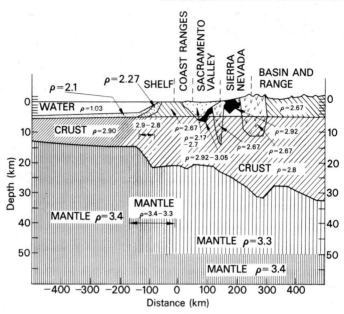

Figure 2.11.1 A geological-geophysical cross-section across the Pacific margin of North America where the trench is absent but where deformation has recently taken place and where seismic activity occurs. Density units are 10^3 kg m^{-3}. *Source:* Thompson and Talwani (1964).

obvious from this diagram that the continental upper crust is far more complex than either the lower crust or the upper mantle, or, for that matter, the oceanic crust. But is the continental upper crust really far more complex than the lower crust and upper mantle, or does it just appear so because our present techniques lack the sophistication required to define the finer structure? We cannot be sure; but perhaps history can provide at least part of the answer. Not so very long ago, the upper mantle was widely regarded as remarkably homogeneous. Today, discontinuities and lateral variations in seismic wave velocity are slowly coming to light. Tomorrow, ...

Further reading

M.H.P. Bott (1971), *The Interior of the Earth*. London, Arnold.
A. H. Cook (1969), *Gravity and the Earth*. London, Wykeham.
G. D. Garland (1965), *The Earth's Shape and Gravity*. Oxford, Pergamon Press.
R. H. Tucker, A. H. Cook, H. M. Iyer and F. D. Stacey (1970), *Global Geophysics*. London, English Universities Press.

CHAPTER THREE

The Earth's Heat and Thermal Properties

3.1 Introduction

In a very real sense, study of the Earth's thermal processes may be regarded as the most important of all branches of geophysics because heat plays a part, and very often a crucial part, in all theories concerning the origin and development of the Earth's interior and surface features. The distortions of the Earth's crust, for example, have at one time or another been attributed to contraction of an Earth which is cooling down, expansion of an Earth which is getting hotter, or to the effects of convection currents in the Earth's mantle. Deeper in the Earth, the origin of the geomagnetic field is usually attributed to thermal convection in the fluid outer core. And on the smaller scale, localized processes such as volcanic action are only too obviously involved closely with heat. Whatever the process, whether proven or speculative, thermal activity is almost certainly bound to find a place somewhere, either directly or indirectly, and with varying degrees of importance.

But if heat is the most crucial parameter relating to the Earth, the study of it forms one of the most speculative branches of geophysics. The reason for this is mainly that the internal properties of the Earth upon which thermal processes are so dependent are largely unknown or difficult, if not impossible, to determine. For example, is heat transmitted through the Earth by conduction, convection or radiation?* It may be that all three processes occur—but in what proportion? The answer to this question is important because the transmission mechanism, among other things, will determine the *rate* at which heat is transmitted. Again, what are the thermal properties of the many and varied materials which constitute the Earth? Even for a simple transmission mechanism such as conduction different materials will transmit heat at different rates. Although the broad structure of the Earth is known, the nature of the materials which form the Earth's various components—crust, mantle and core—are far from known;

and this being the case, it is impossible to know just what their heat
transmission characteristics are. Finally, how is it possible to say just
what the sources of heat in the Earth are?

The study of the Earth's thermal processes must therefore proceed
on a fairly speculative basis although the speculation must be tempered
with common sense and an awareness of the conditions imposed by
knowledge from other branches of geophysics. As in many branches of
science the usual procedure is to set up models which, after consideration, may be rejected as being untenable or, if acceptable in principle,
be modified and refined in the light of known limitations or boundary
conditions. To take a simple example—if we know that the Earth's
mantle is solid, any model which predicts anywhere in the mantle
a temperature above the melting point can hardly be completely valid.
In practice, of course, the nature of the relevant material will not be
known, or known only vaguely, and so its melting point will not be
very well defined. The boundary condition imposed on the thermal
model by virtue of the fact that the mantle must remain solid will thus
not be very precise. But this is the nature of the problem; and the lack
of precision may be regarded as the essential difference between physics
as practised by physicists in the laboratory and physics as applied by
geophysicists to the Earth.

3.2 The basic thermal data

One of the chief aims of studying the Earth's thermal behaviour is to
try to determine how temperature varies with depth in the Earth and,
if possible, how the temperature distribution has changed with time.
Clearly, however, the temperature deep in the Earth cannot be measured
directly; and the geophysicist must be content with observations made
at or near the Earth's surface. In practice, such measurements may be
made at the bottom of the deepest mine or of the longest borehole that
man is technically able to drill. This may mean depths of up to a few
kilometres; but even so, such depths are small compared to the Earth's
radius and thus even the deepest measurements are really hardly more
more than surface measurements.

In practice, what is important is not the surface temperature or
near-surface temperature itself but the near-surface temperature
gradient; that is, the change in temperature (ΔT) over a short vertical
(radial) distance (z) near the Earth's surface. In other words:

$$\text{temperature gradient} = \frac{\Delta T}{z} \qquad (3.2.1)$$

In general, temperature is observed to increase with depth. The average
temperature gradient is 0.03 °C per metre near the Earth's surface

although this average conceals a considerable variation. Most temperature gradients lie in the range 0–0.4 °C per metre; but on occasions even higher values have been observed.

The reason why the near-surface temperature gradient is important is that this is one of the parameters necessary to calculate the quantity of heat flowing upwards through the Earth's surface. It is found experimentally that the quantity of heat flowing *by conduction* through an area of one square metre in one second—that is, the rate (q) at which heat is conducted through an area of one square metre—is proportional to the temperature gradient at the area of flow. So:

$$q \propto \frac{\Delta T}{z} \qquad (3.2.2)$$

Or, removing the proportionality:

$$q = \frac{k\Delta T}{z} \qquad (3.2.3)$$

where k is a constant.

The rate at which heat flows must depend not only upon the temperature gradient but also upon the nature of the material through which the heat is being conducted. k is thus interpreted as a property of the rock concerned and is called the *thermal conductivity* of the rock. The definition of thermal conductivity may be obtained from equation (3.2.3). Rewriting this equation to give k:

$$k = \frac{qz}{\Delta T} \qquad (3.2.4)$$

If we set the temperature gradient equal to 1, $\Delta T/z = 1$ and $z/\Delta T = 1$, so that:

$$k = q \qquad (3.2.5)$$

In other words, thermal conductivity, k is the quantity of heat flowing across an area of one square metre in one second in a region where the temperature gradient is 1 °C per metre. This definition is illustrated further in Figure 3.2.1.

Units: In SI units the unit of heat energy is the joule (J), the unit of area is the square metre (m^2) and the unit of time is the second (s). q is thus measured in joules per square metre per second ($J\,m^{-2}\,s^{-1}$) or, because joules per second = watts, in watts per square metre ($W\,m^{-2}$). The temperature gradient unit will be degrees per metre ($K\,m^{-1}$, which is numerically the same as °C m^{-1}). Thus from equation (3.2.4):

$$k = \frac{qz}{\Delta T}$$

and so:

$$[\text{units of } k] = [\text{units of } q] [\text{units of } z/\Delta T]$$

$$\equiv [\text{W m}^{-2}] [\text{K}^{-1} \text{ m}]$$

$$\equiv \text{W m}^{-1} \text{ K}^{-1} \text{ (watts per metre per degree)}$$

In heat flow studies, however, it is convenient to use 'working units' based on the cgs (centimetre–gram–second) system. In this case the unit of heat is the calorie (cal); but because the observed heat flow is very small it is usual to work in microcalories (μcal) where 1 microcalorie = 10^{-6} calorie. The full unit for rate of flow of heat is thus μcal cm^{-2} s^{-1}. To avoid having to write this out in full many times it will, in this chapter, be abbreviated to h.f.u. (heat flow unit). The numerical factors for conversion of one set of units to the other are:

Quantity	SI unit	Working unit	Conversion factor†
heat flow, q	W m^{-2}	μcal cm^{-2} s^{-1}	0.0418
temperature gradient, $\Delta T/z$	K m^{-1}	°C cm^{-1}	100
thermal conductivity, k	W m^{-1} K^{-1}	μcal cm^{-1} s^{-1} °C^{-1}	4.18×10^{-4}

† To convert 'working unit' to SI unit multiply by this number.

Equation (3.2.3) illustrates the essential and important point that in order to determine the heat flow through the Earth's surface it is necessary to make two separate measurements—the near-surface temperature gradient and the thermal conductivity of the rock. In

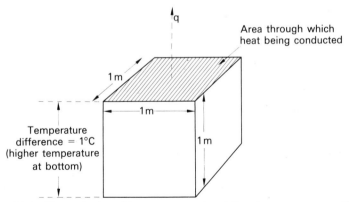

Figure 3.2.1   The conduction of heat across a surface. When the temperature gradient is unity, as it is in the diagram, the rate of heat flow (q) across the surface is equal to the thermal conductivity (k) of the material forming the block, assuming that none of the heat flows out of the sides of the block.

this chapter we shall be concerned with these measurements and their implications; but anticipating the results somewhat, it is worth noting at this stage two things which have a general bearing on the context. The first is that of the various energy processes relating to the Earth, the rate of loss of heat energy from the Earth's interior is far greater than the energy involved in any other purely terrestrial process—it is, for example, some thousand times greater than the energy released by earthquakes. The four most important energy transactions which affect the Earth are shown in Table 3.2.1, from which it may be seen that the geothermal heat loss is exceeded only by the solar energy received by the Earth.

Table 3.2.1 The principal energy transactions affecting the Earth.

Process	Energy: joules per year
solar energy received (and re-radiated)	10^{25}
geothermal heat loss	10^{21}
energy lost by slowing of Earth's rotation	3×10^{19}
energy released by earthquakes	10^{18}

But the second point of considerable importance is that although the solar energy received by the Earth is some 10 000 times greater than the geothermal energy, the former hardly penetrates the Earth and is mostly re-radiated back into space. The heat from the Sun is the main source of energy for processes occurring on and above the Earth's surface and controls the Earth's surface temperature. But its influence on the Earth's interior is negligible because the thermal conductivity of rocks is extremely low and so heat conducts through rocks extremely slowly. Thus on land, daily variations at atmospheric temperature produce changes of less than 1 °C at a depth of 1 m and are not felt there for over half a day after the atmospheric change has taken place. Only seasonal variations are felt below a few metres and at a few tens of metres temperature changes are very small and over a year late.

What all this means is that the low thermal conductivity of rock prevents the measurement of heat escaping from the Earth's interior being completely swamped by solar heat entering and leaving the Earth, except in the upper few tens of metres. But by the same token, if the temperature gradient produced by the Earth's internal heat is to be measured free from any effects whatsoever from solar heat, it must be done so at depths of at least 30 m and preferably below 100 m. Another consequence of low thermal conductivity, however, is that the heat we now observe at the Earth's surface may well have begun its journey many millions of years ago. If heat is transmitted in the Earth only by conduction, a sudden change in temperature at the

Earth's centre, for example, would take 200000 million years to be felt at the surface. To put it another way, whatever the Earth's temperature distribution is now it will be the combined result of all large-scale thermal events which have taken place in the Earth over the past many millions of years. In short, it is likely to be extremely difficult to interpret the heat flow data even when they have been obtained.

Finally, it should be emphasized that the use of equation (3.2.3) to determine heat flow makes the assumption that heat near the Earth's surface is being transmitted by conduction. This is probably quite valid for the solid upper crust; but it should not therefore be supposed that everywhere in the Earth heat is transmitted solely by conduction. We shall have cause to consider the implications of other forms of heat transfer later.

3.3 The measurement of terrestrial heat flow

Historically, the first determinations of terrestrial heat flow were made on land; ocean floor measurements were not begun until 1950. In many ways, however, measurements at sea are both easier to make and interpret and this explains why there are now far more ocean floor values than continental values of heat flow available. But wherever heat flow is measured there are some uncertainties involved; and each possible source of error must be carefully considered before the final results may be interpreted.

Measurement of temperature gradient

In theory, all that is required to measure temperature gradient is to have two thermometers placed a known distance apart. In practice, however, for a reason we shall come to later, it is more usual to have several temperature-measuring devices suitably spaced down the borehole on land, or within the sediment on the ocean floor, so that the variation of temperature gradient with depth may also be determined. On land the thermometers used are either mercury thermometers which record maximum temperatures reached or thermistors*, and are lowered down the required borehole which may have been specially drilled for the purpose or which may have originally been bored for some other exploratory purpose. Because drilling on land is an expensive business, many of the continental heat flow determinations have been made in pre-existing holes originally drilled by, for example, petroleum companies for oil exploration. Obviously this saves both money and time; but the disadvantage is that holes drilled for a specific purpose such as the search for oil are likely to lie in regions where, on geological grounds, the probability of finding oil is quite high. In this sense the sites may not be representative of continents as a whole and this is likely to pose problems in the interpretation of heat flow data in terms of continents in general.

On the ocean floors where sediments are comparatively soft the drilling of a borehole is unnecessary. An apparatus which both allows the measurement of temperature gradient in ocean sediments and enables sediment sample to be collected for later thermal conductivity measurement is shown in Figure 3.3.1. The hollow barrel together with outrigged thermistors is simply allowed to drop into the sediment which is usually easily penetrated.

Sources of error in temperature gradient measurement

The apparent simplicity of temperature gradient measurement conceals some serious problems which may introduce significant, and often unknown, errors into the temperature gradients directly observed, although in some cases sources of error may be eliminated with suitable precautions. The main problems encountered in the determination of temperature gradient are these:

1. Continents: Temperature gradients on land are usually measured in boreholes; but the process of drilling the hole in the first place disturbs the thermal equilibrium at the site. Friction from the drill produces heat which may take some time to dissipate; and although water used to cool the drill during the drilling operation will carry some of the extra heat away, details of the effect are unknown. In practice, once a borehole has been drilled it takes several times the time taken to drill the borehole for the original thermal equilibrium to be re-established throughout the complete length of the hole. However, the lower regions of the hole may reach equilibrium rather quicker so that measurements there may be begun but a few days after drilling. Even the upper sections of the hole may be used before thermal equilibrium is re-established as long as the measurements are repeated at various times after drilling has ceased. In this case, the change of temperature with time is used in conjunction with a mathematical formula to determine the true equilibrium temperature.

Ocean floors: On the ocean floor the disturbance of thermal equilibrium is much less severe. In the Ewing probe, for example, the thermistors are housed in fine tubes mounted away from the main corer. Because of their small mass, these probes come to thermal equilibrium with their surroundings very quickly, only about half a minute being required for them to come within a few percent of the final temperature. The temperature gradient can thus be measured in two to four minutes

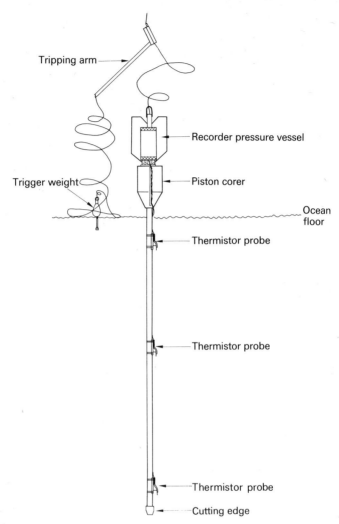

Figure 3.3.1   The Ewing technique for temperature gradient measurement and sample collection on the ocean floor. When the trigger weight hits the ocean floor, the main apparatus is released and falls freely under its own weight to penetrate the sediment. The sample core for later thermal conductivity measurement is collected in the central hollow barrel which can achieve a penetration of up to 20 m. The outrigged probes which house the thermistors are hollow stainless steel tubes about 0.3 cm in outside diameter with a wall thickness sufficient to withstand pressures up to 1000 atmospheres. The probes are mounted on fins which hold the probes about 7–10 cm out from the core barrel wall; and the tips of the probes project about 2.5–4 cm ahead of the fins. *Source:* Langseth (1965), with modification.

—well before the thermal disturbances generated by the penetration of the main coring tube reach the positions of the probes.

2. *Continents:* To avoid the effects of solar radiation, temperature gradients on land must be measured below at least 30 m and preferably below 100 m.

Ocean floors: In this case solar effects are usually absent because of the shielding effect of up to several kilometres of sea water which produce a nearly constant temperature at the ocean floor. Deep waters of the ocean originate from the horizontal spreading of cold, dense waters which originally sank at high latitudes; and because this process is associated with the freezing of ice at the high latitudes, the temperatures of deep waters everywhere are within a few degrees of 0 °C and have probably remained so for a considerable time. There are, however, a few areas where this is not so. In the Mediterranean, for example, temperatures are not directly influenced by the spread of water from high latitudes because the Mediterranean basin is enclosed by topographic sills which rise higher than the deep waters of the larger oceans. Here the effects of temperature are less certain; but in most areas significant temperature variations may be ruled out.

3. *Continents:* Because the Earth's surface departs from a plane of constant temperature, variations in topography will cause irregularities in heat flow. This effect is only important in mountainous regions; and even there most disturbing influences are those within a 2 km radius of the borehole. Sometimes the errors introduced are positive and sometimes negative (higher than normal heat flow in valleys, lower than normal heat flow on peaks). The best way to avoid having to make complicated corrections is thus to make several measurements of temperature gradient in the area—that is, in different boreholes—and take an average. In this way, positive and negative errors will hopefully cancel out. But for single boreholes in mountainous areas the effect of topography may be significant.

Ocean floors: Here too topography may seriously affect temperature gradients as may the uneven distribution of sediments on the ocean bottom. Where topographic variations are known, mathematical corrections (not always very satisfactory) may be made. Very often, however, the topography in the vicinity of the measuring site is just not known.

4. *Continents:* Variations in heat flow will also have been caused by differential changes over geological time—for example, uplift, erosion, glaciation and climatic changes. Mathematical corrections for some of these may be applied; but they are tedious and not very satisfactory

because in many areas the geological and climatic histories are not accurately known.

Ocean floors: Similar effects may be produced on the ocean floor by, for example, variations in sedimentation rate or erosion. Over most of the ocean floor, average sedimentation rates are too low to affect surface heat flow; but exceptions may occur near continents where sedimentation rates are very high—for example, the Gulf of California, the Pacific coast of North America and the Gulf of Mexico. If rapid deposition or erosion has occurred, the upper layers of sediment may not be in thermal equilibrium with those below. Sometimes these effects may be detected by an examination of sediment cores—contorted sediments, for example, indicate turbulent deposition.

These are just some of the problems likely to be encountered in obtaining accurate measurements of temperature gradient—the list is far from exclusive. On land, for example, the flowing of underground waters may introduce errors. Sometimes this effect may be detected by the appearance of water in the drill hole but is not obvious when inlet and outlet points lie below the surface. Errors may also arise in boreholes near oceans or large lakes; that is, near regions of large mass water flow. Results may also be affected by local sources of heating; for example, the oxidation of ore bodies or local concentrations of radioactive material. Finally, as with any scientific measurement, there will be errors of measurement and instrumental errors.

The general point to remember in connection with the determination of temperature gradient in any area is that a group of determinations is likely to give a more valid result than a single determination, for by using more than one hole, errors and spurious effects are more likely to be averaged out. At the same time, the precise locations of boreholes will depend on the problem to be investigated, of which there are three main types: (i) measurement of average heat flow over a large area to investigate regional or worldwide variations, (ii) measurements on prominent geological features— such as ridges, trenches and continental margins—to investigate anomalies, and (iii) closely spaced measurements to investigate local features. From the above consideration of error sources, it is clear that ocean floor determinations generally pose the least severe problems quite apart from the advantage that oceanic holes may be put down more or less at will (but suffer from the difficulty of close navigational positioning) whereas continental holes are expensive.

Measurement of thermal conductivity

To determine heat flow, the thermal conductivities of the rock materials involved are required as well as the temperature gradients. In the

Ewing probe for use at sea the required samples are collected with the apparatus also used to measure the temperature gradient. On land, samples may be taken from the borehole itself or, where the borehole cores are no longer available (if, for example, the hole was previously drilled for some other purpose), from close by. The chief problem with sampling can easily be foreseen—the difficulty of sampling representatively. The number of samples to be taken will depend on how variable the rock is over the distance within which the temperature gradient is measured. Any given borehole is likely to pass through a variety of rock types; and the greater this variety the greater will be the number of thermal conductivity measurements required to give a good average value for the complete hole. Moreover, even where the rock *appears* to be uniform throughout, marked variations in thermal conductivity can occur.

Although methods are now available for measuring thermal conductivity *in situ*, measurements are more frequently made in the laboratory. Numerous types of apparatus are available. A particular scientist's choice of equipment will depend upon his own idea of what constitutes a suitable compromise between reliability, accuracy and convenience, including cost and the time required for measurement, for the particular job involved. However, the thermal conductivity apparatus most used for continental samples is some form of what is known as the 'divided bar' apparatus. The principle of the method was first applied by C. H. Lees in 1892 although since that time the Lees apparatus has undergone numerous modifications. The version shown in Figure 3.3.2 was developed by A. E. Beck.

The principle of the Lees–Beck apparatus is that the thermal conductivity of the rock sample is compared with that of a standard material such as brass (known) under steady state conditions. The apparatus comprises two brass rods a few centimetres long between which is placed the rock sample in the form of a disc having a cross section to match the rods. Very small thermistors are placed at intervals along each rod for temperature measurement. The outer ends of the rods are sprayed with water from baths each thermostatically controlled to within 0.01 °C; but one bath (the lower one in the diagram) is maintained at a temperature 20 °C higher than the other. Heat will thus flow from the hot end, along the lower brass rod, through the rock disc, along the upper rod and so out at the cooler end. The idea is to get all the heat flowing along in this way; and so an insulating layer of polythene is used to prevent the escape of heat from the sides as far as possible.

When the steady state is reached—that is, when all thermistors reach a constant (but not all the same) temperature (which takes about ten minutes)—the heat entering the lower rod must be equal to the heat leaving the upper rod apart from minor unavoidable side losses.

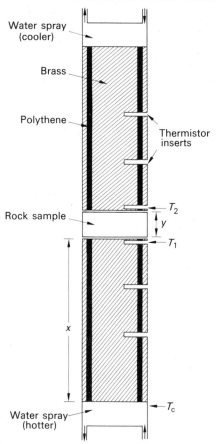

Figure 3.3.2   The Lees–Beck divided bar apparatus for measuring the thermal conductivity of rock (stylized).

This must be so because once the thermistors reach steady temperatures this is an indication that the net amount of heat in the brass rods and rock disc is no longer changing. In other words, the amount of heat flowing through the rods must equal the amount of heat flowing through the sample of rock in the same time.

Now equation (3.2.3) shows that the rate of flow of heat (q) through unit cross-sectional area is given by:

$$q = \frac{k\Delta T}{z} \tag{3.2.3}$$

where k is the thermal conductivity of the material and $\Delta T/z$ is the temperature gradient in it. Thus for the brass (denoted by subscript b):

$$q_b = k_b \left(\frac{\Delta T}{z}\right)_b \qquad (3.3.1)$$

and for the rock sample (denoted by subscript r):

$$q_r = k_r \left(\frac{\Delta T}{z}\right)_r \qquad (3.3.2)$$

But as we have shown above, q_b must be equal to q_r; and so:

$$k_b \left(\frac{\Delta T}{z}\right)_b = k_r \left(\frac{\Delta T}{z}\right)_r \qquad (3.3.3)$$

which, rearranged, becomes:

$$k_r = k_b \left[\left(\frac{\Delta T}{z}\right)_b \Big/ \left(\frac{\Delta T}{z}\right)_r\right] \qquad (3.3.4)$$

In order to measure k_r it is thus necessary to determine each of the three terms on the right hand side of equation (3.3.4):

(i) The temperature gradient in the brass rods, $(\Delta T/z)_b$, may be measured. In terms of the symbols shown in Figure 3.2.2 it is $(T_c - T_1)/x$. The bath temperature (T_c) is known, the temperature T_1 is measured by thermistor, and the distance x is known after measurement.

(ii) The temperature gradient in the rock, $(\Delta T/z)_r$, may also be measured. In terms of the symbols shown in Figure 3.2.2 it is $(T_1 - T_2)/y$. The temperatures T_1 and T_2 are measured by thermistor, and the rock thickness y is known after measurement.

(iii) The thermal conductivity of brass (k_b) is already known.

The biggest problem with this apparatus is that it is essential in theory, but impossible in practice, to make a perfect contact between the brass and the rock. The difficulty is that there is a thin air film between each end of the rock disc and the corresponding brass rod; and thus the temperature difference $(T_1 - T_2)$ is not really the temperature difference across the rock sample but the temperature difference across the rock sample *and* the two air films. This effect may be reduced to negligible proportions by applying an axial pressure which forces the rock and brass closer together and by using a contact medium of higher conductivity than air (for example, silicone grease, liquid detergent or 'Vaseline'). Otherwise, additional experiments may be carried out to determine the quantitative error introduced by the air films.

The Lees–Beck apparatus is particularly suitable for hard continental rock although it may also be used for softer sediments as long as the sediment is held to a disc shape with a plastic ring. In most cases, however, sediment thermal conductivities are measured using a needle probe. In this method, a very thin needle inserted into the sediment is heated by an internal heater wire at a known and constant rate. The needle (see Figure 3.3.3) is usually 0.5–0.9 mm in outside diameter and 6.4 cm long. The rate of rise in temperature of the needle is measured with a small thermistor placed inside the needle and at its mid-point.

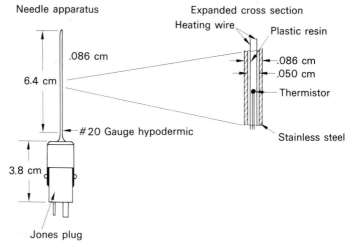

Figure 3.3.3 The needle probe for measuring the thermal conductivity of sediment. *Source:* Langseth (1965).

After the heater has been running for about ten seconds, the temperature T (°C) recorded by the thermistor varies with time (seconds) according to the formula:

$$T = \frac{Q}{4\pi k}\ln(t) + C \tag{3.3.5}$$

where Q is the heat applied to the needle per centimetre of its length per second (cal cm^{-1} s^{-1});

k is the thermal conductivity of the sediment (cal cm^{-1} s^{-1} °C^{-1});

C is a constant.

If the temperature is plotted against the natural logarithm of time, a straight line results with a gradient of $Q/4\pi k$. Since Q is known, k may be calculated from this gradient. An example of such a graph is shown in Figure 3.3.4.

Problems associated with thermal conductivity determination

1. The chief problem is to ensure that the thermal conductivity obtained is quite representative of the borehole or ocean core in question. For one thing, there is not necessarily any correlation between variations

in the appearance of rock and variations in thermal conductivity. A single borehole may pass through several different types of rock each of which differs in thermal conductivity; but equally, a section of rock which visually appears quite uniform may exhibit marked variations

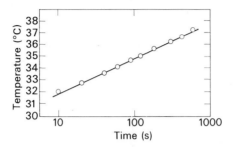

Figure 3.3.4 Calculation of thermal conductivity from the needle probe method. Temperature is plotted as a function of the logarithm of time. (In the graph shown, time is plotted directly on a logarithmic scale.) A straight line results, from which k may be calculated. The temperature rise is usually recorded for about four minutes. *Source:* Von Herzen, Maxwell and Snodgrass (1962).

in thermal conductivity, partly because the various proportions of its constituent minerals may vary.

Because thermal conductivity may vary along a core, a decision has to be made as to how many samples constitute a representative selection. An aid to this decision is to plot the observed temperature gradient as a function of depth in the hole. If it is assumed that the heat flow is constant along the length of the borehole, then any changes in temperature gradient may be presumed to be due to changes in thermal conductivity. The number of changes observed on the temperature gradient–depth curve will thus give some indication of how many samples need to be measured to obtain a good average value of thermal conductivity for the whole section. Ultimately, however, the scientist must make a subjective assessment of the number of samples required.

Finally, it is worth emphasizing that high precision in the measurement of thermal conductivity is less important than making a large number of measurements. However accurate a single measurement is, it is no good at all if it is not representative. It is far better to make a very large number of rapid, if slightly less accurate measurements. And here again it is worth noting that the oceans have an advantage in that the average thermal conductivity of oceanic sediment is remarkably constant throughout the world. Comparative figures for the three major oceans are shown in Table 3.3.1.

2. A second, but perhaps less important, point is that thermal conductivity should strictly be measured under the same conditions under

Table 3.3.1   Thermal conductivities (k) of oceanic sediments. *Source:* Lee and Uyeda (1965).

Ocean	Number of values, N	Mean k†	Standard deviation†
Atlantic	106	2.09	0.19
Indian	180	1.98	0.25
Pacific	300	1.95	0.20
All	586	1.98	0.22

† Units: mcal cm^{-1} °C^{-1} ($= 10^3$ μcal cm$^-$ s^{-1} °C^{-1}).

which the relevant rocks were transmitting the Earth's heat. Thus for samples brought up from depth for thermal conductivity determination in the laboratory, corrections should be applied for the pressure and (more importantly) temperature at the point from which the samples were collected. This particularly applies to ocean floor samples (*in situ* at 0 °C, 700–1000 atmospheres) for which corrections are small but not necessarily insignificant:

(i) effect of pressure on $k = +1$ percent for each 2000 metres depth;
(ii) effect of temperature on $k = -6$ percent for the change 25 °C to 4 °C.

From these figures it can be seen that the effects of temperature and pressure are opposed and thus tend to cancel out. As it becomes possible to drill deeper and deeper holes, however, the effects of removing the rock from its natural surroundings may become more serious in that, for example, the release of pressure may produce irreversible changes in rock structure.

3.4 Calculation and analysis of heat flow rate

Once both thermal conductivity and temperature gradient have been measured, it becomes possible to calculate the rate of heat flow according to equation (3.2.3). There are several different ways in which this may be done although they usually give similar results.

Ideally one has two sets of basic data:

(a) a series of temperature gradients along the length of the borehole;
(b) a series of thermal conductivity measurements covering all lithological units within the section and all variations whether or not they visually correlate with lithological units.

The simplest way of proceeding is then to divide the section into lithological units. For each unit the thermal conductivity values are

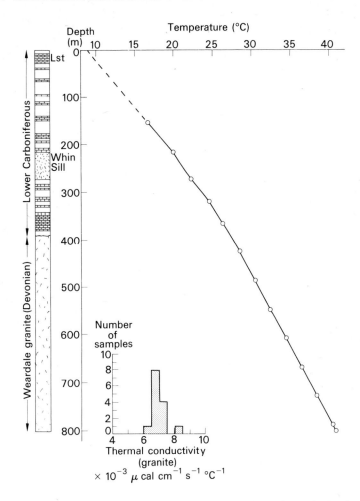

Figure 3.4.1 The determination of heat flow in the Rookhope borehole, Stanhope, County Durham. The temperature–depth distribution was obtained using a thermistor probe three years after drilling was complete. Thermal conductivity measurements were only made on the granite at depths between 427 and 792 m. The data for the borehole are:

observed temperature gradient over 427–792 m $= (32.45 \pm 0.10) \times 10^{-5}\,{}^{\circ}\text{C cm}^{-1}$
calculated correction for topography $= -(1.55 \pm 0.50) \times 10^{-5}\,{}^{\circ}\text{C cm}^{-1}$
corrected temperature gradient $= (30.90 \pm 0.51) \times 10^{-5}\,{}^{\circ}\text{C cm}^{-1}$
average thermal conductivity $= (7000 \pm 200)\,\mu\text{cal cm}^{-1}\,\text{s}^{-1}\,{}^{\circ}\text{C}^{-1}$
heat flow by equation (3.2.3) $= (2.16 \pm 0.07)\,\mu\text{cal cm}^{-2}\,\text{s}^{-1}$ (h.f.u).

Source: Bott (1971).

averaged; and the heat flow rate is calculated by multiplying mean thermal conductivity by temperature gradient according to equation (3.2.3). The mean rate of heat flow for the whole is then calculated by averaging the rates for the separate lithological units. An experimental example of heat flow measurement in a borehole in England is shown in Figure 3.4.1.

By 1969 about 3000 heat flow values had been obtained, of which over eighty-three percent were from the ocean floor. (The proportion of the Earth's surface covered by ocean is about seventy-one percent; so there are about twice as many values per unit area of ocean as there are of continent.) The analysis of heat flow data is usually based either on individual measurements or on average values for each 5° latitude by 5° longitude segment of the Earth's surface. The idea of using mean values within each 5° × 5° area rather than individual values in order to, for example, calculate mean values for large areas of the Earth's surface is simply an attempt to compensate for the fact that the distribution of observations over the Earth's surface is not very uniform. If localized averaging is first carried out, so the argument goes, the large-area averages later calculated from them will come closer to the truth. Mathematically speaking this is probably true, although the lack of uniformity is so marked that it is doubtful whether averages calculated in this way are really much better than averages calculated from individual values.

This lack of uniformity is well illustrated by Figure 3.4.2 which shows the heat flow averages for 5° × 5° areas where observations are available at all. Coverage is extremely poor in Africa, South America and Antarctica and is not particularly good in any continental area. Because of the lack of uniformity, in order to contour the heat flow values over the Earth's surface a mathematical 'smoothing' must be carried out; although it must be recognized that even this process can only be perfect if the data are distributed uniformly in the first place. One recent example of this smoothing process is shown in Figure 3.4.3 whence it can be seen that there are various 'centres' of regional extent over which the heat flow is comparatively low in some cases and high in others. Diagrams such as this are useful when it comes to comparing the world heat flow distribution with similar distributions for other quantities such as gravity or topography. For most purposes, however, it is more useful to look at the data on a rather smaller scale and to compare the smaller scale averages one with another.

But before we do this it is worth trying to obtain some idea of what the magnitude of instrumental error is likely to be. Because of the wide variety of apparatus in use, this is difficult; but it is quite important because if we are to compare heat flow averages between different regions, it is clearly useful to know whether the differences in heat flow as observed may be explained solely as instrumental error or whether

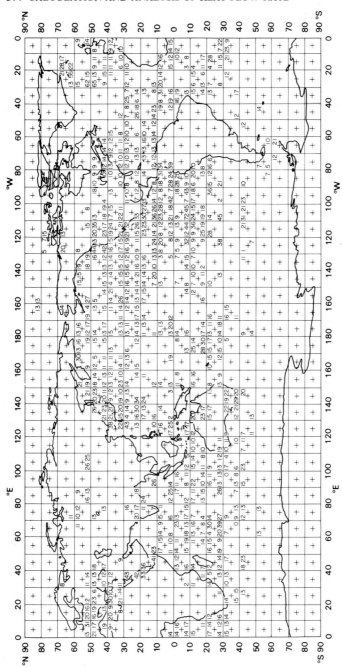

Figure 3.4.2 Distribution of heat flow throughout the world as averaged in 5° latitude by 5° longitude areas. Units are 10^{-1} μcal cm^{-2} s^{-1}; that is, a figure 13 on the diagram is equivalent to 1.3 h.f.u. *Source*: Horai and Simmons (1969).

they reflect more fundamental processes at work in the Earth. The best way of estimating instrumental error is to make a repeat set of measurements in the same borehole and under the same conditions; but this is seldom done. However, a rough estimate of measurement error may be made by analysing (i) the few repeat measurements, together with (ii) measurements which have been made in closely

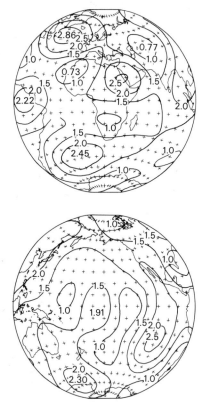

Figure 3.4.3 Worldwide heat flow contours (units: h.f.u.) obtained mathematically. *Source:* Horai and Simmons (1969).

spaced holes—say, holes within 10 km of each other. Let us suppose that for each of such heat flow 'pairs', one member has heat flow x and the other has heat flow y. Then the difference in heat flow, $(x - y)$, for the members of each pair will give some indication of the measurement errors involved; if there were no such errors, for example, x should always be equal to y and then $x - y = 0$. The average values of $(x - y)$ for 74 heat flow pairs on land and 49 heat flow pairs on the ocean floor are shown in Table 3.4.1.

From Table 3.4.1 it would appear that measurement errors are lower on continents than at sea although it is doubtful whether the difference is significant. Under the circumstances the best thing to do is probably to take the larger of the two figures—that pertaining to the ocean floor—because we are mainly interested in estimating the maximum possible error to which heat flow data may, on average, be subjected. We shall not do so here but it is possible to show mathematically that an average $(x - y)$ value of 0.04 h.f.u. with a standard

Table 3.4.1 Statistics for pairs of heat flow stations which are less than 10 km apart. *Source:* Lee and Uyeda (1965).

	Number of pairs	Average $(x - y)$ value	Standard deviation
Land	74	0.01	0.15
Ocean	49	0.04	0.47

deviation of 0.47 h.f.u. corresponds to an average error in mean heat flow for a region of 0.2 h.f.u. In other words, on this basis—and it is a fairly crude sort of basis—regional heat flow differences may be considered significant (that is, not solely due to measurement error) if they are greater than about 0.2 h.f.u.

3.5 Heat flow over the ocean floor

As we have seen, the bulk of heat flow values have been obtained from the ocean floor, largely because ocean floor measurements are generally cheaper and easier to make than continental measurements. In one sense, however, this is an ideal circumstance, for the key processes of global tectonics are chiefly related to the ocean floors; the availability of such data thus enables us to examine and compare both the theoretical and observed consequences of the dynamic Earth from the thermal point of view. At mid-oceanic ridges, for example, where material from the mantle is supposedly upwelling to form new ocean floor we would expect, *a priori*, heat flow to be higher than average because mantle material is hotter than the Earth's crust. Likewise, at oceanic trenches, where cooler crustal material purports to sink, a lower than average upward flow of heat is to be expected. But are these expectations confirmed by observation?

In this section we shall examine the relationship of heat flow to such features as ridges, trenches and ocean basins, largely to see how well such relationships accord with the tenets of the new global tectonics. But, first, what are the overall averages for the various oceans and how do these averages compare with each other? The relevant figures are presented in Table 3.5.1 and histograms of heat flow values from the three main oceans are plotted in Figure 3.5.1. If the value of 0.2 h.f.u.

Table 3.5.1 Average values of heat flow for the oceans, continents and world-wide. N = number of observations; q = heat flow in h.f.u.; S.D. = standard deviation in h.f.u. *Source:* Horai and Simmons (1969).

	N	q	S.D.
Pacific Ocean	1445	1.78	1.15
Atlantic Ocean	461	1.34	0.88
Indian Ocean	398	1.54	1.18
All oceans†	2348	1.64	1.11
All continents	474	1.65	0.89
World	2822	1.65	1.08

† Includes 44 values from the Arctic and Antarctic Oceans.

presented in the previous section is to be taken as a yardstick, there appear to be significant differences between oceanic mean values, especially between the Pacific and Atlantic. Unfortunately, these differences could arise from non-uniform sampling rather than be fundamental differences between oceans. Because of this, it cannot be really said that oceanic average heat flows differ significantly from each other; and certainly there are no discernible differences in the shapes of the histograms.

Ocean basins

Ocean basins are characterized by relatively smooth topography, deep water, a crust of normal thickness, and aseismicity. Heat flow values in ocean basins are comparatively uniform (a relatively low scatter as represented by the comparatively low standard deviation—see Table 3.5.2), the average value of 1.27 h.f.u. is somewhat lower than

Table 3.5.2 Average values of heat flow for the main provinces of the continents and ocean floors. N = number of observations; q = heat flow in h.f.u.; S.D. = standard deviation in h.f.u. *Source:* Sass (1971).

	N	q	S.D.
Ocean basins	683	1.27	0.53
Mid-oceanic ridges	1065	1.91	1.48
Ocean trenches	78	1.17	0.69
Precambrian shields	214	0.98	0.23
Post-Precambrian non-orogenic areas	96	1.48	0.41
Palaeozoic orogenic areas†	88	1.44	0.41
Mesozoic–Cenozoic orogenic areas†	159	1.77	0.57

† Post-Precambrian orogenic areas.

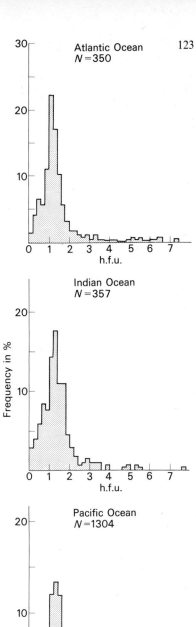

Figure 3.5.1 Histograms of heat flow values from the Atlantic, Indian and Pacific Oceans. *Source:* Langseth and Von Herzen (1970).

the oceanic and world averages, and the histograms of values shown in Figure 3.5.2 (a) are nearly symmetrical. According to the new global tectonics, ocean basins are generally regions where the oceanic lithosphere is spreading horizontally (that is, from the tectonic point of view they are the most 'normal' part of the ocean floor) and thus the heat flow values are generally consistent with this picture.

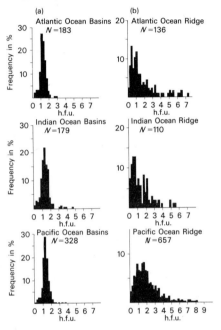

Figure 3.5.2 Histograms of heat flow values from (a) the basins, and (b) the ridges of the Atlantic, Indian and Pacific Oceans. *Source:* Langseth and Von Herzen (1970).

Ocean ridges

Ocean ridges have a rugged topography and shallow water and may be seismic (most) or aseismic (very few). As far as the seismic ridges are concerned, heat flow values are very scattered; but it is difficult to decide whether the scatter is due mainly to true variations or to disturbances, for several of the sources of error discussed above are particularly applicable to ridges. For example, topographic errors and errors arising from uneven sediment thicknesses are especially relevant. Moreover, because sediments on ridges are fewer, the average penetration of the temperature gradient probe is probably less and so measurement errors are likely to be greater than in ocean basins. Further, the volcanism associated with the ridge axes can be expected to induce the circulation of water within the sediments.

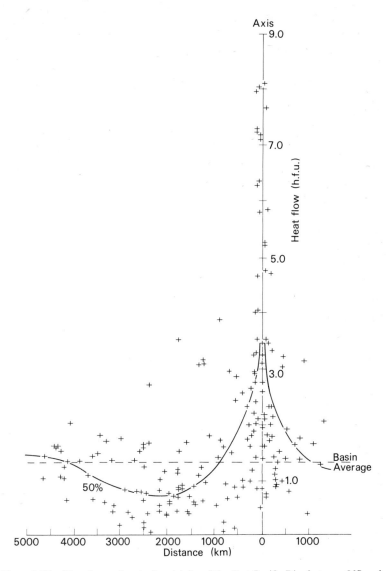

Figure 3.5.3 Heat flow values in the vicinity of the East Pacific Rise between 5 °S and 20 °S plotted as a function of distance from the axis. *Source:* Langseth and Von Herzen (1970).

Nevertheless, it seems reasonable to suppose that the histograms of ridge heat flow values shown in Figure 3.5.2 (b) are skew partly because of real regional heat flow variations over the ridges. In Figure 3.5.3 heat flow values from the East Pacific Rise are plotted as a function of distance from the ridge axis; and it seems clear from this that immediately above the axis itself heat flow is very high indeed. A similar conclusion may be drawn for the mid-Atlantic Ridge, the data for which are plotted slightly differently in Figure 3.5.4. These high values are, of course, consistent with the presence of hot mantle material immediately beneath ridge axes.

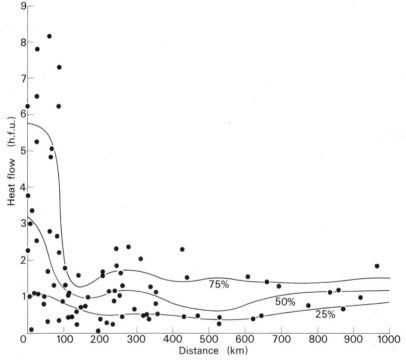

Figure 3.5.4   Heat flow values in the vicinity of the mid-Atlantic Ridge plotted as a function of distance from the axis. The percentages shown refer to the proportions of the points lying below the corresponding lines. *Source:* Lee and Uyeda (1965).

At the same time, however, it is interesting—and surprising—to note that there are regions on the flanks of both the East Pacific Rise and the mid-Atlantic Ridge where heat flow is extremely low—lower than the average for ocean basins. For example, much of the western flank of the East Pacific Rise south of the equator has a heat flow of only half the basin average. The average value of heat flow over ridges

of 1.91 h.f.u. (Table 3.5.2) appears to be rather higher than the world
or overall oceanic average (Table 3.5.1); but when the high scatter
of values is taken into account the difference cannot be considered
significant.

Ocean trenches

Ocean trenches are associated with island arc systems, very deep water
and strong seismicity. Because of the deep water the measurement of
heat flow over trenches is both difficult and hazardous, so there are
comparatively few observations. The histogram of heat flow values

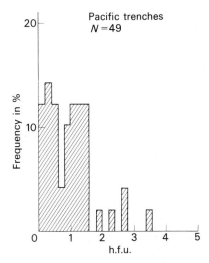

Figure 3.5.5 Histograms of heat flow
values from Pacific trenches. *Source:*
Langseth and Von Herzen (1970).

from the Pacific trenches is shown in Figure 3.5.5, from which it is
apparent that the distribution is bimodal. That part of the distribution
centred around 1.2 h.f.u. is similar to that for ocean basins; but that
part of the distribution centred around about 0.4 h.f.u. is entirely
characteristic of trenches. These low values come from a very narrow
zone in the floor of the trench and from the trench's landward wall.
Again they are consistent with the ideas of sea floor spreading; but
again, in view of the large scatter of values (though much lower than
for ridges), the ocean trench heat flow average of 1.17 h.f.u. (Table
3.5.2) may not be significantly lower than elsewhere.

Oceanic heat flow and global tectonics

The general, simplified theory of sea floor spreading envisages the
upwelling of mantle material along the axes of mid-oceanic ridges to

form new lithosphere which spreads laterally away from the ridges and subsequently sinks at trenches. In these very general terms, these processes imply a higher than average upward heat flow along active ridge axes where magma is rising, a lower than average heat flow along trenches where colder lithosphere is sinking, and about an average or 'normal' heat flow over ocean basins where the lateral spreading takes place. In general, the average heat flow values quoted in Table 3.5.2 support this view. The average for ocean basins is, to be sure, somewhat lower than the overall world average; but the ridge average is higher and the trench average is much lower than the world average. At the same time, it is difficult to be sure that these differences are really significant because the standard deviations are large, because heat flow observations are not very uniformly distributed throughout the world, and because it is difficult to know whether or not such factors as topography, sediment thickness and sedimentary water circulation introduce significant systematic errors. What is more certain is that within a narrow zone of a few hundred kilometres across each ridge axis individual heat flow values are significantly higher than average, and that within a narrow zone across each trench values are significantly lower than average. In this sense the consistency of heat flow variations with the sea floor spreading process would seem to be proved.

It is important to realize, however, that the simplified theory of sea floor spreading is just that—simplified—and that in practice the processes involved are likely to be much more complex. That this must be so is well illustrated by the fact that at ridge flanks the heat flow is lower than in ocean basins—a phenomenon which the simple theory does not predict. If it really be true that the overall ridge average heat flow (that is, over the axes and flanks together) is no different from the world average or basin average, this would suggest a round-about and swings situation—that the excess heat appearing at ridge axes is derived from the flanks. This, in turn, implies that the material appearing at the axes to form new lithosphere is derived from beneath the flanks. But these ideas are very tentative and no satisfactory explanation of the low heat flow over ridge flanks has yet been produced.

Other complexities must also obtain in trench regions. Figure 3.5.6 shows a heat flow profile stretching from Japan across the Pacific to the East Pacific Rise, from which the relationship between ridge flank and ocean basin heat flows is quite evident. It is equally evident, however, that to the landward side of the very low heat flow values associated with the Japan trench, heat flow rises to well above the ocean basin average. This is characteristic of regions landward of trench–island arc systems and is thought to be due to a combination of volcanic activity, frictional heating by the lithosphere as it descends, and some

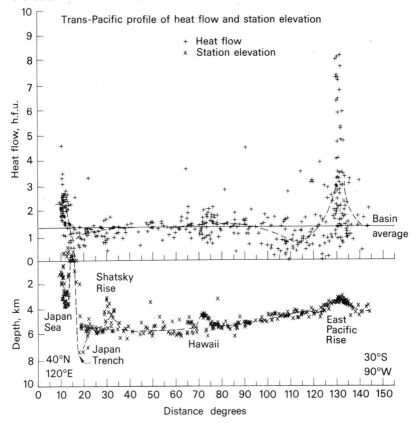

Figure 3.5.6 Profile of heat flow (top) and station elevation (bottom) from Japan across the Pacific to the East Pacific Rise. *Source:* Langseth and Von Herzen (1970).

process which concentrates heat-producing radioactive elements in the upper part of the lithosphere in this region.

3.6 Heat flow over continents

Measuring heat flow on land is not only technically more difficult than making measurements at the ocean floor but the results are more difficult to interpret because of greater geological complexity. In order to avoid, or at least assess, the effect of some of the disturbances which are likely to make heat flow observations unrepresentative of the regional pattern, knowledge of the local geology is required. Moreover, the total number of continental heat flow observations is still so low that problems of non-uniform sampling are even more severe than for ocean floors. The average heat flow for each of the five major continents is shown in Table 3.6.1, but no differences can be shown to exist. North America, Australia and Asia are very close to the world average, though Europe is slightly higher. Africa is appreciably lower; but there are few observations and the low value could thus easily arise from statistical bias.

Table 3.6.1 Average values of heat flow by continent. N = number of observations; q = heat flow in h.f.u.; S.D. = standard deviation in h.f.u. *Source:* Horai and Simmons (1969).

	N	q	S.D.
Africa	32	1.08	0.69
Asia	83	1.55	0.62
Australia	44	1.57	0.53
Europe	164	1.84	1.10
North America	151	1.63	0.77

However, more significance may be placed on the heat flow averages for the various different large-scale geological provinces. The locations of these provinces—Precambrian shields, post-Precambrian non-orogenic areas and post-Precambrian orogenic areas (Palaeozoic and Mesozoic–Cenozoic)—throughout the world are shown in Figure 3.6.1 and the heat flow averages are given in Table 3.5.2.

Where Precambrian rocks are exposed in large continental areas they are called shields and are usually areas of low relief which have been very stable since the Precambrian. Heat flow is consistent with this long-term stability in that it is low and very uniform (low standard deviation). However, over the eighty percent of the continental surface outside the Precambrian shields, heat flow is both higher and more scattered. It is highest and most scattered in the severely disturbed orogenic regions especially in the areas of Mesozoic and Cenozoic orogeny. In the latter areas the average heat flow is somewhat higher than the world average; but in the less disturbed non-orogenic areas heat flow is slightly lower than the world average.

To see how these world-wide phenomena relate within a single continent, consider two examples—North America and Australia:

North America

In the north-east of North America lies the Canadian Shield (see Figures 3.6.1 and 3.6.2) which comprises ancient Precambrian rocks—mainly granites and gneisses but also various types of old folded sediments and lavas. Over the ages this shield has worn down to a low

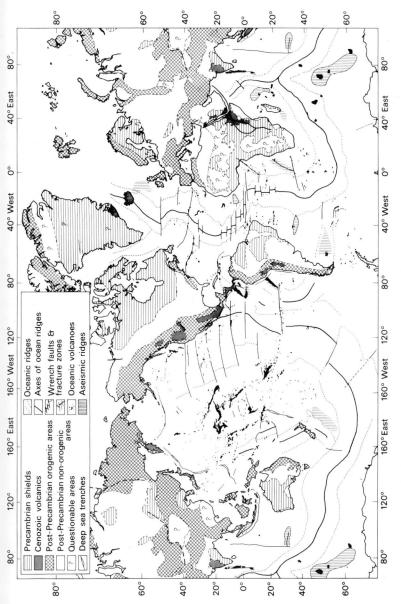

Legend:

- Precambrian shields
- Cenozoic volcanics
- Post-Precambrian orogenic areas
- Post-Precambrian non-orogenic areas
- Questionable areas
- Deep sea trenches
- Oceanic ridges
- Axes of ocean ridges
- Wrench faults & fracture zones
- Oceanic volcanoes
- Aseismic ridges

Figure 3.6.1   The major geological features of the Earth. *Source*: Lee and Uyeda (1965).

relief surface which passes southward and southwestward beneath
the post-Precambrian sedimentary rocks of the Interior Lowlands
(the central white strip in Figure 3.6.1). In the southeast of the country
lies the Appalachian mountain system formed during the Paleozoic;
and extending along the entire Pacific coast is the Cordilleran mountain
system which is of post-Paleozoic origin.

In the Canadian Shield the heat flow is, as expected, low (21 observations give an average of 1.09 h.f.u.). Heat flow in the Interior Lowlands

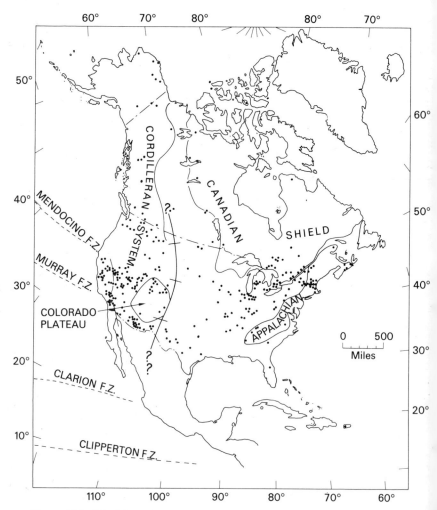

Figure 3.6.2 The four main provinces of North America. The points are heat flow
stations (up to August 1967). *Source:* Simmons and Roy (1969).

(post-Precambrian non-orogenic area) is considerably higher (26 values, 1.49 h.f.u. average) and is, if the difference is statistically significant, rather a surprise because the only significant geological difference between the two regions is a thin cover of Paleozoic and later sediments in the Interior Lowlands. Even more surprising, in a way, is the fact that heat flow in the Appalachians (32 values, 1.32 h.f.u. average) is similar to that in the Interior Lowlands where there is a marked difference in geology. On the other hand, in the Cordilleran system (post-Precambrian orogenic area) heat flow is predictably high (20 values, 1.83 h.f.u. average) and very variable.

Australia

Australia is a country of moderate relief, lacks young mountains and comprises about two-thirds Precambrian rocks (see Figure 3.6.1). In the west lies the Australian Shield which is mostly buried under desert sands; and along the east coast is a series of eroded ranges and table lands which have been raised comparatively recently, geologically speaking. Between these highlands and the shield is a broad depression (Interior Lowlands) in which relatively soft Mesozoic and Cenozoic sediments overlie Paleozoic and Precambrian rocks. For the past 200 million years Australia has remained comparatively stable although volcanic activity in the east was quite widespread during the Miocene.

In the Australian Shield heat flow is unexpectedly high (10 values, 1.50 h.f.u. average) and rather higher than that in the Interior Lowlands (13 values, 1.20 h.f.u. average). In the eastern highlands, however, the heat flow is expectedly high (21 values, 1.83 h.f.u. average).

North America and Australia

In geophysics one has to make the best of the data at hand—data which are come by with difficulty and expensively and thus slowly. In the above two subsections we have tried to interpret the few data available; but even so it was probably little more than an object lesson in statistics. Earlier we showed that on the world scale there are probably significant differences in heat flow between the different types of large-scale geological province. But on the continental scale this general picture tends to break down—not necessarily because the fundamental relationships are not valid but rather because the statistics are poor.

That these problems are probably due to lack of sufficient data is well illustrated by Table 3.6.2 which compares heat flow averages obtained from analyses made in 1965 and 1969. As can be seen there are vast differences between the two sets of data because it is doubtful whether either analysis is based on sufficient data to give reliable averages. In the cases marked with an asterisk, agreement between

Table 3.6.2   Comparison of heat flow averages for analyses carried out in 1965 and 1969. N = number of observations; q = heat flow in h.f.u.; asterisk has significance described in text. *Sources:* Lee and Uyeda (1965), Horai and Simmons (1969).

	1965 analysis		1969 analysis	
	N	q	N	q
Canadian Shield (North America)	10	0.88*	21	1.09*
Cordilleran system (North America)	9	1.73*	20	1.83*
Eastern Highlands (Australia)	2	2.03*	21	1.83*
Interior Lowlands (Australia)	7	2.04	13	1.20
Interior Lowlands (North America)	8	1.25	26	1.49
Appalachians (North America)	12	1.04	32	1.32
Australian Shield (Australia)	7	1.02	10	1.50

the two analyses is good and the values are more or less consistent with world averages. In other cases, however, agreement is poor on both counts—which leads one to suspect that it has been possible to place the asterisks where they are by sheer good fortune.

But as well as being an object lesson in statistics, this is also a good illustration of a problem the geophysicist faces. It is a salutary warning on the dangers of concluding too much too soon where a body as complex as the Earth is concerned.

3.7 The equality of continental and oceanic heat flows

Table 3.5.1 clearly shows that the average heat flow values for continents and ocean floors are almost identical. This is, arguably, the most important single result to emerge from all heat flow studies carried out so far. Moreover, it came as a complete and utter surprise. The heat now reaching the Earth's surface was widely believed to be due largely to the presence of radioactive elements in the Earth's crust. But whereas the continental crust is about 35 km thick on average, the average thickness of the oceanic crust is only about 5 km. So on this basis the heat flow over continents was expected to be considerably higher than that over the ocean floors. That the heat flows are, in fact, about equal suggests that a higher proportion of the oceanic heat derives from below the crust (that is, from the upper mantle). This, in turn, suggests that there are differences between the upper mantle beneath the continents and that beneath the oceans. In short, the equality of continental and oceanic heat flows is likely to have important implications for the temperature and general behaviour of the upper mantle. Before we consider these, however, we must ask where the heat comes from in the first place.

3.8 Sources of heat in the Earth

If the average heat flow through the Earth's surface is 1.65 h.f.u. (μcal cm^{-2} s^{-1}), multiplying this figure by the total surface area of the Earth (5.1×10^{18} cm^2) will give the total internal heat (Q) flowing from the Earth each second. Thus it is that:

$$Q = 8.4 \times 10^{12} \text{ cal s}^{-1} \equiv 3.5 \times 10^{13} \text{ J s}^{-1} \equiv 3.5 \times 10^{13} \text{ W.}$$

This, it must be remembered, is the heat transmitted through the Earth's upper crust and surface by *conduction* (see equation (3.2.3)). Because the Earth's upper crust is solid and at a comparatively low temperature, it is safe to say that transmission of heat by radiation or convection in this region is negligible. On the other hand, some comparatively small amount of heat will be brought to the Earth's surface by, for example, volcanic lava, hot water and steam.

But what is the source of the conducted heat? There are various possibilities:

Heat produced during the Earth's formation: At one time it was widely believed that the Earth had originally formed as a hot body and has since been gradually cooling down. Under these circumstances the heat currently flowing across the Earth's surface could be regarded as the result of this cooling. It is now clear, however, that the Earth formed initially as a cool body by accretion—a progressive collision and coalescence of grains and particles in space to form the larger body. Even so, heat could still be produced in this type of Earth formation in at least two ways: (i) by the impact of the various materials as they collided with a growing Earth, and (ii) as a result of compression during the accretion process. For each of these mechanisms it is possible to make a rough calculation of the heat likely to be produced; in each case it can be shown that the heat produced is unlikely to be sufficient to account for the present heat flow:

(i) As small bodies hit the Earth during its growth period, their kinetic energy would be converted largely to heat as they came to rest. Most of this heat would be dissipated in the vicinity of the impacts and would be radiated out into space without affecting the Earth's deep interior. But some of the energy at impact would go to set up seismic waves in the Earth which might travel to considerable depths. As these waves gradually died out their energy would again be dissipated as heat. If the energy trapped in this way was 0.1 percent of the original energy available at impact, the internal temperature of the Earth would be raised by 30 °C. This is far too small to account for the thousands of degrees temperature known to exist in the Earth's deep interior.

(ii) As the Earth grew by the accretion of smaller particles, the inner
material would be gradually compressed and the internal pressure
would rise giving an increase in temperature. A simple application
of the laws of thermodynamics shows that at moderate depths
within the Earth the temperature gradient produced in this way
would be 0.15 °C per kilometre. In fact, the temperature gradient
is about 30 °C per kilometre, showing that the heat of compression
is also insufficient to explain the present heat flow.

But whilst neither of these two processes is itself sufficient to explain
the large amount of heat now flowing through the Earth's surface, this
does not necessarily mean to say that *none* of the observed heat flow
derives from the heat produced at the Earth's formation. As we showed
in section 3.2, because the thermal conductivity of Earth material is
very low, heat is conducted through the Earth very slowly and a
change in temperature at the Earth's centre would take at least 200 000
million years to be felt at the Earth's surface. This is, of course, very
much longer than the age of the Earth itself. What this means is that
we must take very serious account of the heat produced during the
Earth's formation when we come to interpret the currently observed
heat flow in terms of the temperature distribution within the Earth.
Such heat may be quite small in quantity but it stays within the Earth
for a very long time.

   Finally, there is another possible source of heat at the Earth's formation but one even more difficult to assess. During the early history of
the Earth three very short-lived radioactive isotopes are thought to
have been present—Al^{26}, Cl^{36} and Fe^{60}. Of these, the most important
is Al^{26} which has a half-life of 0.73 million years and would thus have
acted as a significant heat source for about 10 million years. The other
two isotopes have half-lives of about 0.3 million years and would
thus have acted as effective heat sources for only about 4 million years.
All these isotopes have long since decayed away; but if they really
were present at the Earth's formation, they would or would not have
had a significant effect depending on just how long the Earth took to
accrete fully. If, for example, accretion was fairly rapid, taking place
over about 20 million years, Al^{26} would have been present for a considerable part of this time and would have been a significant source
of heat. If, on the other hand, accretion took place over a 100 million
year period, the three isotopes would have acted as heat sources only
within the inner ten percent of the original Earth.

Heat produced from the Earth's rotation: Because of gravitational
interaction with the Moon, and to a lesser extent the Sun, the rate of
rotation of the Earth is gradually decreasing. What the Earth's period
of rotation was at the time of the Earth's formation is not known with

certainty; but suggestions have ranged from two to ten hours compared with the twenty-four hour period of today. The energy lost by this slowing down is quite considerable. Part is dissipated by the production of tides in the oceans, part by the production of tides in the solid Earth, and part is used to increase the orbital energy of the Moon as it recedes from the Earth. As far as the Earth is concerned, the energy which goes to produce tidal motions is finally dissipated as heat; but just how much heat is produced will depend on the proportion of energy going into solid Earth tides on the one hand and oceanic tides on the other. If all the energy released in the Earth during an increase in rotational period of from three to twenty-four hours were dissipated via solid Earth tides, the internal temperature of the Earth would rise by about 2000 °C; but if ninety percent were dissipated via the oceanic tides the corresponding temperature increase would be 200 °C. What the real partition of energy between the two types of tide is, is not known, however. The current loss of rotational energy is small compared with the currently observed loss of heat energy; but the effect would have been more significant when the Moon was much closer to the Earth.

Heat produced during differentiation of the Earth: It is now believed that the Earth formed by cold accretion from relatively homogeneous material. But today the Earth is structured into core, mantle and crust. Thus at some time in its history, the initially homogeneous Earth must have differentiated out into its present constituent layers. When this took place is still a matter for debate. Some hold to the view that the core, for example, has been growing steadily in size over most of the Earth's life; others argue that the core formed relatively rapidly during an early stage in the Earth's history. Either way, the formation of the core by the concentration of high density iron–nickel close to the Earth's centre would release large quantities of gravitational energy, some of which is likely to be dissipated finally as heat. Calculations show that about six percent of this heat would be required to melt the iron–nickel core but that the other ninety-four percent would be available to raise the Earth's temperature by about 1500 °C. The total heat released during core formation is about the same as the total heat released by the decay of radioactive elements (to be discussed next) throughout the whole life of the Earth. In other words, it is likely to be an extremely important source of heat in the Earth.

Heat released by the decay of long-lived radioactive elements: When radioactive isotopes decay they release energy which is dissipated as heat. All such isotopes do this; but the only ones which are significant heat sources in today's Earth are those which are abundant and/or which have half-lives comparable to the age of the Earth (in contrast to the three short-lived isotopes mentioned above, all of which have now completely decayed away). In practice, only four isotopes are now important—U^{238} (uranium), U^{235} (uranium), Th^{232} (thorium) and K^{40} (potassium). The rate of heat production for each of these isotopes (determined experimentally) is shown in Table 3.8.1. Also shown are the abundances of these isotopes at various times in the past *relative to present day abundances* (= 1.00), these being obtained easily from

Table 3.8.1 The half-lives, rates of heat production and abundances (relative to present = 1.00) for four important long-lived radioactive isotopes. *Source:* Bott (1971).

Isotope	Half-life (1000 My)	Heat production (cal g^{-1} year^{-1})	Abundances in past relative to present					
			0 My	1000 My	2000 My	3000 My	4000 My	4500 My
U^{238}	4.50	0.71	1.00	1.17	1.36	1.59	1.85	2.00
U^{235}	0.71	4.3	1.00	2.64	6.99	18.50	48.80	80.00
Th^{232}	13.9	0.20	1.00	1.05	1.11	1.16	1.22	1.25
K^{40}	1.3	0.21	1.00	1.70	2.89	4.91	8.35	10.90

the well-known laws of radioactive decay. Actual present-day abundances of these radioactive isotopes in the Earth are, in the last analysis, impossible to determine because the interior of the Earth is inaccessible —a situation which simply adds a further element of uncertainty to heat flow studies. However, the concentrations within various rock types may be determined quite easily by experiment (Table 3.8.2).

Although past and present abundances of radioactive elements in the Earth cannot be known precisely, there seems little doubt that the four isotopes listed above could easily account for all of the heat observed to be flowing through the Earth's surface. This does not necessarily mean that all the observed heat *is* derived from radioactivity

Table 3.8.2 Uranium, potassium and thorium in various rock types. *Source:* MacDonald (1965).

	Average concentration (parts per million)			Ratios	
	U	K	Th	K/U	Th/U
Granite	4.75	37 900	18.5	0.8×10^4	3.90
Intermediate	2.00	18 000	—	0.9×10^4	—
Basalt	0.60	8400	2.7	1.4×10^4	4.50
Eclogite: low U	0.048	360	0.18	0.7×10^4	3.75
Eclogite: high U	0.25	2600	0.45	1.0×10^4	1.80
Peridotite	0.016	12	—	0.8×10^4	—
Dunite	0.001	10	—	1.0×10^4	—
Chondrite	0.012	845	0.0398	7.0×10^4	3.32

because, as we have shown above, there are other possible sources, both major and minor, which could make a contribution. The fact is, however, that the other possible major sources of heat are difficult to assess and so—rightly or wrongly—radioactive elements have received closer attention because they are easier to handle quantitatively in this context. Science, as well as politics, is the art of the possible. It may well be, of course, that radioactivity is indeed the main source of the Earth's observed heat flow; but no one can know for sure. This stricture should be borne in mind continuously in what follows.

3.9 Temperature distributions in the Earth

Almost at the beginning of this chapter we said that one of the chief aims towards which heat flow studies are directed is the determination of the temperature distribution within the Earth. From what we have said since, however, it is clear that hard evidence with which to proceed upon such a course is difficult, if not impossible, to obtain. Perhaps the best one can do under these circumstances is to try to determine what factors influence the Earth's temperature distribution and, if possible, what the relative effects of these factors are likely to be. What this means in practice is the setting up of possible thermal models of the Earth which are restricted by certain known boundary conditions. Whether it will ever be possible to determine the precise distribution of temperature within the Earth is a moot point; but with the few data available it is actually possible to make a little progress.

First, however, it might be useful to summarize the certainties and uncertainties which may be brought to the problem. We do know the following:

1. That a large amount of heat of internal origin is escaping from the Earth's surface. Observation suggests that this is about 3.5×10^{13} watts; but the data upon which this figure is based are not very uniformly distributed over the Earth's surface and are subject to sources of uncertainty. Even so, because the average heat flow from the Earth is based upon several thousand individual observations, the figure is probably quite accurate.

2. That the rate of heat flow through continents is about the same as that through the ocean floor. There may be factors at work which make this equality more apparent than real; but for the moment it must be accepted at face value.

3. That heat flow is calculated upon the assumption that heat is transmitted by conduction. This is a fair assumption as far as the Earth's upper crust is concerned because temperatures there are relatively low and the thermal conductivities of crustal materials are low. If con-

duction is the main transfer mechanism throughout the whole Earth, however, heat produced at the Earth's centre would take at least 200 000 million years to reach the surface. In short, the Earth has a high thermal inertia.

4. That on a regional geological scale, variations in heat flow are broadly consistent with the general tenets of the new global tectonics.

5. That there are many possible sources of heat in the Earth, some relating to the Earth's origin and some to its subsequent history. Because of the Earth's high thermal inertia, heat present at the time of the Earth's formation could still be contributing to the currently observed surface heat flow. Of heat produced subsequent to the Earth's formation, a major contribution could have been made by core construction or even by the Earth's decreasing rate of rotation. On the other hand, radioactivity could produce sufficient heat to account fully for that observed to be escaping from the Earth's surface.

But the following are not, or sometimes only partly, known:

A.   How heat is transmitted throughout the whole Earth. Conduction may be satisfactory to explain heat flow in the crust but at greater depths where temperatures are higher, radiation could easily play a significant part. Moreover, global tectonics implies mass fluid flow and hence the likelihood of heat transfer by convection.

B.   The thermal properties of the whole Earth. We do not even know how thermal conductivity varies with depth in the Earth. Other unknown parameters include heat capacity, expansion characteristics, and density.

C.   The precise origin or origins of heat in the Earth.

D.   The distribution of heat sources within the Earth.

E.   The time relationships between thermal events in the Earth's history. Because the Earth's thermal inertia is high, contributions to the Earth's observed surface heat flow could come from events at any time in its history; and the present heat flow will generally be an integrated effect of all such events. Conversely, because heat flow may lag considerably behind heat production, it is not possible to use current heat flow to deduce current heat production in the Earth.

Radioactivity models of the Earth

Recent attempts to determine the temperature distribution throughout the Earth have been based on the assumption that most of the Earth's currently observed heat flow derives from radioactive elements, because it is hardly possible to make any progress otherwise. But what is the distribution of radioactive elements in the Earth? A useful starting point here is to assume that on average the composition of the Earth is the same as that of chondritic meteorites, or chondrites.* The reason for this is that chondrites are apparently the most fundamental natural material known to man in the sense that their composition is the nearest we have been able to get to the primordial non-volatile matter of the solar system. The abundances of the non-volatile elements in chondrites are also very similar to abundances in the Sun. The implicit point here is that when the Earth formed, it probably accreted from these very basic materials. To be sure, the Earth may have differentiated into core, mantle and crust since its formation; but on the face of it, there seems no reason why the Earth's composition should not still be similar to chondritic *on average*.

From the heat flow point of view, the simple chondritic Earth model is also attractive for another reason. Taking the concentrations of the three radioactive elements in chondrites to be $U = 1.1 \times 10^{-8}\,\mathrm{g\,g^{-1}}$ (that is, grams of uranium per gram of chondrite—for convenience, wherever concentrations are mentioned in future these units will be omitted), $Th = 4.0 \times 10^{-8}$ and $K = 8.0 \times 10^{-4}$ (these are experimentally determined values), it turns out that a chondritic Earth would produce radioactive heat at the rate of $7.4 \times 10^{12}\,\mathrm{cal\,s^{-1}}$. This compares with the observed value of $8.4 \times 10^{12}\,\mathrm{cal\,s^{-1}}$. In other words, the chondritic Earth would produce almost all the observed heat. To put it another way, the chondritic Earth would lead to a surface heat flow of 1.42 h.f.u. compared to the observed world average of 1.65 h.f.u. When it is remembered that the small additional amount of heat required could be derived from that present at the time of the Earth's formation, the chondritic Earth model appears very attractive in this overall way.

Is this, then, the answer? Is it not possible to accept the chondritic Earth model as valid, being the simplest and most reasonable model which is consistent with the observed heat flow? Unfortunately, many people have rejected the chondritic Earth model on other grounds. One of the chief arguments against the model is that the K/U ratio observed in crustal rocks is much lower than the K/U ratio observed in chondrites. As may be seen from Table 3.8.2, the K/U ratios in a wide variety of terrestrial rocks are remarkably constant at about 1.0×10^4 even though the absolute concentrations of U, Th and K cover a very wide range. In chondrites, by contrast, the K/U ratio is 7.0×10^4. Arguing from these facts, there are two possibilities:

(i) That because the K/U ratio is so constant in a wide variety of very different rocks, it is probable that the corresponding K/U ratio (1.0×10^4) is typical of the Earth as a whole;

(ii) That the K/U ratio in the Earth's mantle is very much higher than that in the crust so that *on average* the Earth still remains in chondritic composition with an overall K/U ratio of 7.0×10^4.

The problem with (ii) is that if the K/U ratio in the mantle is higher than in the crust, K must have preferentially differentiated from the crust into the mantle with respect to U. In other words, if it is assumed that the Earth still has an overall chondritic K/U ratio of 7.0×10^4, then at some time in the Earth's history K must have moved downwards from the crust to the mantle to leave a lower K/U ratio of 1.0×10^4 in the crust and a very much higher K/U ratio in the mantle. Those who reject the chondritic Earth model argue that such a process is not possible because there is no known way in which it could occur. This is not, of course, the same as saying that it could not have happened. Nevertheless, this and other factors have led many people to suppose that the chondritic Earth model can no longer be valid and accordingly it has fallen into disfavour.

So if option (ii) is to be rejected, option (i) must be accepted—and we are left to consider a model for the Earth in which the K/U ratio is taken as 1.0×10^4 throughout. Further, as can be seen from Table 3.8.2, the Th/U ratio for terrestrial rocks is also quite constant—and so we may adopt the average value for Th/U of 3.7 (which, as it happens, is not very different from that for chondrites). In other words, for our 'working model' we have K/U $= 1.0 \times 10^4$ and Th/U $= 3.7$.

But these are the ratios—what about the actual concentrations of the various radioactive elements? At this point we must return to the observed heat flow because whatever model we end up with it *must* be able to produce the heat flow actually observed. Now, we can do a little calculation:

Average rate of heat flow over Earth's surface
$$= 1.65 \ \mu\text{cal cm}^{-2} \text{ s}^{-1} \text{ (h.f.u.)}$$
Therefore, total rate of heat flow from Earth
$$= 8.4 \times 10^{12} \text{ cal s}^{-1} \text{(section 3.8)}$$

Mass of Earth's crust and mantle $\quad = 4.1 \times 10^{27} \text{ g}$

If all the heat is produced in the crust-mantle:

$$\text{Rate of heat production in crust-mantle} = \frac{\text{total rate of heat produced}}{\text{mass of crust-mantle}}$$

$$= \frac{8.4 \times 10^{12} \text{ cal s}^{-1}}{4.1 \times 10^{27} \text{ g}}$$

$$= 2.0 \times 10^{-15} \text{ cal g}^{-1}\text{s}^{-1}$$

Now, if $K/U = 1.0 \times 10^4$ and $Th/U = 3.7$, the combined rate of heat production for $(U + Th + K)$ is 5.5×10^{-8} cal s^{-1} for each 10^4 g of the $(U + Th + K)$ material (experimental result):

If 5.5×10^{-8} cal s^{-1} is produced by 10^4 g of $(U + Th + K)$,

$$2.0 \times 10^{-15} \text{ cal s}^{-1} \text{ is produced by} = \frac{2.0 \times 10^{-15} \times 10^4}{5.5 \times 10^{-8}} \text{ g, of } (U + Th + K)$$

$$= 3.6 \times 10^{-4} \text{ g of } (U + Th + K)$$

But as we have seen above, 2.0×10^{-15} cal s^{-1} is produced by 1 g of crust-mantle:

2.0×10^{-15} cal s^{-1} is produced by 1 g of crust-mantle,

and

2.0×10^{-15} cal s^{-1} is produced by 3.6×10^{-4} g of $(U + Th + K)$

so that

1 g of crust-mantle must contain 3.6×10^{-4} g of $(U + Th + K)$.

But 10^4 g of $(U + Th + K)$ contains 1 g of U because $K/U = 1.0 \times 10^4$ and $Th/U = 3.7$:

Therefore, 3.6×10^{-4} g of $(U + Th + K)$ contains $\dfrac{3.6 \times 10^{-4}}{10^4}$ g of U

$$= 3.6 \times 10^{-8} \text{ g of U}$$

Therefore, 1 g of crust-mantle contains 3.6×10^{-8} g of U. In other words:

Concentration of U in crust-mantle $= 3.6 \times 10^{-8}$ g g^{-1}

What this means is that if the Earth's crust and mantle has $K/U = 1.0 \times 10^4$ and $Th/U = 3.7$ (this is the model we are testing), then the concentration of uranium in the crust + mantle must be 3.6×10^{-8} in order to account for the observed heat flow *as long as the present heat flow arises from the present heat production*. But we know that in reality, because the Earth has a high thermal inertia, the heat flow lags behind heat production—the heat we are observing now is produced not by the present concentrations of radioactive elements but by some past concentrations.

The above calculation shows that if the present heat flow arises from present heat production in a crust-mantle with $K/U = 1.0 \times 10^4$ and $Th/U = 3.7$, then the U concentration in the crust-mantle must be 3.6×10^{-8}. However, if the present heat flow arises from heat production at some time in the past, the corresponding U concentration required would be *lower*. The reason for this is that radioactive isotopes decay with time—and so the proportion of radioactive U isotope in 1 g of U element would have been greater in the past. In other words, the quantity of U element containing a given quantity of heat-producing U isotope in the past would have been smaller than the quantity of U element containing the *same* quantity of heat producing U isotope today.

From the laws of radioactive decay it can easily be shown that if the present heat flow was produced *on average* from the radioactive isotopes present 1000 million years ago, the required U concentration at that time would have been 3.3×10^{-8}. And:

.........2000 million years ago........2.9×10^{-8}
.........3000 million years ago........2.4×10^{-8}, and so on.

Thus assuming that there is no contribution from the heat present at the Earth's formation, the present surface heat flow may be accounted for by an average crust-mantle U concentration of 2.4–3.6×10^{-8}. Of course, if appreciable initial heat is still being received at the Earth's surface the required U concentration would be lower.

In summary, if the chondritic Earth model is to be rejected, the next most reasonable model has:

$$K/U = 1.0 \times 10^4$$

$$Th/U = 3.7$$

and $U = 2.4$–$3.6 \times 10^{-8} \, g \, g^{-1}$

or less, depending on the initial heat still contributing to the surface heat flow.

The situation involved here may be put another way. Although the chondritic Earth model is consistent with currently observed surface heat flow, this fact alone does not necessarily make the model valid. For as we have shown above, at least one other model can also explain the observed heat flow quite satisfactorily.

Thermal models of the Earth

No one would pretend that the simple radioactivity models presented above necessarily bear much relationship to the real Earth; in this sense they are little more than academic, but essential, 'doodling'. Nevertheless, they do illustrate an important point of principle— that *there is no unique model which can account for the observed surface heat flow*. But in the real Earth there are other boundary conditions to be taken into account, other complexities to be considered, if models are to be used to determine the temperature distribution in the Earth.

In addition to the question of how the radioactive elements are distributed throughout the Earth, attention must be given to (a) the initial temperature distribution and the formation of the Earth, and (b) how heat is transmitted in the Earth's interior.

Many people have attempted to come to terms with these problems and thus develop more complex thermal models of the Earth. In order to illustrate the principles involved in such development we shall concentrate here on a set of models first considered by G. J. F. Mac-Donald during the early 1960s. MacDonald took account of the following:

The initial temperature distribution: As we have said before, because of the Earth's high thermal inertia, heat present at the Earth's formation may still be contributing to the surface heat flow observed today. Calculations show, for example, that if the average initial temperature of the Earth was 1500 °C, the initial heat would be contributing fifteen to twenty percent of the present heat flow. For this reason the Earth's initial temperature distribution will play an important, though not dominant, part in determining the subsequent temperature distribution, including the present one. Of course, the initial temperature distribution cannot be known and so a plausible assumption must be made. In his models, MacDonald assumed that initially temperature increased linearly with depth from 0 °C at the Earth's surface to 1000 °C at 600 km and then remained at 1000 °C from that depth to the Earth's centre.

The heat transfer mechanism: At relatively low temperatures in solid material heat is transmitted mainly by conduction; but at high temperatures such as those obtaining in the Earth's deep interior, radiation becomes a real possibility. In his models, MacDonald therefore considered both conduction alone and conduction and radiation together. Global tectonics also implies fluid motion in certain parts of the Earth, especially in the upper mantle, and hence the possibility of heat transfer by convection. However, MacDonald took no account of convection, although the effects of convection will undoubtely modify his solutions.

The distribution of radioactivity: MacDonald considered three different distributions which we shall call Models A, B and C. For each model, $K/U = 1.0 \times 10^4$ and $Th/U = 3.7$, as in the simple models described above.

MODEL A: THE UNIFORM MODEL

U is distributed uniformly throughout the crust-mantle.

MODEL B: THE OCEANIC MODEL

All radioactivity is concentrated in the Earth's upper 1500 km but more strongly in the upper 465 km. The U content of the upper 465 km is 18.2 times greater than that in the region below; that is:

$$\frac{U\,(0\text{--}465\ km)}{U\,(465\text{--}1500\ km)} = 18.2$$

MODEL C: THE CONTINENTAL MODEL

Again all radioactivity is concentrated into the upper 1500 km but this time there are three different concentration regions as follows:

$$U\,(0\text{--}45\ km) : U\,(45\text{--}465\ km) : U\,(465\text{--}1500\ km) = 40.0 : 3.29 : 1$$

The determination of the temperature distributions which would be produced by models having the above characteristics is a complicated mathematical problem which we shall not go into here. We are more interested in the results, which emerge in two stages.

The first stage involves a determination of how heat flow varies with average U concentration in the crust-mantle, for we must always take account of the condition that any valid thermal model must be consistent with the observed heat flow. The results of this part of the analysis are shown in Figure 3.9.1. Figure 3.9.1 (a) shows how the heat flow produced by Model A varies with average U concentration, with and without the effects of radiation. As can be seen from the curves, for U concentrations up to 7.0×10^{-8} the heat flow never reaches the observed average heat flow of 1.65 h.f.u. In other words, in order to account for the observed heat flow by Model A, we would require improbably high U concentrations. This applies whether or not radiation plays any part, although if radiative transfer occurs (upper curve) the U concentration required is lower than for conduction only (lower curve). Accordingly, we must conclude that Model A is unlikely to obey even the heat flow boundary condition and cannot therefore be a valid representation.

Similar curves for Models B and C are plotted in Figure 3.9.1 (b) for conduction and radiation together and in Figure 3.9.1 (c) for conduction only. In each case we can see here that reasonably low U concentrations can account for the observed heat flow. Reading from the curves:

Model B (average observed heat flow over ocean floors = 1.64 h.f.u.):

(i) with radiation, U concentration required = 5.5×10^{-8}
(ii) without radiation, U concentration required = 4.9×10^{-8}.

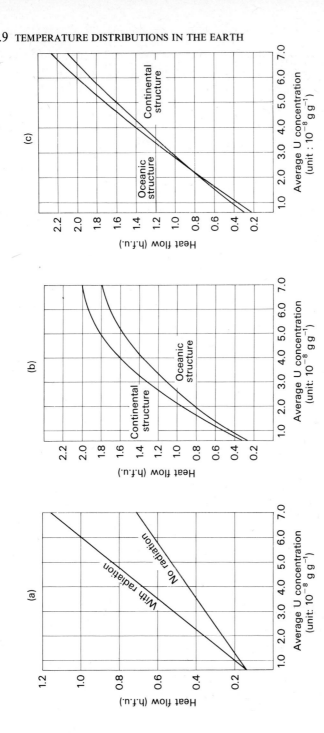

Figure 3.9.1 The variation of heat flow with average U concentration: (a) for Model A, with and without radiation, (b) for Models B and C, with radiation, and (c) for Models B and C, without radiation. *Source:* MacDonald (1965).

Model C (average observed heat flow over continents = 1.65 h.f.u.):

(i) with radiation, U concentration required = 4.2×10^{-8}
(ii) without radiation, U concentration required = 5.3×10^{-8}.

In other words, with or without radiative heat transfer, the observed heat flow over continents and ocean floors may be accounted for by U concentrations in the range $4.2–5.5 \times 10^{-8}$.

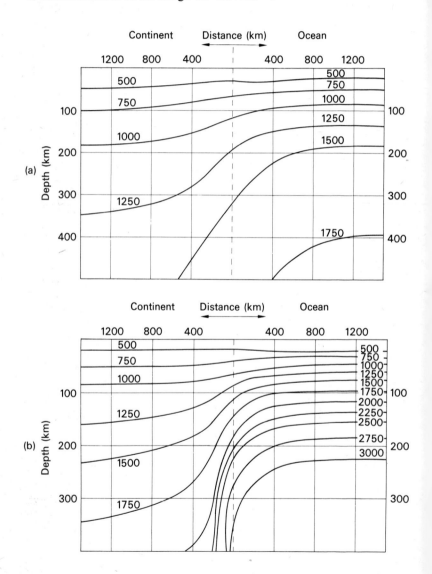

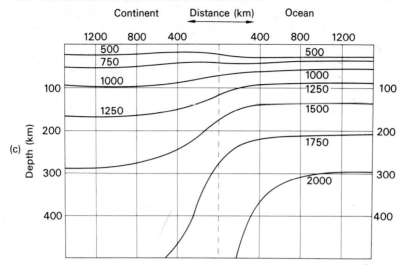

Figure 3.9.2 The distribution of temperature beneath ocean floors and continents as predicted by Models B and C respectively: (a) for an average U concentration of 3.3×10^{-8} g g^{-1}, with radiation, (b) for an average U concentration of 3.3×10^{-8} g g^{-1}, without radiation, and (c) for an average U concentration of 5.5×10^{-8} g g^{-1}, with radiation. *Source:* MacDonald (1965).

Three examples of temperature distributions predicted by Models B and C at an oceanic–continental boundary are shown in Figure 3.9.2: for (a) an average U concentration of 3.3×10^{-8} with radiation, (b) an average U concentration of 3.3×10^{-8} without radiation, and (c) an average U concentration of 5.5×10^{-8} with radiation. From these curves the following conclusions may be drawn:

(i)   Apart from within a very narrow surface layer, temperatures beneath the oceans are always higher than beneath the continents at a corresponding depth.

(ii)   Temperatures rise very rapidly in the upper 200 km.

(iii) Comparison of Figures 3.9.2 (a) and (b) shows that for the same average U concentration the inclusion of radiative heat transfer has pronounced effects. To put it the other way round, ignoring radiation leads to much higher temperatures, especially beneath the ocean floors—so much so that it is necessary to consider seriously the possibility of melting at depth.

Because the precise nature of the mantle is unknown, it is very difficult to say just at what temperature the mantle will melt and how the melting temperature will vary with depth. The best evidence we have, however, suggests that melting points will lie somewhere within the hatched region of Figure 3.9.3. Comparison of the sub-oceanic temperatures of Figures 3.9.2 (b) with the melting point region of Figure 3.9.3 clearly shows that if heat is transmitted solely by conduction, temperatures in the mantle beneath the oceans generally will be far in excess of the mantle melting point and that the mantle will thus be completely liquid below about 70 km. But seismological data indicate that this cannot be so. There is thus strong support here for the view that at depth, radiation is a very important mechanism for the transfer of heat.

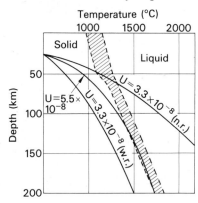

Figure 3.9.3 The vertical temperature distributions for Model B at U concentrations of 3.3×10^{-8} g g^{-1} (with radiation), 3.3×10^{-8} g^{-1} (without radiation), and 5.5×10^{-8} g g^{-1} (with radiation). The hatched region is the probable melting zone for mantle material. *Source:* MacDonald (1965), with modification.

(iv) The vertical temperature distributions beneath the oceans for U concentrations of 3.3×10^{-8} (with radiation) and 5.5×10^{-8} (with radiation) are also compared with the melting zone in Figure 3.9.3. The curve for a U concentration of 3.3×10^{-8} falls well to the 'solid' side of the mantle melting zone and so poses no conflict with a solid mantle. But the curve for a U concentration of 5.5×10^{-8} is particularly interesting because this is just the concentration that Model B (oceanic model) requires to explain the observed heat flow. As can be seen, the vertical temperature distribution curve just brushes the melting zone in the vicinity of 150 km depth. It is at just about this depth that the asthenosphere begins—a zone which is not absolutely fluid but which has some flow properties and which may be presumed to be close to the mantle melting point at the relevant depths. In short, in general terms the curve is remarkably consistent with what is known of upper mantle properties.

An essential point to remember about these models is that they are just that—models. This means to say they are man-made abstractions based on numerous assumptions and containing many uncertainties. Hopefully, the assumptions bear some relationship to the real world; some of them certainly do. Moreover, the results must be consistent with known boundary conditions—for example, that the mantle is solid and that the world average heat flow as observed at the Earth's surface is 1.65 h.f.u. At the same time, because the models are necessary oversimplifications, too much faith should not be placed in them. Nor should it be thought that these are the only possible models yet available; other people have other ideas about what constitutes the best thermal model of the Earth. Nor should it be assumed that any one single conclusion drawn from the models is necessarily valid, for what seems reasonable one day may be rejected the next. This point is aptly illustrated by the problem of radiation. MacDonald's models lead to the idea that radiation is important; but more recent experimental studies suggest that the contribution of radiation to heat transfer in the mantle has been greatly overestimated. Finally, of course, MacDonald completely ignored convection.

The best one can hope for is that such models can give a broad feeling about what is happening in the Earth, some indication of the various factors involved, and perhaps even produce some generalizations about the Earth's behaviour. In the country of the blind the one-eyed man is king.

3.10 The equality of continental and oceanic heat flows

As noted in section 3.7, the observed equality of heat flow between the ocean floors and the continents contradicted expectations. Assuming that radioactive elements are concentrated in the crust, most people assumed that oceanic heat flow would be the lower because the oceanic crust is much thinner. In fact, the situation is even more extreme than that because not only is the oceanic crust much thinner than the continental crust, it is formed largely of rock types with lower concentrations of radioactive elements. Table 3.8.2 shows that, volume for volume, continents (generally granitic) produce far more radioactivity-induced heat than do the ocean floors (generally basaltic).

In order to get a more quantitative view of the situation, suppose that the continental crust (35 km thick) is made up entirely of granite with the radioactive element content shown in Table 3.8.2. In this case, heat produced in the continental crust would lead to a surface heat flow of 2.5 h.f.u., much higher than that observed. To put it another way, 23 km of granite alone would produce the observed heat flow of 1.65 h.f.u.—or a 35 km thick crust comprising 22 km granite and 13 km basalt would also give 1.65 h.f.u. If, on the other hand, the continental crust were formed entirely of intermediate rock (Table 3.8.2), the surface heat flow would be 1.1 h.f.u. The average composition of the continental crust cannot be determined precisely; but what the above calculations do show is (i) that it is quite possible that continental heat flow can be explained entirely by radioactivity in the crust, and

(ii) that if any of the continental heat flow is derived from beneath the crust, this contribution is unlikely to exceed 0.5 h.f.u. The oceanic crust, by contrast, cannot contain its own heat sources. Five kilometres of basalt give a surface heat flow of only 0.05 h.f.u., showing that most of the ocean floor heat flow must derive from below the oceanic crust.

These results seem to indicate that the mantle beneath the continents must in some way be different from that beneath the oceans. In particular, the oceanic mantle will have a higher temperature—a conclusion which was also derived from the MacDonald models. But if this difference exists, why does it? Two explanations have been offered—together with a third which attempts to account for the equality of heat flow without invoking mantle differences:

Different heat source distributions: Perhaps the most obvious possibility is that radioactive elements are distributed differently beneath oceans and continents—this is why MacDonald considered two models with different distributions, one of which he termed 'oceanic' and the other 'continental'. The suggestion here is that the mantle has undergone vertical differentiation under the continents, thereby concentrating most of the radioactive minerals in the crust, but not appreciably beneath the oceans. This differentiation would presumably have happened at the time that the granitic material of the continents was produced. Unfortunately, there are two important objections to this hypothesis:

(i) The mantle under the ocean floor will be less dense than that under the continents, partly because it is hotter and thus thermally expanded and partly because it still presumably contains the lighter materials which the continental mantle lost by differentiation into the crust. But if this density difference exists it should be reflected in the geoid (Chapter Two). However, the geoid shows no distinction between oceanic and continental areas.

(ii) Because the continental crust is old—that is, much of the granitic differentiation took place several thousand million years ago—the presumption must be that continents and oceans are permanent. This is difficult to reconcile with the global tectonics with its drifting continents and its spreading sea floors.

The effect of convection: The validity of the new global tectonics leads naturally to the possibility that heat may be transferred around the upper mantle by means of convection because large mass flows in the upper mantle are involved. The suggestion here is that heat is carried through the oceanic upper mantle by the convection which gives rise to sea floor spreading, although heat would still be transmitted up through the lithosphere by conduction. In the continental upper mantle, on the other hand, convection is assumed to be absent or at least very small. The general picture is thus that as mantle material rises beneath mid-oceanic ridges it discharges heat and continues to do so as it moves laterally away from the ridges. By contrast, continental heat flow is, in most cases, still accounted for mostly by radioactivity in the crust.

If heat flow is intimately bound up with convection—as it must surely be—then it follows that the observed heat flow should put constraints on possible types of convection in the mantle. In other words, in trying to determine the form of convection which takes place in the mantle, we must reject any models which are not consistent with the observed heat flow.

When convection in the mantle was first suggested, it was customary to think of it in terms of large convection cells spreading throughout the whole mantle. Nowadays, however, convection is widely thought to be limited to the upper few hundred kilometres of the mantle, in particular to the semi-fluid asthenosphere. The ways in which heat flow may put constraints on the latter type of convection have been illustrated by M. H. P. Bott. For example, when sea floor spreading was first thought of, it was implied that the convection current effectively came up to the ocean floor itself so that the oceanic lithosphere travels at the same rate as the convection current underlying it. Figure 3.10.1 shows the pattern of heat flow which would be expected from

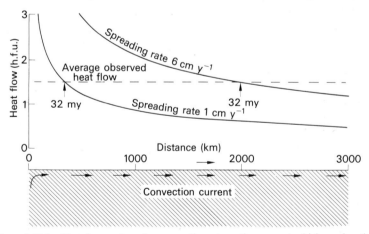

Figure 3.10.1 Heat flow pattern from a cooling convection current which reaches the Earth's (ocean floor) surface, for current velocities of 1 cm year $^{-1}$ and 6 cm year $^{-1}$. The current emerges at the origin and thereafter flows horizontally, its thermal conductivity being 0.0077 cal cm $^{-1}$ s $^{-1}$ °C $^{-1}$. Radioactive heat sources are assumed to be absent, but the initial temperature at all depths below the origin is set at 1100 °C. Radiation is assumed to be negligible. *Source:* Bott (1971).

this type of model for two different rates of sea floor spreading and assuming that the initial temperature beneath the ridge crest is 1100 °C (the approximate temperature of basalt magma). Here the heat is transmitted in the mantle by convection but up through the lithosphere layer by conduction.

The predicted pattern of heat flow is different from that actually observed, mainly in that the observed heat flow is more uniform. It is true that the observed heat flow is high over ridges; but even so, the average heat flow out to a spreading distance of 32 million years is still much less than that predicted from the model. Beyond 32 million years the observed heat flow is greater than the model predicts. We may thus conclude that the idea of an oceanic lithosphere moving at the same rate as the convection cell beneath cannot be correct.

If this model is replaced by one in which the lithosphere is stationary (which does not, of course, accord with the sea floor spreading hypothesis), a much more uniform pattern of heat flow may be predicted. Figure 3.10.2 shows the case for a 60 km thick stationary layer with

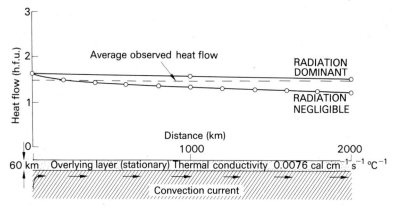

Figure 3.10.2   Heat flow pattern from a cooling convection current in the upper mantle with a stationary overlying layer 60 km thick, with no significant radiation and with radiation dominant. Radioactive heat sources are assumed to be absent. *Source:* Bott (1967), with modification.

and without the effects of radiation adding to the conduction. In this model, if transfer of heat upward through the stationary layer is by conduction alone, the velocity of the underlying convection current would have to be as high as 20 cm year^{-1} although if radiation is dominant this velocity could be reduced to 4 cm year^{-1}. In either case, however, the predicted heat flow pattern is much too uniform. In particular the model does not predict high heat flow over the ridge although this could be explained easily by assuming that heat is carried to the surface beneath ridges by magma.

In practice, the truth probably lies somewhere between these two models—a fairly fast convection current below a lithosphere which is moving in the same direction but much more slowly. As the models get closer to reality they also get more complicated—we shall pursue them no further here. The general point to be emphasized, however, is that no convection model may be considered acceptable unless it can explain the observed pattern of heat flow.

But there is one further interesting point to be made in connection with convection models for heat flow. If oceanic heat flow is to be explained mainly in terms of convection and continental heat flow by radioactivity (two entirely different and apparently unconnected processes) why should they be equal at all? Is this a fortuitous situation which has led scientists up the garden path, or is there still some fundamental control which keeps the two heat flows about the same? At the moment we do not know.

Apparent equality: There is a third theory for equal continental and oceanic heat flows which says that the two are not really equal at all but only appear so. There is, of course, no doubt that the two heat flows are about equal as measured; but what if there is some external process operating which artificially reduces the continental heat flow, for example? This idea has recently been developed by I. K. Crain who postulated that such a process might be glaciation.

There is abundant evidence that the Earth has undergone periods of widespread glaciation, the latest of which may have ended as recently as 10 000 years ago. During this last glacial period, the temperature at the base of the ice sheet—that is, at the continental surface—was probably in the range 0 °C to −8 °C and no longer dominated by the heat from the Sun. When the ice retreated, however, the surface temperature would again come to be influenced mainly by the Sun; but because of the low thermal conductivity of crustal rocks, the deeper crust which had been cooled during a long period of glaciation would 'thaw out' only very slowly—a process likely to take many thousands of years. The heat flow, which during the ice age had been reduced by the effect of the lower ice temperature, would thus still be reduced to some extent.

Crain has calculated that if glaciation ended 10 000 years ago, producing a comparatively rapid rise in temperature of 10 °C at the continental surface, the effect to be observed today would be an apparent increase in heat flow with depth over the few thousand metres of a borehole. But is such an increase actually observed? It is difficult to test the idea in a single borehole because the effect is small. However, Crain has tried to detect the average effect in a number of boreholes in the Appalachian region of North America. As Figure 3.10.3 (a) shows, the heat flow does in general appear to increase with depth in the boreholes in the way predicted (dashed line). (Note that this is not the general increase in *temperature* with depth in the Earth on the scale of kilometres; we are here talking about *heat flow* over depths negligible compared with the Earth's radius.)

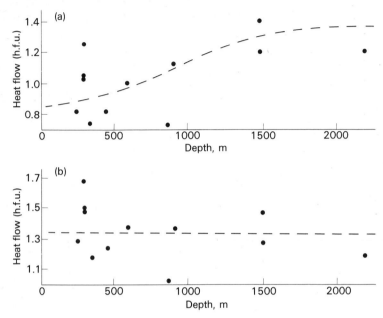

Figure 3.10.3 The possible effect of glaciation on heat flow. In (a) the dashed line is the predicted heat flow variation with depth; and the data points are as observed (uncorrected). In (b) the dashed line and the data points have been corrected for glaciation effects. *Source:* Crain (1968).

When the observed borehole data are 'corrected' for the supposed effects of glaciation, the curve in Figure 3.10.3 (b) is obtained; that is, heat flow becomes constant again as one would expect it to be. These figures also show that over about the upper 1500 metres the observed heat flow is lower than it should be, supposedly due to the effects of glaciation. In numerical terms, the observed 1.12 h.f.u. average for the Appalachian boreholes investigated by Crain becomes 1.46 h.f.u. after correction. Taken over all continental surfaces, this would mean that average continental heat flow is actually some thirty percent higher than that observed—and thus so much higher than the oceanic average. Ocean floor values will not, of course, be affected by glaciation.

Whether something which seems to work in the Appalachian region can be taken to obtain over all the Earth's continents is uncertain. Moreover, K. Horai has recently calculated the effect of glaciation in a different way from Crain, from which he concludes that the maximum correction should be no more than 0.1–0.2 h.f.u. At the moment, all that perhaps can be said is that the glaciation hypothesis has not yet been adequately assessed but remains a possible explanation.

Stated in the above way, it might appear that the three explanations —variations in the distribution of radioactivity, convection, and apparent equality—are mutually exclusive. This is by no means necessarily the case. From what we now know about global tectonics, it seems inconceivable that convection does not play a significant part; but this certainly does not imply that the other two explanations are not even partly valid. In the meantime, the whole problem of the equality of continental and oceanic heat flows remains one of the central issues in heat flow studies.

3.11 General remarks

Mark Twain once wrote: 'There is something fascinating about science. One gets such wholesale returns of conjecture out of such a trifling investment of fact.' Twain was writing last century about the geography of the Mississippi; but from the tone we have set in this chapter, his

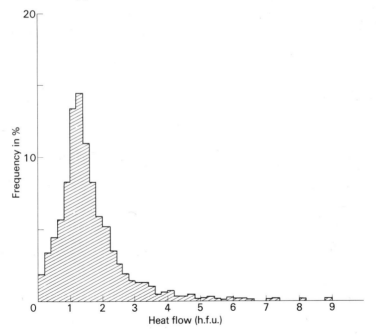

Figure 3.11.1   Histogram of the Earth's surface heat flow values. *Source:* Langseth and Von Herzen (1970).

remark would perhaps not be inappropriate in the context of today's study of the Earth's thermal properties. This is not to denigrate heat flow studies in any way. The investment in fact is trifling only in the sense that the Earth is so large a body that in a short period of time man can hardly do more than get a trifling amount of data from it. It is possible to summarize all heat flow data in one simple diagram (see Figure 3.11.1); but in human terms, the effort which has gone into retrieving them is quite considerable. Moreover, it must also be remembered that the study of the Earth's heat flow is a very young branch of science. Almost every useful heat flow observation has been made since 1950.

At the same time, one must recognize that trying to determine the thermal characteristics of the Earth's interior is an exercise in attempting to determine the near-indeterminable. Basically, the only hard data we have (and those imperfect) relate to the Earth's surface heat flow—and so the essential problem is no more nor less than trying to define a curve using only a single point. The aims of this chapter have thus been twofold—first, to describe how that single point is obtained and the difficulties encountered in obtaining it, and secondly, to illustrate the *sort* of intellectual reasoning which must substitute for direct physical access in extrapolating the surface data downwards towards the Earth's deep interior. At the same time, we have also been able to show, in a general way, that the observed heat flow accords with our ideas of global tectonics and can, moreover, make its own contribution to the elucidation of global tectonic processes.

Further reading

M. H. P. Bott (1971), *The Interior of the Earth*. London, Arnold.
W. H. K. Lee (Ed.) (1971), *Terrestrial Heat Flow*. Washington, American Geophysical Union.
J. H. Sass (1970), Terrestrial heat flow, *Comments on Earth Sciences: Geophysics*, **1**, 8–13.
J. H. Sass (1971), Tectonic and geochemical implications of heat flow data, *Comments on Earth Sciences: Geophysics*, **1**, 87–94.
J. H. Sass (1971), The Earth's heat and internal temperatures, in I. G. Gass, P. J. Smith and R. C. L. Wilson (Eds.), *Understanding the Earth*. Sussex, Artemis Press and Cambridge, Mass., M.I.T. Press.

CHAPTER FOUR

Earthquakes: Characteristics, Prediction and Modification

4.1 Introduction

Many, perhaps most, academic geophysicists regard earthquakes simply as sources of elastic waves, and the worldwide earthquake distribution shown in Figure 1.5.1 as an indicator of plate boundaries. But as G. D. Garland has pointed out, these 'rather coldly scientific applications' should not be allowed to obscure the 'very great impact these terrestrial phenomena can have on human existence', both individual and collective. T. Rikitake has suggested that 'those who are living in non-seismic countries like western Europe would hardly be able to realize the terror of great earthquakes. It is difficult to explain how one feels when one experiences violent quakes of the ground on which one stands. Perhaps even a scientist who is professionally concerned with seismology is terrified when he is attacked by an earthquake of a large intensity.' On the larger scale, it has been estimated that during historic time over 14 million people have lost their lives in earthquakes or because of earthquake after-effects such as landslides, fires and tsunamis (large sea waves resulting from seismic disturbance, sometimes, though incorrectly, called tidal waves). The economic cost of historic earthquakes in terms of both death and property damage can hardly be envisaged.

There can be no correlation between the magnitude (see section 4.2) of an earthquake and the death and destruction it causes because so many other factors enter into the problem. The great Alaskan earthquake (magnitude 8.5) of 28 March 1964, for example, killed only 178 people, whereas the 29 February 1960 shock (magnitude 5.8) in Morocco killed 10 000–15 000 and the Yugoslavian earthquake (magnitude 6.0) of 26 July 1963 killed 1100. This lack of correlation is equally well illustrated by Table 4.1.1 which lists all the earthquakes

Table 4.1.1 Major earthquake activity, 1971. Earthquakes of magnitude 7.0 or greater and others which caused fatalities.

Date	Location	Killed	Magnitude M_s	Comments
3 January	South Atlantic Ridge		7.1	
10 January	West Iran	1	8.1	24 houses on pillars collapsed
16 January	Zaire Republic		5.0	damage
4 February	Northern Sumatra		7.1	damage in north Sumatra
6 February	Central Italy	20	4.6	270 injured; $41.6 million damage
8 February	South Shetlands		7.0	
9 February	Southern California	65	6.5	1000 injured; $550 million damage
2 May	Andreanof Islands		7.1	small local tsunami
12 May	Turkey	57	5.9	100 injured; extensive damage
22 May	Turkey	812	6.7	2000 injured; extensive damage
16 June	Java	1	5.2	6 injured; $390 000 damage
17 June	Chile	1	7.0	damage to several villages
9 July	Chile	84	7.5	447 injured; 40 000 homeless
14 July	New Britain	2	7.9	5 injured; some damage; local tsunami
15 July	Italy	2	5.2	100 injured; significant damage
19 July	New Ireland		7.1	
26 July	New Britain		7.9	locally damaging tsunami
27 July	Ecuador	1	7.5	3 injured; significant damage
2 August	Hokkaido, Japan		7.0	local tsunami
5 August	Central mid-Atlantic Ridge		7.0	
9 August	Northern Iran	1	5.3	39 injured; significant damage
5 September	Sakhalin Island		7.1	local tsunami
16 September	Banda Sea		7.0	
25 September	East New Guinea		7.0	
15 October	Peru	5	5.7	major damage
27 October	New Hebrides	1	7.1	major damage
21 November	Santa Cruz Islands		7.1	
24 November	Off East Coast Kamchatka		7.3	
15 December	Kamchatka		7.8	local tsunami

in the single year 1971 which had magnitudes equal to or greater than 7.0, or which caused fatalities. To take but one comparison, the California shock (magnitude 6.5) of 9 February killed 65 people and contrasted sharply with the South Shetlands earthquake (magnitude 7.0) of the previous day which apparently caused no fatalities at all.

The fact is, of course, that as much depends on where and when an earthquake takes place as on what its strength is. The Alaskan shock of 1964 took place in an area which is comparatively sparsely populated; but the much smaller Californian shock of 1971 occurred not far from the centre of one of the world's largest cities. Other factors which enhance the lack of correlation between magnitude and destruction include the depth of the earthquake focus (all destructive earthquakes are comparatively shallow events), the resistance (or lack of it) of buildings (the more modern buildings of, say, California—despite the surprising lack of attention given to the design of earthquake-proof constructions—tend to be more earthquake-resistant than those in the older Mediterranean countries), local geological and soil conditions, and even the time of day (fewer deaths are likely to result during the night, when most people are asleep in low-rise dwellings, than during the day, when many may be at work in high-rise office blocks).

To describe the effects of an earthquake in terms of this diversity of factors, Båth has devised a term which he calls *specific destruction* (f_0) and which is essentially a measure of the number of deaths per unit of seismic energy. According to Båth's definition, specific destruction is given by:

$$f_0 = \log \frac{c(N+1)}{E} \qquad (4.1.1)$$

where N = number of people killed,
$\quad\quad E$ = seismic wave energy (see section 4.2),
and $\quad c$ = a constant.

Combining this with equation (4.2.7), which expresses the relationship between seismic wave energy (E) and earthquake magnitude (M_s), gives:

$$f_0 = \log(N+1) - 1.44\,M_s + 12.82 \qquad (4.1.2)$$

In these terms, the ten most destructive earthquakes occurring through 1964 are listed in Table 4.1.2. What is particularly striking about this list is that of the 'top ten' earthquakes no less than nine occurred in the Mediterranean–Middle East belt, in spite of the fact that, as Figure 1.5.1 shows, the most seismically active region in the world is the circum-Pacific belt. This imbalance in destructiveness is further illustrated by Table 4.1.3 which shows the average values of f_0 for the most seismically active regions. What is quite clear is that if

Table 4.1.2   The ten most destructive earthquakes up to 1964 in terms of the specific destruction, f_0. *Source:* Båth (1967a).

Date	Region	f_0
1960	Morocco	8.6
1857	Italy	7.5
1915	Italy	7.2
1963	Yugoslavia	7.2
1960	Iran	7.0
1908	Italy	6.9
1962	Iran	6.8
1949	Ecuador	6.8
1930	Italy	6.6
1935	Pakistan	6.5

anything is to be done about earthquake destruction, the Mediterranean–Middle East area has a priority claim, although this is not to belittle the dangers which exist in other highly populated regions such as Japan and the west coast of North America.

But can anything be done? Is it possible, for example, that earthquakes may be predicted, thus allowing death, though not property damage, to be avoided? During the past few decades, considerable effort has been devoted to the problem of earthquake prediction, especially in Japan and the United States, but with very little (though some) success. On the other hand, a series of more or less accidental phenomena has generated hope that some earthquakes may be avoided altogether by suitably modifying the tectonic environment.

Table 4.1.3   The average specific destruction, f_0, for the world's most seismically active regions. The average standard deviation for the average f_0 values is ± 1.0. *Source:* Bath (1967a).

Region	Average f_0	Number of earthquakes
Mediterranean	6.3	11
Iran–Pakistan–Afghanistan	6.0	6
Central Asia	4.8	6
South America	4.7	7
Japan–Formosa	4.6	11
India	4.3	3
New Zealand	3.3	2
North America	2.8	6

4.2 Earthquake characteristics

In general terms, an earthquake may be regarded as a sudden release of strain energy in a comparatively localized region of the Earth's crust or upper mantle. But having said that, it must be admitted that the ultimate causes of earthquakes are very far from understood. It is quite clear from Figure 1.5.1, however, that the production of earthquakes is closely related to global processes such as sea floor spreading and plate tectonics. It is thus reasonable to assume that a full understanding of earthquake phenomena can only be developed within the framework of the new global tectonics.

Types of waves

In Chapter Two we discussed the behaviour of P and S waves, the body waves which pass through the body of the Earth. However, earthquakes also produce *surface waves* which are restricted to the vicinity of the Earth's free surface. There are two main types of surface waves: (i) *Rayleigh waves*, in which the motion of the surface particles is confined to the vertical plane containing the direction of wave propagation, and (ii) *Love waves*, in which the particle motion is in a horizontal direction perpendicular to the direction of wave propagation. Both body and surface waves are illustrated schematically in Figure 4.2.1.

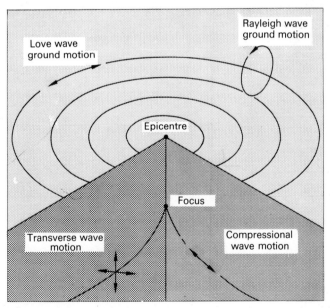

Figure 4.2.1 Schematic representation of the basic types of wave produced by an earthquake. *Source:* Davies (1968).

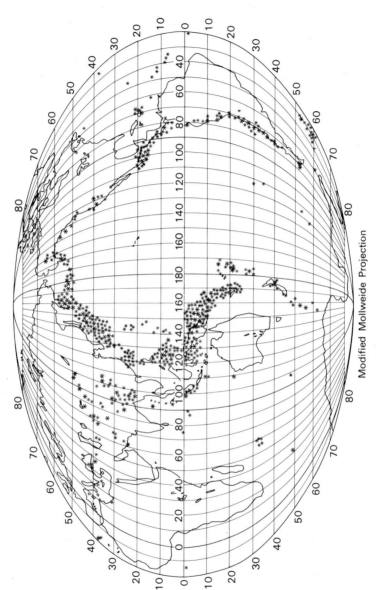

Modified Mollweide Projection

Figure 4.2.2 World map of large shallow earthquakes. The larger stars represent events of magnitude 7.7 or higher occurring during the period 1904–1952. The smaller stars represent events within the magnitude range 7.0–7.7 occurring from 1918–1952. *Source:* Gutenberg and Richter (1954).

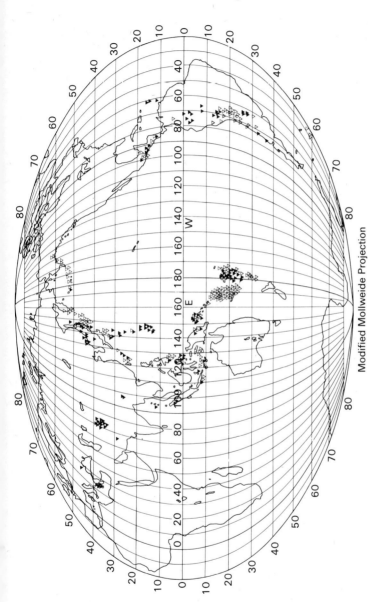

Modified Mollweide Projection

Figure 4.2.3   World map of large intermediate and deep earthquakes for the period 1904–1952. Open triangles represent intermediate events of magnitude 7.0–7.7 (smaller triangles) and magnitude equal to or greater than 7.7 (larger triangles). Closed triangles represent deep events of magnitude 7.0–7.7 (smaller triangles) and magnitude 7.7 or greater (larger triangles). *Source*: Gutenberg and Richter (1954).

Depth of focus

All earthquakes occur within about the upper 700 km of the Earth; none have been detected below 720 km. (The deepest shock ever

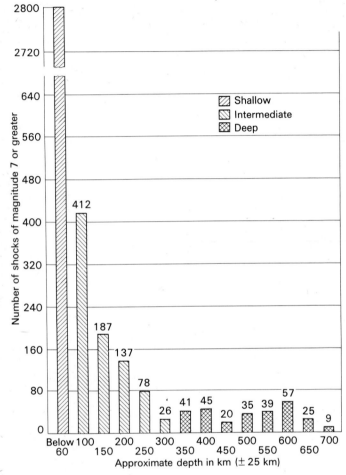

Figure 4.2.4 The variation of earthquake frequency with depth of focus for events between 1904 and 1945. *Source:* Howell (1959).

recorded occurred at 720 km beneath the Flores Sea, East Indies, on 29 June 1934.) The classification of earthquakes on the basis of depth of focus is:

shallow focus	0–70 km
intermediate focus	70–300 km
deep focus	below 300 km

The worldwide distribution of large earthquakes (magnitudes 7.0+) is shown in Figures 4.2.2 (shallow events) and 4.2.3 (intermediate and deep events). Seventy-five percent of shallow earthquakes, ninety percent of intermediate earthquakes and nearly all deep earthquakes occur around the margin of the Pacific, in the circum-Pacific belt. Most of the remaining large earthquakes occur beneath the Alpine–Himalayan belt. As Figure 1.5.1 shows, earthquakes are also concentrated along the oceanic ridge system. These are generally shallow focus events; but are also comparatively small (typical magnitudes 4.0–6.0) and thus do not show up on Figure 4.2.2. In fact, the world's earthquakes are heavily biased in favour of shallow events as Figure 4.2.4. demonstrates. Over seventy-five percent of the energy released by earthquakes derives from shallow focus events and only about three percent from deep focus events. Moreover, it is usually the shallow events which produce the damage at the Earth's surface. Few shocks at depths greater than 100 km cause damage, although a notable exception was the Rumanian earthquake of 10 November 1940 which, though occurring at a depth of 160 km, caused considerable damage and killed about 1000 people.

Below any given region, earthquakes are not necessarily limited to a particular depth nor even to a narrow depth range, although where earthquakes occur throughout a wide depth range they need not be distributed uniformly. For example, Figure 4.2.5 shows earthquakes beneath the Japanese area as a function of focal depth. The depth range is very wide; but as Table 4.2.1 demonstrates, earthquakes are preferentially distributed within certain level ranges. For deep earthquakes, for example, there are significantly more within the 300–400 km range than within any other 100 km interval. By contrast, in the San

Table 4.2.1 The number (N) of earthquakes within various depth ranges beneath Japan, including only events of magnitude greater than 6.0 within the period 1926–1956. *Source:* Wadati (1967).

Depth (km)	N	Depth (km)	N
0–10	82	100–120	7
10–20	76	120–150	5
20–30	27	150–200	10
30–40	78	200–250	10
40–50	28	250–300	9
50–60	46	300–350	19
60–70	4	350–400	11
70–80	6	400–450	10
80–90	3	450–500	10
90–100	13	500+	8

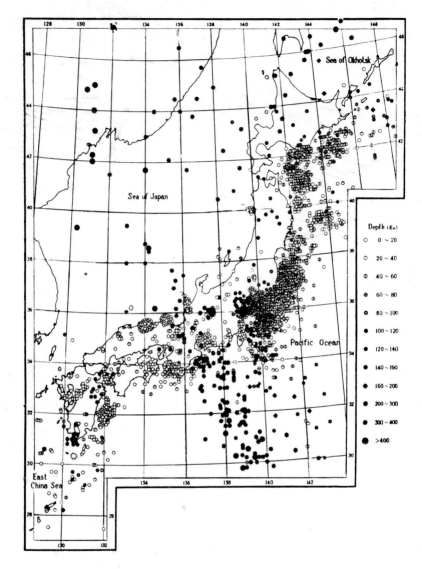

Figure 4.2.5   Earthquakes beneath the Japanese region distinguished by depth of focus. *Source:* Wadati (1967).

Andreas Fault zone of the western United States earthquakes are limited to the upper 15 km. Then again, in South America there are no events at all between 300 km and 550 km.

169

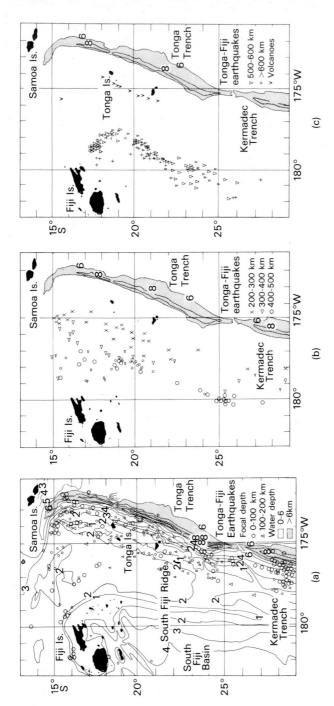

Figure 4.2.6 Earthquake epicentres in the Tonga–Fiji region: (a) for shallow focus events, (b) intermediate, and (c) deep. The contours in (a) show the water depth in kilometres. Note that towards the north the earthquake belt bends, mirroring the trench–arc system. This implies that the earthquake belt and the trench–arc system are both results of the same underlying tectonic processes. *Source*: Sykes (1966).

The most intense seismic activity occurs beneath arcuate features which generally comprise a trench–island arc association. In such cases, the earthquake foci are found to lie roughly along a plane which dips at about 45° away from the ocean side and which sometimes even extends beneath the continent. Figure 4.2.6 shows the geographic relationship of shallow, intermediate and deep earthquake epicentres to the Tonga trench. It is clear from these distributions that as the shocks become deeper they lie further from the trench, a relationship which is even more dramatically demonstrated in Figure 4.2.7. This

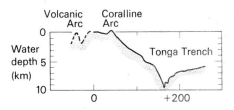

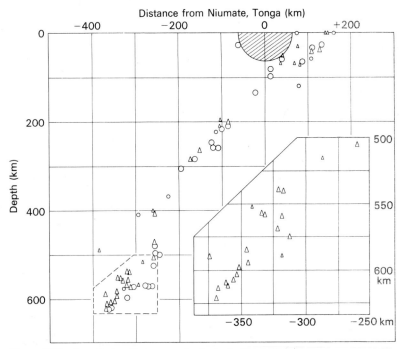

Figure 4.2.7 A vertical section perpendicular to the Tonga trench showing earthquake foci for the year 1965. The circles represent foci projected from within 150 km to the north of the section; the triangles represent foci projected from within 150 km to the south. *Source:* Isacks, Oliver and Sykes (1968).

is particularly strong evidence in favour of ocean floor spreading which envisages the downflow of oceanic lithosphere beneath trench–arc systems.

Magnitude

The magnitude of an earthquake is an absolute measure of its size, which is related to the seismic energy released and which is determined from the amplitudes of the elastic waves generated. There are several different magnitude scales; but each one may be defined by the general equation:

$$M = \log \frac{A}{T} + a f(\Delta, h) + b \qquad (4.2.1)$$

where M = magnitude,
  $\log$ = logarithm to the base 10,
  A = maximum amplitude of wave, measured in microns
      (1 micron is 10^{-6} m),
  T = period of wave, measured in seconds,
  $f(\ )$ = function of (a quantity which depends on .....),
  Δ = distance from point of measurement of amplitude to the
      epicentre, measured in degrees,
  h = focal depth of earthquake, measured in kilometres,
  a, b = constants which must be determined empirically.

The function f (which takes account of the diminution of amplitude with distance due mainly to spreading and gradual absorption of the wave) may be determined by a combination of experiment and theory. Once f is known, equation (4.2.1) may be applied to any wave.
   The concept of earthquake magnitude was first introduced by Richter to measure the size of shallow earthquakes in California. For this purpose, he defined magnitude in terms of the maximum wave amplitude (A) observed at a distance of 100 km. This quantity is now known as the *local magnitude*, M_L, but has never been widely used outside California. However, the basic idea was later extended for use at greater distances from the epicentre (but still for shallow earthquakes) by defining the magnitude M_S which is based on the maximum amplitude (A) of surface waves having a period (T) of about twenty seconds. A third magnitude, m_b, known as the *body wave magnitude*, makes use of the amplitude (A) of body waves at large distances from the epicentre and for events at any depth. M_S (surface waves) and m_b (body waves) are the two magnitude measurements now in general use.†

   † Unless otherwise stated, earthquake magnitudes quoted in this chapter refer to M_S.

The three magnitude scales may be related to each other by the following equations:

$$m_b = 1.7 + 0.8\,M_L - 0.01\,M_L^2 \qquad (4.2.2)$$

and

$$m_b = 0.63\,M_S + 2.5 \qquad (4.2.3)$$

However, it should always be remembered that equations such as these are based on empirically determined functions and constants and are thus open to disagreement and refinement or even radical change. Equations (4.2.2) and (4.2.3) contain numerical values determined by Gutenberg and Richter. More recently, however, Båth has suggested that for shallow focus earthquakes equation (4.2.3) should be replaced by:

$$m_b = 0.56\,M_S + 2.9 \qquad (4.2.4)$$

Båth also suggests that for shallow focus earthquakes:

$$M_S = \log\frac{A}{T} + 1.66 \log \Delta + 3.3 \qquad (4.2.5)$$

But whatever magnitude definition is adopted and whatever numerical values are used, it is worth remembering that a magnitude scale is always a logarithmic (to the base 10) scale.

It should be clear from what has been said above that the magnitude of an earthquake, in spite of its essentially absolute nature, is not quite so certain a quantity as a simple table of magnitudes (for example, Table 4.1.1) might imply. Båth has recently summed up the situation in this way:

'As magnitude is a quantity characteristic for each shock, determinations from different stations and also from different waves at the same station should agree within error limits, i.e. within about ±0.2–0.3 units. Unfortunately, variations are often larger because of a number of reasons, such as inaccurate seismographs, not well known station corrections [constants], use of surface waves also for shocks of greater depth than normal without proper correction for depth etc.

'Pasadena and Berkeley [seismic stations] magnitudes usually agree well with each other and with magnitudes from Uppsala, Kiruna, Strasbourg, Praha and some other places, the latter having been adjusted to the Pasadena system or some average "world system". Palisades reports magnitudes which are often too low, and the U.S. Coast and Geodetic Survey magnitudes are consistently low (by about 0.7 units). The Moscow magnitudes used to be low, as they were exclusively based on surface waves, but this has recently been corrected.' (*Source*: Båth (1967b).)

Energy

Once an earthquake's magnitude has been determined, its elastic wave energy (E) may be calculated to a first approximation by:

$$\log E = 11.8 + 1.5\,M_S \quad \text{(Gutenberg and Richter)} \qquad (4.2.6)$$

$$\log E = 12.24 + 1.44\,M_S \quad \text{(Båth)} \qquad (4.2.7)$$

where E is measured in ergs (1 erg $= 10^{-7}$ J). The average annual release of energy by earthquakes is about 10^{18} J, most of which comes from the few really large shocks. However, it should be noted that all the energy released by an earthquake does not go to produce elastic waves; a great deal is dissipated as heat.

Intensity

Before the concept of absolute magnitude was developed, the size of an earthquake was expressed in terms of a more subjective, less 'scientific' quantity known as *intensity*, which is based on the observation of the direct effects of the earthquake at the surface. The intensity is determined by assessing the degree to which shaking is perceptible

Table 4.2.2 The Rossi–Forel earthquake intensity scale.

I.	Shocks so weak as to be registered only by one type of seismograph and confirmed only by practical observers. Not perceptible on seismographs generally.
II.	Shocks registered by seismographs generally. Confirmed only by persons who are in a condition of rest.
III.	Shocks noticed by many persons. Strong enough for the duration and direction of shocks to be estimated.
IV.	Shocks noticed by persons who are in a state of activity. Movable objects, windows, and doors shaken. Cracking sounds in houses.
V.	Shocks generally noticed by the entire population. Large objects, beds, and other pieces of furniture are set in motion. Ringing of some doorbells.
VI.	General awakening of people who are asleep. General ringing of doorbells, swinging of chandeliers, stopping of clocks, visible swaying of trees and bushes. Shocks strong enough to cause people to desert their houses in terror.
VII.	Overturning of movable objects, falling of plaster from walls and ceiling, ringing of church bells. No damage to structures. Shocks powerful enough to cause general terror.
VIII.	Throwing down of chimneys, appearance of cracks in the walls of buildings.
IX.	Partial or complete destruction of certain buildings.
X.	Great catastrophe. Ruined buildings, overturning of earth layers, appearance of clefts in the earth, landslips.

to people (for example, by sending out post-earthquake questionnaires to those concerned), the amount of damage to man-made structures, and the extent of visible deformation of the Earth itself. The intensity thus defined is 'measured' in terms of arbitrary scales.

Intensity scales have been in use since 1811. One of the most important was the so-called Rossi–Forel scale introduced towards the end of the nineteenth century—a scale with ten intensity grades ranging from barely perceptible shocks to visible deformations of the Earth (see Table 4.2.2). Later this was modified to a twelve-grade scale by Mercalli in order to improve the discrimination at the higher intensity end of the scale. A modified version of the twelve-grade Mercalli scale (the Modified Mercalli Scale) is now used (see Table 4.2.3).

Intensities, once determined, are usually displayed in the form of *isoseismal maps*, an example of which is shown in Figure 4.2.8. If the ground were completely uniform and if the energy were radiated out

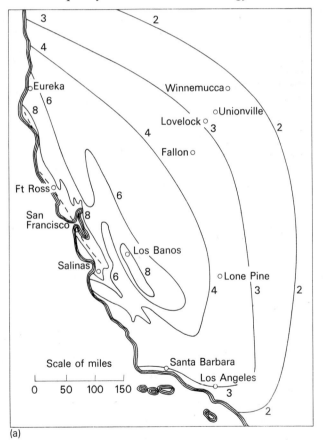

(a)

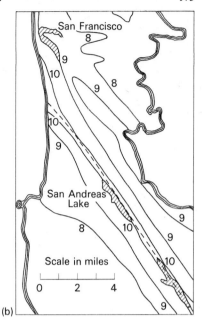

Figure 4.2.8 Isoseismal map of the 1906 San Francisco earthquake: (a) shows the wider region; (b) shows the epicentral area. The numbers denote intensity on the Modified Mercalli Scale. The dotted line represents the San Andreas fault. *Source:* Lawson (1908).

(b)

uniformly in all directions, the *isoseismal lines* would be circles, although this is never the case in practice. Although the intensity is greatest near the epicentre and generally decreases outwards, there are irregularities depending upon crustal conditions. Moreover, the shape of isoseismal lines is also strongly dependent on the distribution of population in the area where the earthquake is likely to be felt; if there are no people, no shock can be felt.

The intensity grade may be taken as a rough measure of the ground acceleration produced by the earthquake. A general relationship between the maximum intensity (I_0) on the Modified Mercalli Scale and the maximum acceleration may be written as:

$$I_0 = p \log a_0 + q \tag{4.2.8}$$

where a_0 is the acceleration in cm s^{-1} and p and q are constants determined empirically to be in the ranges 2.0–3.0 and 1.5–3.5, respectively. The precise values of p and q probably vary from region to region. For example, for earthquakes in California, Gutenberg and Richter concluded that:

$$I_0 = 3 \log a_0 + 1.5 \tag{4.2.9}$$

In spite of the apparent lack of sophistication of intensity measures, intensity studies are still carried out today because they are useful in

Table 4.2.3 The Modified Mercalli earthquake intensity scale.

Scale degree	Effects on persons	Effects on structures	Other effects	Rossi-Forel equivalent	Equivalent shallow magnitude
I.	Not felt except by few under favourable circumstances			I.	
II.	Felt by few at rest		Delicately suspended objects swing	I–II.	2.5
III.	Felt noticeably indoors. Standing cars may rock		Duration estimated	III.	
IV.	Felt generally indoors. People awakened		Cars rocked. Windows, etc., rattled	IV–V.	3.5
V.	Felt generally	Some plaster falls	Dishes, windows broken. Pendulum clocks stop	V–VI.	
VI.	Felt by all. Many frightened	Chimneys, plaster damaged	Furniture moved. Objects upset	VI–VII.	
VII.	Everyone runs outdoors. Felt in moving cars	Moderate damage		VIII.	5.5
VIII.	General alarm	Very destructive and general damage to weak structures. Little damage to well-built structures	Monuments, walls down. Furniture overturned. Sand and mud ejected. Changes in well-water levels	VIII–IX.	6
IX.	Panic	Total destruction of weak structures. Considerable damage to well-built structures	Foundations damaged. Underground pipes broken. Ground fissured and cracked	IX.	
X.	Panic	Masonry and frame structures commonly destroyed. Only best buildings survive. Foundations ruined	Ground badly cracked. Rails bent. Water slopped over banks	X.	
XI.	Panic	Few buildings survive	Broad fissures. Fault scarps. Underground pipes out of service	X.	8.0
XII.	Panic	Total destruction	Acceleration exceeds gravity. Waves seen in ground. Lines of sight and level distorted. Objects thrown in air	X.	8.5

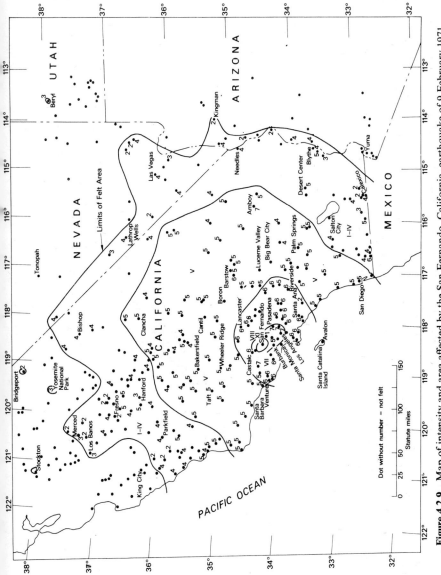

Figure 4.2.9 Map of intensity and area affected by the San Fernando, California, earthquake of 9 February 1971. *Source:* Scott (1971).

assessing ground damage, preparing earthquake risk maps, and so on. An isoseismal map for a very recent event is shown in Figure 4.2.9, which relates to the San Fernando, California, earthquake of 9 February 1971.

Of course, magnitude and intensity scales assess quite different aspects of an earthquake; and the scales are thus independent. Even so, there seems to be a correlation between magnitude and maximum intensity I_0 for shallow shocks which is quite well represented by the empirical relationship:

$$M_s = 0.67\,I_0 + 1.7\log h - 1.4 \qquad (4.2.10)$$

where the logarithm is to the base 10 and h = focal depth in km.

Aftershocks and foreshocks

Large magnitude earthquakes are usually followed by a number of smaller shocks (*aftershocks*) occurring fairly close to the focus of the main shock. Aftershocks are probably related to mechanical readjustment taking place in the crust or mantle following the release of energy by the main shock. Immediately after the main event, the frequency of aftershocks is usually high but falls off gradually with time—for very large events, often over a period of several years. Also, aftershock activity is greater for shallow than for deep earthquakes. The magnitude of the largest aftershock in a series is very often about 1.0 less than the magnitude of the main shock; and some of the larger aftershocks may be accompanied by aftershocks of their own. The pattern of aftershocks from the San Fernando earthquake is shown in Figure 4.2.10.

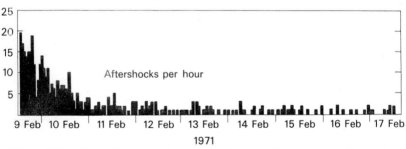

Figure 4.2.10   Hourly frequency of occurrence of aftershocks from the San Fernando (1971) earthquake, as measured by a seismic station about 318 km away in Nevada. The days are GMT. *Source:* Espinosa, Engdahl, Tarr and Brockman (1971).

Some large earthquakes are also preceded by smaller shocks (*foreshocks*). However, because foreshocks have characteristics similar to those of other shocks, they cannot actually be identified as foreshocks until the main shock has taken place.

Causes

The ultimate causes of most tectonic earthquakes must be related to the processes embodied in the new global tectonics—but are still poorly understood. In the meantime, however, it is possible to make some progress in understanding by considering the more immediate processes producing earthquakes.

The traditional explanation of earthquakes is the *elastic rebound theory* proposed by H. F. Reid in the aftermath of the great San Francisco earthquake of 1906. In simple terms, the fault from which an earthquake derives is regarded as the common boundary between two blocks of the crust. If crustal forces operate in such a way as to try to move the blocks relative to each other, horizontally and in the direction of the fault, no such movement will take place in the first instance because of friction and cementing. Thus initially the blocks remain locked, but as crustal forces persist, a state of strain builds up in the blocks in the vicinity of the fault. Ultimately, the restraints will be overcome and the two blocks will suddenly slip with respect to each other, producing the earthquake. This event reduces the pre-earthquake strain to zero; but if the crustal forces continue, strain will build up again to a second shock.

The principle of the elastic rebound theory is illustrated in Figure 4.2.11. In (a) the fault is initially in an unstrained state with the imaginary line AOB drawn perpendicularly across it. As the A block tries to move relative to the B block in the directions indicated by the arrows (under

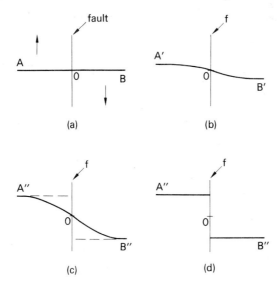

Figure 4.2.11   The elastic rebound theory of shallow earthquakes.

the action of crustal forces), the material at A moves to A' and that at B moves to B'; but the fault remains locked at O as shown in (b). Diagram (c) shows the situation obtaining immediately before the slip occurs, by which time A has reached A" and B has reached B". By (d) the earthquake has occurred by fault slip; and the whole region is again in an unstrained state but with a displacement of the original imaginary line across the fault. In the particular case studied by Reid the fault was, of course, the San Andreas fault, which is now regarded as a transform fault related to the East Pacific Rise spreading system. Here the oceanward side is moving northwestwards relative to the landward side. The relative displacement produced by the 1906 earthquake (about 6.3 m) was actually measured from stations on each side of the fault.

Although the elastic rebound theory has been generally accepted for many years, it is not entirely clear that such acceptance is fully justified. For one thing, some people have protested that, because the theory is derived from the behaviour of the 1906 earthquake, it can hardly be regarded as an explanation for a typical earthquake. Justification in principle for such a criticism comes from the modern view that whereas the San Francisco earthquake occurred along a transform fault, many more earthquakes occur along oceanic ridge and trench–island arc systems. In fact, the greatest difficulty with the elastic rebound theory comes in just such regions as trenches where some earthquakes are deep. A theory involving fault slip requires a position to arise where the shearing stress of the rock exceeds the frictional stress. At depths of several hundred kilometres, however, the frictional stress may be at least a hundred times greater than the shearing stress—thus unlikely ever to be overcome. The maximum depth at which friction stress may be overcome by shearing stress could, in fact, be as low as 300 m.

One way out of this problem would be to postulate the presence of some lubrication mechanism, such as fluid (magma, for example) in the rock pores along the fault boundary between the blocks, whereby the frictional forces may be reduced and thus overcome. But it seems unlikely that such a mechanism could increase the maximum depth at which faulting may take place to more than about 25 km, although some would put this figure as high as 60 km. Accordingly, although faulting may be taken to explain earthquakes up to this depth, some other mechanism must be sought for deeper shocks. Several possible mechanisms have been suggested, some of which appeal to non-elastic processes—that is, processes in which the application of stress produces a *permanent* deformation (as opposed to an elastic process in which the original state is recovered when the stress is removed).

Finally, assuming elastic processes, it is possible to calculate the strain energy released by an earthquake. Figure 4.2.12 shows the total global strain release from all large ($M_S \geqslant 8.0$) shallow shocks (which

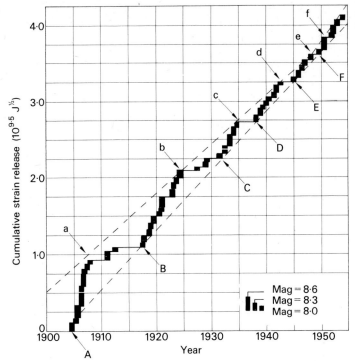

Figure 4.2.12 Global strain release (cumulative) for large ($M_S \geqslant 8.0$) shallow earthquakes over the period 1904–1954. Strain release is here defined as the square root of the energy released. The basic unit is thus $(joule)^{\frac{1}{2}}$ or $(J)^{\frac{1}{2}}$. *Source:* Benioff (1955).

account for the bulk of the energy released from all earthquakes) plotted as a function of time over the period 1904–1954. The resulting curve is step-like, indicating bursts of energy (Aa, Bb, Cc, etc.), alternating with relatively quiet periods (aB, bC, cD, etc.,) with a successive decrease in the strength of the bursts. This seems to imply that the Earth is gradually becoming less active; but the period covered is really too short to enable any predictions to be made about long-term future activity.

Mechanisms

The first wave to reach a seismic detector from an earthquake is the *P* wave. However, if the records from many detectors (stations) for a particular earthquake are examined, the *P* wave is found to reach some stations as a compression (ground movement away from focus) and some stations as a dilatation (ground movement towards the focus). Moreover, the distribution of compressions and dilatations forms a systematic pattern. The *P* wave pattern for a fault source is shown in Figure 4.2.13. It has four 'lobes' of alternate compression ($+$) and dilatation ($-$), where the perimeter (envelope) of the lobes represents

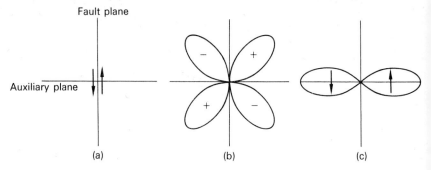

Figure 4.2.13   A Type I (single couple) earthquake source (a) with P wave radiation pattern (b) and S wave radiation pattern (c). Compression is indicated by $+$ and dilatation by $-$.

the amplitude of the waves. Thus in all directions at 45° to the fault the wave amplitude is maximum, but is zero along and normal to the fault.

It is easy to see that once the *P* wave pattern has been determined, it is possible to construct both the fault plane and the *auxiliary plane* perpendicular to it; and this method may be used to find the fault and auxiliary planes for faults which are not visible at the Earth's surface. However, it is also easy to see that the *P* wave pattern gives an ambiguous answer. It is possible to construct the two planes from it; but it is not possible to say which is the fault plane and which is the auxiliary plane. At this point it is necessary to consider the *S* wave pattern. For the simple fault source shown in Figure 4.2.13, the *S* wave pattern possesses two lobes as shown in (c). *S* wave amplitude is zero along the fault plane and maximum at right angles to it. There is no ambiguity here and so the fault plane may be determined uniquely. The fault source shown in (a) is known as a single couple or Type I source.

Unfortunately, it turns out that most earthquakes give rise to an *S* wave pattern which has not two lobes as in Figure 4.2.13 (c) but four lobes as in Figure 4.2.14 (c). In other words, the ambiguity inherent in the *P* wave pattern is reflected in the *S* wave pattern; and so the latter cannot in practice be used to distinguish between the fault and auxiliary planes. To make this distinction it thus becomes necessary to use other information, such as a knowledge of the local geology, to select the more likely fault plane. The *S* wave pattern in Figure 4.2.14 (c) is consistent with the type of source shown in Figure 4.2.14 (a) (i). This is known as a double couple or Type II source and implies two superimposed fault motions at right angles.

On the face of it, a fault such as the San Andreas forms a Type I

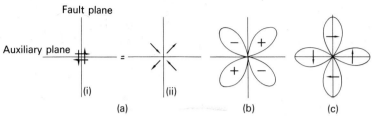

Figure 4.2.14 A Type II (double couple) earthquake source (a) with P wave (b) and S wave (c) radiation patterns. Mathematically, the force arrangements in (i) and (ii) are equivalent.

source which should lead to a two-lobe S wave pattern. The fact that such faults give four-lobe S wave patterns thus tended to discredit the whole elastic rebound theory for many years. However, it has since been shown theoretically that an apparently simple fault such as the San Andreas acts as a Type II source. That this is so experimentally follows from the form of the S wave pattern; but it turns out that even in theory the forces effectively operate at 45° to the fault as in Figure 4.2.14 (a) (ii). Mathematically, (i) and (ii) are equivalent.

Seismologists interested in travel times (see Chapter Two) regard the earthquake as a point source, a good first approximation for that particular purpose. In reality, however, the focal region must have dimensions of several kilometres and possibly, for large earthquakes, even of up to 50 km. More sophisticated models of earthquake mechanisms must therefore take into account the finite source size.

Finally, it must be said that plotting the P and S wave radiation patterns is not quite so easy as it sounds. This is particularly true of the S wave pattern which must be deduced from a seismic record which has already been disturbed by the previous arrival of P waves. As might be expected, therefore, there is not only disagreement among seismologists on the nature of the earthquake mechanism, there is very often disagreement about what the radiation patterns actually are in any given case. It thus seems likely that not a few of the reported patterns may be of dubious merit and thus that geological conclusions drawn from them may not be valid.

4.3 Some historic earthquakes

The effects of earthquakes on countries, communities, individuals, artefacts and geological environments make a fascinating, if lengthy, study in their own right. Unfortunately, we cannot here do full justice to the impact that earthquakes have had upon society because time and space forbid it; but a few notes will serve to illustrate some of the diverse results that real earthquakes have produced.

Table 4.3.1 List of destructive earthquakes. For additional notes see Appendix Three. *Source:* Båth (1967a)

No.	Date	Origin time GMT	Latitude degrees	Longitude degrees	Magnitude M_S	Region	Number of people killed
1	1556 Jan 23					China: Shansi	830 000
2	1693 Jan 9					Italy: Sicily	(60 000)
3	1703 Dec 31					Japan: Odowara, Tokyo	5230
4	1730 Dec 30					Japan: Hokkaido	137 000
5	1737					India: Calcutta	300 000
6	1755 Nov 1				$(8\frac{3}{4})$	Portugal: Lisbon	60 000
7	1759 Oct 30					Syria	30 000
8	1783 Feb 5					Italy: Calabria	30 000
9	1797 Feb 4					Ecuador, Peru	40 000
10	1812 Mar 26					Venezuela: Caracas	20 000
11	1857 Dec 16		40.3 N	16.0 E	$(6\frac{1}{2})$	Italy	12 000
12	1868 Aug 13					Peru, Ecuador	40 000
13	1883 Jul 28					Italy: Casamicciola (Ischia)	2300
14	1891 Oct 28					Japan: Mino–Owari	7270
15	1896 Jun 15					Japan: Riku–Ugo	27 120
16	1897 Jun 12	11.06	26 N	91 E	8.7	India	
17	1899 Sep 10	21.41	60 N	140 W	8.6	Alaska: Yakutat Bay	
18	1902 Dec 16					Turkestan	4500
19	1905 Apr 4	00.50	33 N	76 E	8.6	India: Kangra	19 000
20	1905 Sep 8	01.43	38.8 N	16.1 E		Italy: Calabria	(2500)
21	1906 Jan 31	15.36	1 N	$81\frac{1}{2}$ W	8.9	Colombia	1000
22	Mar 16	22.42	23.5 N	120.7 E		Formosa: Kagi	1300
23	Apr 18	13.12	38 N	123 W	8.3	California: San Francisco	700
24	Aug 17	00.04	33 S	72 W	8.6	Chile: Santiago, Valparaiso	20 000
25	1907 Jan 14	20.40	17.9 N	76.7 W		Jamaica: Kingston	1600
26	Oct 21	04.23.36	38 N	69 E	8.1	Central Asia	12 000
27	1908 Dec 28	04.20.24	38 N	$15\frac{1}{2}$ E	7.5	Italy: Messina, Reggio	83 000
28	1911 Jan 3	23.25.45	$43\frac{1}{2}$ N	$77\frac{1}{2}$ E	8.7	North Tien-Shan	450
29	1912 Aug 9	01.29	$40\frac{1}{2}$ N	27 E	7.8	Marmara Sea (west coast)	1950
30	1915 Jan 13	06.52.42	42 N	$13\frac{1}{2}$ E	7.0	Italy: Avezzano	29 980
31	Oct 3	06.52.48	$40\frac{1}{2}$ N	$117\frac{1}{2}$ W	7.6	Nevada: Pleasant Valley	(0)
32	1920 Dec 16	12.05.48	36 N	105 E	8.6	China: Kansu, Shansi	100 000
33	1922 Nov 11	04.32.36	$28\frac{1}{2}$ S	70 W	8.4	Peru: Atacama	600
34	1923 Sep 1	02.58.36	$35\frac{1}{4}$ N	$139\frac{1}{2}$ E	8.3	Japan: Tokyo, Yokohama	99 330
35	1925 Mar 16	14.42.12	$25\frac{1}{2}$ N	$100\frac{1}{4}$ E	7.1	China: Yunnan	5000
36	1927 Mar 7	09.27.36	$35\frac{3}{4}$ N	$134\frac{3}{4}$ E	7.9	Japan: Tango	3020

Table 4.3.1 List of destructive earthquakes. For additional notes see Appendix Three. *Source:* Båth (1967a)—continued.

No.	Date	Origin time GMT	Latitude degrees	Longitude degrees	Magnitude M_S	Region	Number of people killed
37	1927 May 22	22.32.42	$36\frac{3}{4}$ N	102 E	8.3	China: Nan-Shan	200 000
38	1929 May 1	15.37.30	38 N	58 E	7.1	Iran: Shirwan, Kutshan, Budshnurt	3300
39	Jun 16	22.47.32	$41\frac{3}{4}$ S	$172\frac{1}{4}$ E	7.8	New Zealand: Buller, Murchinson	17
40	1930 Jul 23	00.08.37	41 N	$15\frac{1}{2}$ E	6.5	Italy: Ariano, Melfi, Calitri	1430
41	1931 Feb 2	22.46.42	$39\frac{1}{2}$ S	177 E	7.9	New Zealand: Hawke's Bay, Napier, Hastings	255
42	1933 Mar 2	17.30.54	$39\frac{1}{4}$ N	$144\frac{1}{2}$ E	8.9	Japan	2990
43	1934 Jan 15	08.43.18	$26\frac{1}{2}$ N	$86\frac{1}{2}$ E	8.4	India: Bihar–Nepal	10 700
44	1935 Apr 20	22.01.54	$24\frac{1}{4}$ N	$120\frac{3}{4}$ E	7.1	Formosa	3280
45	May 30	21.32.46	$29\frac{1}{2}$ N	$66\frac{3}{4}$ E	7.5	Pakistan: Quetta	30 000
46	1939 Jan 25	03.32.14	$36\frac{1}{4}$ S	$72\frac{1}{4}$ W	8.3	Chile	28 000
47	Dec 26	23.57.21	$39\frac{1}{2}$ N	$39\frac{1}{2}$ E	7.9	Turkey: Erzincan	30 000
48	1943 Sep 10	08.36.53	$35\frac{1}{4}$ N	134 E	7.4	Japan: Tottori	1190
49	1944 Dec 7	04.35.42	$33\frac{3}{4}$ N	136 E	8.3	Japan: Tonankai, Nankaido	1000
50	1945 Jan 12	18.38.26	$34\frac{3}{4}$ N	$136\frac{3}{4}$ E	7.1	Japan: Mikawa	1900
51	1946 Nov 10	17.42.53	$8\frac{1}{2}$ S	$77\frac{1}{2}$ W	7.4	Peru: Ancash	1400
52	Dec 20	19.19.05	$32\frac{1}{2}$ N	$134\frac{1}{2}$ E	8.4	Japan: Tonankai, Nankaido	1330
53	1948 Jun 28	07.13.30	$36\frac{1}{2}$ N	136 E	7.3	Japan: Fukui	5390
54	1948 Oct 5	20.12.05	$37\frac{1}{2}$ N	$58\frac{1}{2}$ E	7.6	Turkmenia: SE of Ashkhabad	
55	1949 Aug 5	19.08.47	$1\frac{1}{2}$ S	$78\frac{1}{4}$ W	6.8	Ecuador: Ambato	6000
56	1950 Aug 15	14.09.30	$28\frac{1}{2}$ N	$96\frac{1}{2}$ E	8.7	India, Assam, Tibet	1530
57	1952 Mar 4	01.22.43	$42\frac{1}{2}$ N	143 E	8.6	Japan: Tokachi	(28)
58	Jul 21	11.52.14	35.0 N	119.0 W	7.7	California: Kern County	11
59	1954 Sep 9	01.04.37	36.3 N	1.5 E	6.8	Algeria: Orléansville	1250
60	1955 Mar 31	18.17.03	8 N	124 E	7.9	Mindanao	430
61	1956 Jun 9	23.13.52	35 N	$67\frac{1}{2}$ E	7.7	Afghanistan: Kabul	220
62	1956 Jul 9	03.11.40	37 N	26 E	7.7	Aegean Sea: Santorin	57
63	1957 Jul 28	08.40.05	$16\frac{3}{4}$ N	99 W	7.8	Mexico	55
64	Dec 4	03.37.47	$45\frac{1}{2}$ N	$99\frac{1}{2}$ E	8.0	Outer Mongolia: Altai–Gobi	30
65	Dec 13	01.44.59	34.7 N	47.9 E	7.1	Iran: Farsinaj, Hamadan, Kermanshah	1130
66	1958 Jul 10	06.15.53	58 N	$136\frac{3}{4}$ W	7.8	S. Alaska, Brit. Columbia, Yukon	5
67	1960 Feb 29	23.40.14	30.5 N	9.7 W	5.8	Morocco: Agadir	10 000–15 000
68	Apr 24	12.14.26	28 N	$54\frac{1}{2}$ E	5.9	Iran: Lar (Girash)	450
69	May 22	19.11.17	$39\frac{1}{2}$ S	$74\frac{1}{2}$ W	8.5	Chile: 36 °S–48 °S	4000–5000
70	1962 Sep 1	19.20.39	35.6 N	50.0 E	7.0	Iran: Qazvin	12 230
71	1963 Jul 26	04.17.17	42.1 N	21.5 E	6.0	Yugoslavia: Skopje	1100
72	1964 Mar 28	03.36.10	61.1 N	147.8 W	8.5	Alaska: Anchorage, Seward	178

Table 4.3.1 is a recent compilation of destructive earthquakes known to have occurred up to 1964. It includes (i) all earthquakes of $M_S > 7.5$ with reported damage even if the damage was comparatively small, and (ii) all earthquakes of $M_S \leqslant 7.5$ if the number of people killed exceeded 1000. One consequence of this limitation is that some recent earthquakes which have received considerable publicity do not appear in the Table, notably:

12 February 1953, Iran, $M_S = 6.5$, number killed $= 970$
18 March 1953, Turkey, $M_S = 7.2$, number killed $= 240$
12 August 1953, Ionian Islands, $M_S = 7.5$, number killed $= 460$
2 July 1957, Iran, $M_S = 7.2$, number killed $= 130$

Moreover, some large shocks such as the Kamchatka earthquake ($M_S = 8.4$) of 4 November 1952 do not appear because no information on the damage is available. Nevertheless, Table 4.3.1 is a pretty good record of the earthquake toll, especially since 1900. Some notes on the events listed in Table 4.3.1 are given in Appendix Three.

Recently, H. M. Iyer has given the following brief descriptions of several historic earthquakes, the selection being made to illustrate different types of earthquake effects (*Source:* Iyer (1970)):

The Lisbon earthquake of 1755

The Lisbon earthquake of 1755 can be considered as a spectacular event of the near past. There were three principal shocks at approximately 9.40, 10.10 and noon on the morning of November 1. Shocks were felt over an extensive area covering southwestern Europe and northeastern Africa. Lisbon suffered severely, about 60 000 out of its 235 000 inhabitants being killed. A noteworthy feature was that the part of the city which was built on soft sediments was almost completely destroyed, while the part of rock foundation suffered less serious damage. When the earthquake struck, rapid small vibrations were felt first. About thirty seconds later, violent rapid movements came and lasted for about two minutes. A minute later, violent upward movements followed and lasted about two and a half minutes. It is presumed that these were the P, S and surface wave phases respectively. The earthquake set up *seiches* in ponds and lakes in Portugal, France, Italy, Holland, Switzerland, Norway and Sweden. (Seiches are sloshing movements in enclosed bodies of water. Such bodies have their own natural frequency of oscillation and, when excited by earthquake waves of the same frequency, they resonate, producing large amplitude seiches.) Historically, the Lisbon earthquake is very important as it produced the impetus for a scientific study of earthquakes.

The New Madrid earthquakes of 1811–1812

These were a series of earthquakes that shook the small town of New Madrid in U.S.A. again and again for about a year, and produced drastic changes on the surface of the earth. Their severity is estimated, not in terms of lives lost, but in terms of the large-scale effects in the area itself and the Mississippi river. The first quake struck at 2.00 a.m. on the morning of 16 December 1811. The inhabitants, about 800 in number, were woken up by the creaking of their log houses, by the furniture being thrown around and by crashing chimneys. Morning brought more shocks, to be followed by more day after day. When the series had ended, their effects were noticeable over an area of about 5000 square miles. The most spectacular effects were confined to the Mississippi river and its tributaries. Some parts of the river bottom subsided to form permanent swamps and lakes. Other parts were elevated. The pressures built up by the movements of the river bed were released in the form of fountains of air, water and sand gushing out to heights of about fifteen feet. Large landslides occurred by the river banks, and several islands in the Mississippi river vanished completely. Temporarily the river changed its course. Large waves moving along the surface waters did great damage. The town was almost completely destroyed by the collapse of the river banks and the waves.

The Assam earthquake of 1897

The earthquake of 12 June 1897 which occurred in Assam, India, is also referred to as the Great Indian earthquake or the Assam earthquake. This earthquake is important, not only because it is estimated to have had a magnitude of 8.7, but also because it was the first scientifically well documented great earthquake. The credit for this goes to R. D. Oldham, who was Director of the Geological Survey of India at the time of the earthquake. He carried out a thorough investigation of the earthquake effects and his monograph is a very valuable source-book in seismology. About 1500 lives were lost in the quake and the city of Shillong completely destroyed. It has subsequently been rebuilt and is an active centre for seismological studies in India.

The San Francisco earthquake of 1906

At 5.12 a.m. on 18 April 1906 the city of San Francisco experienced a sharp tremor, followed by a jerky roar of collapsing man-made structures and a dull booming from the earth itself. Within a minute, the shaking had ceased, but the earthquake earned worldwide notoriety because of the fire that followed, and which did most of the damage.

The losses caused by the fire were estimated to be of the order of 400 million dollars. The earthquake itself caused damage worth less than five percent of this. The reported loss of life was about 700.

However, the importance of the earthquake arises from the fact that it left visible clues as to its cause, and a thorough investigation followed. Visible displacement of the San Andreas Fault was a spectacular feature of this earthquake. The fault broke over a length of about 200 miles, and every town and village within twenty miles on either side of it was damaged. Fences and roads crossing the fault were off-set; water pipes were disrupted. The displacement of the fault was purely horizontal, the Pacific side moving north relative to the continental side. The displacement reached a maximum of 21 feet near Tomales Bay and died to almost nothing at both ends.

In sixty seconds the earthquake crumbled to pieces the pride of the city, the six million dollar city hall. Overturned stoves and blocked chimneys were the causes of the fire. Fire fighting was made difficult as the water mains broke and no water was available. Pumping water from every available source, the city fought the fire for three days before bringing it under control. During this period the fire consumed thirty schools, eighty churches and convents, the homes of a quarter million people, and 450 lives.

The Tokyo earthquake of 1923

On 1 September 1923, an earthquake of magnitude 8.2 devastated the cities of Tokyo and Yokohama. The focus of the earthquake was under Sagami Bay. The earthquake manifested itself with a roar followed by frantic shaking. As in San Francisco, fire started and fire fighting equipments were destroyed. When it was over, Yokohama had lost 27 000 lives, 40 000 people were injured and 70 000 homes destroyed. In Tokyo, 100 000 people were dead, 40 000 injured and 400 000 houses lost. During the month of September the Tokyo seismograph station recorded 1256 shocks of which 237 were felt. The floor level of Sagami Bay changed suddenly, releasing a giant tsunami or seismic sea-wave which piled about thirty feet of water along the shores and caused much destruction. Some visible faulting occurred to the north and east of Sagami Bay.

The Grand Banks earthquake of 1929

This earthquake, which occurred on 18 November 1929, under the ocean, on the continental slope, south of Newfoundland and east of Nova Scotia, did not cause much destruction. It is interesting because it provided direct evidence on the existence of *turbidity currents*, which are fast flowing currents composed of high density mixture of sand, pebbles and sea water, moving down continental slopes. The indication of the current was provided by the breaking of submarine cables in the vicinity of the epicentre in a total of twenty-eight places. The cable breaks did not all occur at the same time, but one after another corresponding to increase in distance, as if some fast moving agency was snapping them. From the times of cable breaks it was estimated that the current was moving at a speed of around 50 knots. Later investigations showed that, on the steep part of the continental slope, the cables were unburied whereas on the flat ocean floor they were buried under deposits of 'sharp and small pebbles'. The hypothesis advanced for the origin of turbidity currents is that, in the vicinity of the earthquake focus, slumping and sliding of material occurred which mixed with sea water and moved as a powerful current.

Two ships which were in the epicentral area felt the quake as violent vibrations, as if the ships had hit submerged material. The earthquake also caused a tsunami which was recorded by tide gauges as far off as the Azores and Bermuda.

The Agadir earthquake of 1960

This earthquake, which struck the city of Agadir, Morocco, just before midnight on 29 February 1960, almost completely destroyed the city and wiped out about a third of its population of 33 000. The earthquake was only 1/6300 as strong as the San Francisco earthquake, but the epicentre was only about two miles outside the city limits. The chief lesson that was learned, in a very painful way, from the earthquake was that the buildings should have had earthquake resistant construction. It was unfortunate that a past disaster in 1751 which had wrecked the city almost entirely, had been completely forgotten.

The Chile earthquake of 1960

1960 was a terrible year for Chile as it experienced a series of earthquakes. The series began with one large shock followed by a series of aftershocks on 21 May 1960. Next day at 3.00 p.m. a large earthquake, twenty times stronger than the initial shock, struck. The earth moved in smooth undulating motions, of periods ten to twenty seconds, for more than three minutes. The shocks produced such serious damage that it will take years before the economy of the country recovers completely.

The Chilean earthquake produced a spectacular tsunami. Shortly after the main earthquake, the inhabitants residing in coastal areas noticed that the sea had begun to recede rapidly. The authorities knew that this was the first ominous sign of the dreaded 'tidal wave' and evacuated the people to higher grounds. In about ten to twenty minutes, the sea returned, thundering into the interior with twenty foot waves, washing away and crushing everything in its path. The sea receded and advanced several times during the afternoon, the third and fourth waves being the highest. Many people lost their lives as they returned to watch after the sea receded for the second time, thinking that the worst was over. The 'tidal wave' travelled across the globe at speeds of the order of 400 miles per hour. At Hilo in the Hawaiian group, 35 foot waves were recorded. Twenty-two hours after the earthquake, the tsunami reached the Japanese coast, more than 10 600 miles away and caused about 70 million dollars' worth of damage.

Another spectacular effect of the earthquake, though not visible to the eye, was that the Earth as a whole was set into oscillations which lasted for about a month. Being an elastic body, it was known that the Earth could go into normal mode oscillations, but the 'ringing' excited by the Chilean earthquake lasted for about a month and was recorded by very sensitive seismographs. The data provided very valuable material for the study of the structure of the Earth.

The earthquake produced extensive damage in the form of land-slides, cracks on the ground, seiches, ground subsidence and rising, flooding, etc. One volcano (the Ruyehue) which has been dormant since 1905, erupted.

4.4 Earthquake prediction

The most obvious way to avoid death by earthquake is to live and work outside the world's seismic zones. Unfortunately, many millions of the world's population choose to ignore this sound advice. In some cases this no doubt reflects a basic ignorance of the risks involved; but this is not the whole story. No such excuse is available to, for example, Californians who can lay a fair claim to comprising the world's most advanced and sophisticated society. Yet San Francisco is one of the most 'at risk' cities in the world—a fact that most San Franciscans must know and which many must even believe. The truth is, of course, that San Francisco is also one of the most pleasant places to live in the whole of North America; and one must assume that knowledgeable citizens of San Francisco have weighed this advantage against the secure knowledge that their city will sooner or later be destroyed with many of them in it. Just when this event will take place no one knows—it could be tomorrow or in one hundred years' time; but take place it will (unless earthquake modification according to the principles described later in this chapter becomes a practical proposition). It has been estimated that a repeat of the 1906 earthquake today would cause damage amounting to over $4500 million. The number of lives to be lost in such an occurrence would, of course, depend on the time of day.

But whatever one might consider to be the rights and wrongs and the sense and nonsense of this situation, many people do live in earthquake zones; and earthquake prediction is thus a matter of considerable human concern. In spite of this, however, the United States still has no national co-ordinated programme of research into earthquake prediction. This is not to say that the research effort is not considerable; but what there is is fragmented and can hardly be described as adequate. Japan, on the other hand, does have a national programme, although again, total expenditure falls far short of the loss to be expected from a single earthquake in a highly populated area. In one sense, the problem of prediction is more urgent for Japan than for the United States because one of the most vulnerable cities in Japan is its capital. This explains why, especially since the great Tokyo earthquake of 1923, Japan has become a leader in earthquake prediction research and has even, in one particular case, had a modified success. In general, however, the problem of earthquake prediction has proved singularly intractable. There seems to be no simple solution to it. The Japanese came to the conclusion over a decade ago that the best hope lies in long-term monitoring of the phenomena associated with earthquakes on the supposition that the patterns of activity obtained may reveal premonitory events. Such monitoring is still in progress and includes the following:

Geodetic measurement

The fact that an earthquake very often produces visible or measurable land deformation leads one to ask whether any deformation, albeit possibly of smaller magnitude than that caused by the earthquake itself, might be produced *before* the earthquake occurs. Attempts to detect such premonitory deformation have been made by carrying out *levelling surveys*. In one region of Japan, for example, a number of levelling surveys have been carried out since 1898 and with increasing frequency since 1958. The results for the five stations concerned are shown in Figure 4.4.1. It appears that at the three northern stations the ground level rose at a fairly constant rate up to 1955 when the rate of rising increased roughly fivefold at two of the stations. After 1959 there was a tendency for the levels to fall, most notably at the second station from the north. The behaviour at the two southern stations was rather different; but again there seems to have been a discontinuity in 1955 and possibly another in 1959. A large earthquake ($M_S = 7.3$) occurred near Niigata on 16 June 1964, producing a large, sudden change in level at the four closest stations. The question is: were the anomalous changes in level from 1955 onwards related to the impending earthquake, or were they fortuitous? The answer is, of course, that more examples are required to prove the point one way or the other.

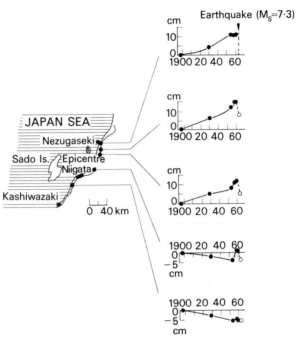

Figure 4.4.1 Anomalous changes in level (height) at five stations prior to the Niigata earthquake of 1964 (closed circles). The open circles indicate the heights immediately after the earthquake. *Source:* Tsubokawa, Ogawa and Hayashi (1964).

Figure 4.4.2 shows the results of a similar survey series carried out in the U.S.S.R. in the vicinity of, and prior to, the Tashkent earthquake of 1966. Stations A and B were close to the epicentre; stations C and D were further away. In each case there was a clear change in the rate of either uplift or subsidence about 1944 and a more rapid change with the onset of the earthquake itself. Thus in this case the premonitory effect, if such it was, appears to have started no less than twenty years or so before the earthquake. Using levelling data from Japan, Yugoslavia, Hungary, Alaska and the U.S.S.R., Mescherikov of the U.S.S.R. concluded that there are three phases of crustal movement: (i) the α-phase, when rates of uplift or subsidence are 'normal', (ii) the β-phase, indicating an impending earthquake, and (iii) the γ-phase, caused by the earthquake itself.

Clearly there is a potential prediction method here, although much more work needs to be carried out to determine the precise nature of the β-phase. It seems to be true, however, that the larger the impending

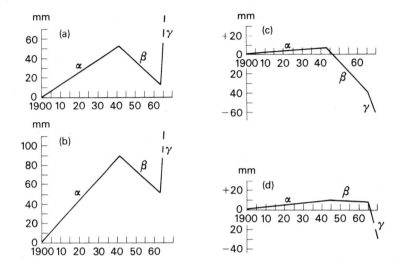

Figure 4.4.2   Anomalous changes in level at four stations prior to the Tashkent earthquake of 1966, showing three phases of crustal deformation. *Source:* Mescherikov (1968).

earthquake, the longer the β-phase is. For the Alaska earthquake of 1964 ($M_S = 8.5$) the β-phase was at least forty years, whereas for an earthquake of $M_S \sim 5$ the β-phase would only be a matter of months.

Tide gauge observation

Prior to the Hamada earthquake of 1872 ($M_S = 7.1$) on the western coast of Japan, the sea was observed to retreat about twenty minutes before the shock—so much so that it was reported that people were able to walk across the exposed sea floor to an island 140 m off the coast, picking up live shells as they went! For most earthquakes, of course, changes in sea level are not quite so spectacular; but the possibility of land deformation prior to an earthquake raises the possibility of there being associated changes in sea level which could be measured and thus used for prediction.

Changes in sea level may be measured with *tide gauges*. The detection of sea level changes prior to earthquakes is complicated, however, by the changes which take place even under normal circumstances; for example, changes due to variations in water temperature, atmospheric pressure and, of course, tides. One way of trying to eliminate the 'normal' factors is to measure the *difference* in sea level between neighbouring tide gauge stations, its being presumed (or at least hoped) that the 'normal' effects apply equally to both stations whereas deformation effects apply to one station more than the other.

Two such stations were in operation in Japan at the time of the 1964 Niigata earthquake—at Nezugaseki and Kashiwazaki (see Figure 4.4.1). Figure 4.4.3 shows how the difference in sea level between the

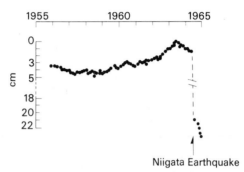

Niigata Earthquake

Figure 4.4.3 Changes in the monthly average sea level at Nezugaseki relative to Kashiwazaki, 1955–1964. *Source:* Tsubokawa, Ogawa and Hayashi (1964).

two stations varied from about 1956 to the time of the Niigata earthquake. It is clear that around the middle of 1963 a significant change in the sea-level movement took place; that is, about one year before the actual shock which caused a much greater change in sea level. Again, there is apparently a premonitory effect here; but again, monitoring must continue in this and other areas to see if the effect is generally observed.

Continuous observation of crustal movement

Levelling surveys are essentially intermittent, whereas in attempting to detect short-term premonitory changes it is clearly an advantage to use some form of continuous measurement. *Tiltmeters* have been used for this purpose. For example, a water-tube tiltmeter, in which the heights of the water surface at two reservoirs about 30–40 m apart are compared, indicates the ground tilt between the reservoirs.

The ground tilting (in two directions) associated with the Matsushiro (Japan) earthquakes of 1965–1966 is shown in Figure 4.4.4, from which it can be seen that the changes in tilt are strongly correlated with

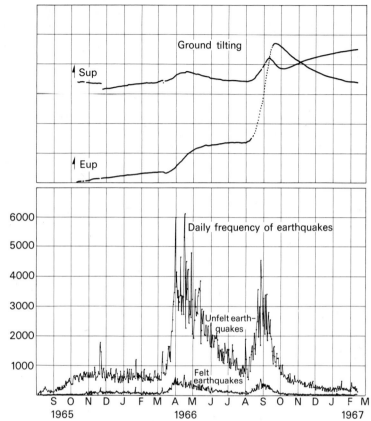

Figure 4.4.4   Changes in ground tilt in the south–north (south up compared to north) and the west–east (east up compared to west) directions, compared with the daily number of felt and unfelt earthquakes during the Matsushiro earthquake series of 1965–1966. Each ordinate division on the upper diagram represents about 12.5 cm. *Source:* Hagiwara and Rikitake (1967).

the growth and decay of seismic activity. But is there any premonitory tilt? Figure 4.4.5 shows an example of tilting immediately prior to, and during, a subseries of the main series of Matsushiro earthquakes. A clear change in the tilting was observed a few hours before the onset of the shocks. On this evidence, therefore, tiltmeter observation would seem to offer prediction possibilities.

Seismic activity

It is reasonable to suppose that, if attempts are to be made to predict earthquakes in any given area, the pattern of seismic activity in the

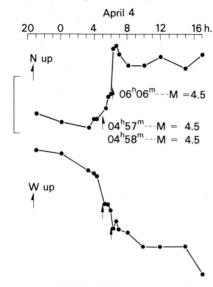

April 4

06^h06^m---M =4.5

04^h57^m---M = 4.5
04^h58^m---M = 4.5

N up

W up

Figure 4.4.5 Changes in ground tilt prior to and during three shocks within the Matsushiro series. A sharp change in tilting began at about 3 a.m. and was followed by three strong shocks occurring northeast of the observation point. The scale on the left represents about 0.25 cm. *Source:* Hagiwara and Rikitake (1967).

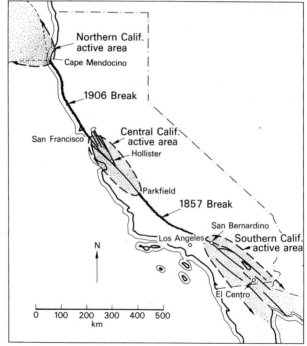

Figure 4.4.6 Areas of contrasting seismic behaviour along the San Andreas fault zone in California. *Source:* Allen (1968).

area may offer useful clues. Along the San Andreas fault in California, for example, areas of quite different seismic behaviour have been identified (Figure 4.4.6). The segments of the fault corresponding to the surface breaks of the great 1906 San Francisco earthquake and the 1857 Fort Tejon shock seem to be 'locked' at present and are currently characterized by very infrequent but very severe earthquakes. At the moment, seismic activity is very low in these regions and there is no fault creep—comparatively quiet steady or episodic slippage. Thus it may be predicted that these are the particularly dangerous segments where severe earthquakes may be expected in the future. In short, it is possible to predict where large earthquakes are most likely to occur but not when they will occur. By contrast, the areas between San Francisco and Parkfield, southeast of San Bernardino and northwest of Cape Mendocino are now 'active', being regions which are characterized by fault creep accompanied by minor to severe (but not the greatest) earthquakes. In such areas the buildup of large amounts of

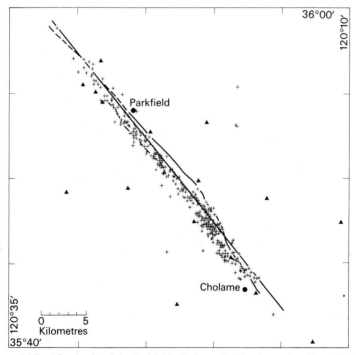

Figure 4.4.7   Aftershocks of the Parkfield–Cholame, California, earthquake of 27 June 1966. Crosses represent the earthquake epicentres; triangles represent seismographs. Zones of surface fracturing which accompanied the main shock are shown by the heavy, interrupted curves. The unbroken line represents the surface outcrop of the 'best' plane fitted to the foci. *Source:* Pakiser, Eaton, Healy and Raleigh (1969).

strain energy is prevented because release takes place in comparatively small doses. This contrasts with the 'locked' regions which are apparently capable of storing large quantities of strain energy until a sudden, violent release takes place.

Detailed seismic studies of the San Andreas and associated faults also indicate marked differences. For example, the aftershocks of the Parkfield–Cholame earthquake of June 1966 (Figure 4.4.7) lay along a narrow, near-vertical zone about 15 km deep which almost coincides at the surface with the mapped fault break. By contrast, most of the aftershocks of the Bear Valley earthquake of 1967 (southeast of Hollister) were closely grouped in an approximately spherical zone about 3 km in diameter centred just west of the San Andreas fault at a depth of about 3 km (Figure 4.4.8). The general microearthquake

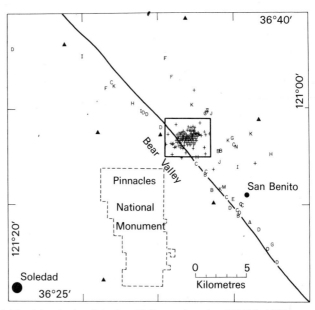

Figure 4.4.8 Aftershocks of the Bear Valley earthquake of 22 July 1967 (crosses inside the small rectangle). Other microearthquakes are represented by letters indicating depth of focus: A, 0–1 km; B, 1–2 km; C, 2–3 km, etc. Crosses outside the small rectangle indicate events with poorly determined focal depths. Most of the Bear Valley aftershocks themselves occurred in the 2–4 km range. The segment of the San Andreas fault shown here is actively creeping. Triangles represent seismograph stations. *Source:* Pakiser, Eaton, Healy and Raleigh (1969).

$(1 \geqslant M_S > 3)$ activity in the fault region south of the San Francisco is shown in Figure 4.4.9. Again there are marked contrasts between different segments of the various faults. In segments which are 'locked' microearthquake activity is sparse; but in other regions microearthquakes tend to act as safety valves, releasing strain energy in small quantities at a time and thus preventing extreme strain buildup.

The essential point to be taken from all this is, of course, that different areas (even within the same tectonic zone) have different seismic characteristics and thus that prediction is likely to mean

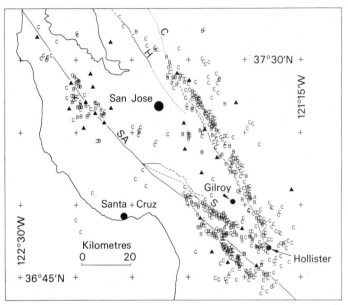

Figure 4.4.9 Microearthquakes within the fault system southeast of San Francisco, March 1968–April 1969. Epicentres are represented by letters indicating the precision of location: A, excellent; B, good; C, fair. Triangles represent seismographs. The faults are: SA, San Andreas; S, Sargent; H, Hayward; C, Calaveras. (*Note:* Figures 4.4.6–4.4.9 may be related geographically by matching place names—but note the different scales. Bear Valley is located near the inferred junction of the San Andreas and Calaveras faults.) *Source:* Pakiser, Eaton, Healy and Raleigh (1969).

different things in different regions. Not that there is yet any convincing method of earthquake prediction in any region, except in the sense that it is now possible (at least in California) to indicate the particular danger areas. On the other hand, it is clear that accurate prediction will hardly be possible unless the long-term seismic patterns of an area are known in considerable detail. Moreover, seismicity studies can also give basic information relating to physical processes. For example, measurements show that the focal depths of microearthquakes in California do not exceed 15 km, whereas the average crustal thickness is 25 km. In other words, the brittle behaviour of rocks along the San Andreas fault must be confined to the upper crust; in the lower crust and mantle, smooth slippage or flow must take place.

Seismic wave velocity

When the rocks forming the Earth's crust are strained, it might be expected that their physical properties will change. For example, is it possible that the same rock in the strained and unstrained states will have different seismic velocities? If so, such differences might be used to measure the buildup of strain prior to an earthquake.

A Russian study of over 800 time–distance graphs for relatively small earthquakes occurring before and after moderately large ($M_S \sim 5$) earthquakes in the Tadjikistan region of Asia between 1958 and 1961 has indicated such a seismic velocity difference. Before the main shocks the average P wave velocity was 5.3 km s^{-1}, whereas afterwards it rose to 6.3 km s^{-1}—a fifteen percent increase. If this increase represents a change in elasticity, the magnitude of the change would need to be thirty percent. It is a moot point whether such a large change is physically reasonable; and in any case no other similar example has yet been reported.

Geomagnetic changes

It is now well established that a stress applied to, or removed from, a rock produces a small change in the rock's remanent magnetization. This is known as the *piezomagnetic effect* and it arises from the distortion of crystal structure. Because seismic events reflect changes in subsurface stress within the Earth, these changes should manifest themselves as changes in the magnetism of the rocks involved and hence in the local geomagnetic field—that is, in the small part of the field arising from the permanent magnetism in the rocks, not the larger part of the field produced deep in the Earth. Continuous monitoring of the local geomagnetic field should therefore lead to the observation of geomagnetic variations which reflect the subsurface stress changes occurring prior to the onset of an earthquake. In this way, the time and location of an impending earthquake might be determined.

One estimate suggests that the stress release from a moderate earthquake might produce a magnetic field change of about 10^{-8} T, in which case one might expect a premonitory change of a few 10^{-9} T. However, there are certain practical problems involved here, namely, those associated with (i) the measurement of exceedingly small magnetic fields and their changes, (ii) the separation of piezomagnetic changes (signal) from the much larger geomagnetic field changes (noise) which are occurring continuously under normal circumstances, and (iii) the avoidance of spurious 'changes' due to mechanical vibrations which jolt the measuring instruments (magnetometers). For some or all of these reasons, most of the correlations between seismic activity reported since 1799 are certainly not valid, and authentic observations are difficult to obtain. One of the very few apparently valid results is shown in Figure 4.4.10.

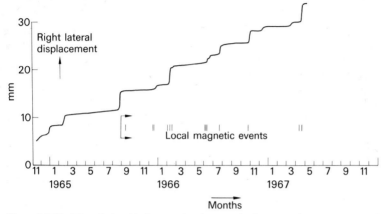

Figure 4.4.10   The relationship between local magnetic changes and creep events on the San Andreas fault at Hollister, 1965–1967. The creep displacements are preceded by magnetic events apparently arising from stress changes in the rocks which herald the subsequent visible creep. *Source:* Breiner (1967).

The state of prediction

From what has been said above, it is clear that the intractable problem of earthquake prediction is far from solved. There are, to be sure, several promising techniques being explored; but none has yet proved successful in the sense that we can now go out and predict the next earthquake in any given area. The long-term monitoring of geophysical phenomena necessary for the understanding of earthquake processes, and, hopefully, for the detection of unambiguous premonitory events, is still under way but seems unlikely to pay off for several decades at least.

On the other hand, it is worth mentioning that Japanese earthquake prediction has marked up one modified success. During the series of earthquakes which struck the Matsushiro area of central Japan during 1965–1966, scientists were able to issue reports to the local people indicating when the occurrences of moderately large earthquakes were most probable. These warnings indicated the dangerous period (usually a range of a few months), rough location and possible maximum magnitude. The scientific basis of the warnings derived from repeated levelling surveys, geodetic measurements, microearthquake and ultra-microearthquake ($M_S < 1$) observations, tiltmeter observations and geomagnetic field monitoring. In short, intelligent guesses were based on a combination of several different types of data. In this way, the particularly violent activity in April 1966 and August 1966 was successfully foretold.

Finally, however, a comment without comment on reactions to this successful exercise: 'In the case of the Matsushiro events, local governments worked hard to prevent possible earthquake damage by repairing school buildings, strengthening fire brigades, and so forth. But those who are engaged in the sightseeing and hotel business were not really pleased with the warnings because of expected shortage of tourists. Great care must be taken to find an adequate way of issuing a warning in the future.' (*Source:*Rikitake (1968).)

4.5 Man-made earthquakes†

The disparity between the energy of a medium to large earthquake and man's ability to react in the face of it is so great that, at first sight, it seems ludicrous to suggest that man may actually come to control earthquakes. Prediction is a clear theoretical possibility (though not yet a practical reality); but the idea of control or modification appears to owe more to the myths of ancient gods. Yet a series of unexpected discoveries made over the past thirty years or so, and more particularly since the early 1960s, has now brought us to the point where some believe the possibility of abolishing earthquakes (at least, large shallow earthquakes) to be more hopeful than prediction. These discoveries concern the effects of reservoirs, nuclear weapons and the injection of fluids into the ground; and what they have done is to show that the release of significant tectonic forces is not the sole prerogative of inanimate nature.

Reservoirs

It is now fairly clear that the loading of reservoirs can, in certain circumstances, give rise to earthquakes. One of the first suggestions that this might be the case came from studies of the Hoover Dam (formerly the Boulder Dam) across Lake Mead in the United States, carried out during the early 1940s. Filling of the lake began in 1935; and the maximum water level was reached in 1941. The first seismograph was installed near the lake in 1938 and immediately began to record hundreds of shocks a year. The pattern of earthquakes in relation to changes in reservoir height and water load is shown in Figure 4.5.1; and Figure 4.5.2 clearly shows that the earthquake

† Magnitudes in this section generally refer to m_6.

epicentres are closely grouped around the lake-dam site. A histogram of earthquake magnitudes for the single year 1942 is shown in Figure 4.5.3, whence it can be seen that the shocks are relatively small, most having magnitudes lower than 3.0.

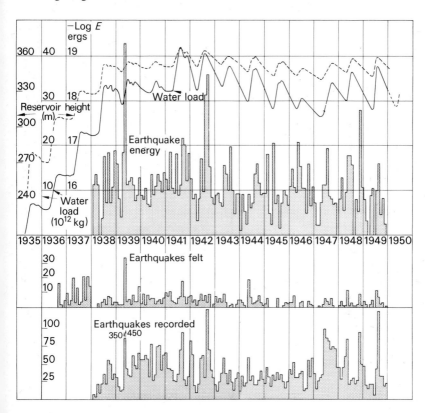

Figure 4.5.1 The relationships between the reservoir height and water load of Lake Mead, and the earthquake energy, the number of felt earthquakes and the number of recorded earthquakes in the Lake Mead area, 1935–1949. The earthquake histograms are given in terms of monthly averages. *Source:* Carder (1970).

The geographical distribution of epicentres strongly implicates the reservoir as the cause of the earthquakes. Unfortunately, it is difficult to prove this hypothesis because the first seismograph was only installed after the filling of the reservoir had begun. Thus it is not possible to compare the seismicity of the area before and after the filling. Nevertheless, the region was considered to be aseismic prior to the construction of the dam. No earthquakes were reported by the few local inhabitants as being *felt* during the fifteen-year period prior to

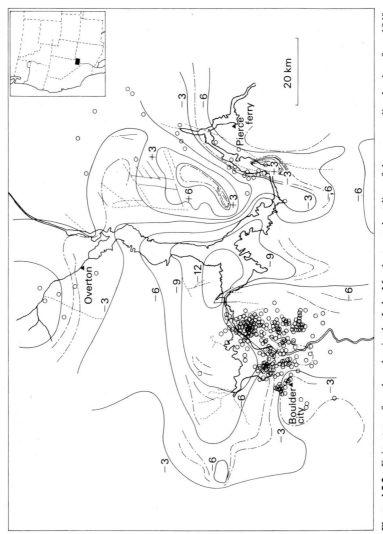

Figure 4.5.2   Epicentres of earthquakes in the Lake Mead area and settling of the surrounding land surface, 1940–1947. The Hoover Dam is about 10 km ENE of Boulder City. The numbers on the settlement contours are centimetres. *Source:* Carder (1970).

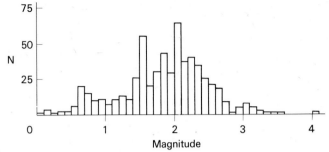

Figure 4.5.3 Histogram of the number of earthquakes, with magnitude, in the Lake Mead area during 1942. *Source:* Jones (1944).

construction, whereas, as Table 4.5.1 shows, 21 felt earthquakes were reported in 1936 and larger numbers in subsequent years.

Table 4.5.1 Number of felt and instrumentally recorded earthquakes in the vicinity of Lake Mead (Hoover Dam), 1935–1942.

Year	Earthquakes felt	Earthquakes recorded
1935	0	†
1936	21	†
1937	116	†
1938	73	317
1939	128	891
1940	43	708
1941	95	578
1942	53	591

† No seismographs installed before 1938.

As far as instrumentally recorded earthquakes are concerned, the following conclusions have been drawn from Figure 4.5.1:

1. A single earthquake of unusually high magnitude (5.0), recorded in May 1939 when the reservoir had been filled to eighty percent capacity, released as much, or more, energy than all the other local earthquakes combined.

2. There is a strong implication that the May 1939 series of shocks was related to the peak load of the previous year, with a triggering effect resulting from the rising water level of 1939.

3. Similarly, the energy and frequency peaks during the summer of 1942 may have been associated with the all-time maximum reservoir

height of the previous year, again with triggering by the rising water load (of 1942).

4. For each year prior to 1945, there was a close association between the energy peak and the load peak.

5. In 1945 and subsequent years, energy peaks were sometimes associated with load minima; and energy maxima were not always associated with frequency maxima.

The general conclusion to be drawn from all this is that the earthquake frequency and energy do not necessarily correlate directly with water load or reservoir level, and thus that the case for a causal connection between earthquakes and water load is not entirely made out on this basis. In the absence of seismic records prior to the filling of the reservoir, the evidence for reservoir-produced earthquakes in the Lake Mead area must remain circumstantial rather than direct. Nevertheless, in the light of subsequent evidence from other reservoirs, a causal relationship between the Lake Mead earthquakes and the loading of the reservoir is now widely accepted as highly probable.

For about twenty years the Lake Mead earthquake series was regarded as of purely academic interest; but during the 1960s this attitude changed. Perhaps the most significant reason for this change was that on 10 December 1967 a large earthquake of magnitude 6.4 occurred in the Koyna region of India, killing 177 people, injuring 2300 others and causing extensive damage to buildings. As destructive earthquakes go, the Koyna shock was not in the big league; but it aroused particular interest and concern, firstly, because it was located in the Indian Precambrian Shield, one of the most stable and least seismic areas of the world, and secondly, because its epicentre lay within a few kilometres of the Koyna Dam.

Filling of the Koyna Reservoir (Lake Shivajisagar), located about 120 km south of Poona, began in 1962 and was completed in 1965. The first tremors in the area were felt in 1963, a few months after filling began, following which five seismographs were installed in and around the lake. As in the case of Lake Mead, no seismographs were operating in the area prior to the filling of the reservoir. However, examination of the records of the Poona seismograph, which had been in operation since 1951, showed that the Indian shield area was not completely aseismic prior to 1963, for there were rare occurrences of feeble tremors. But from 1963 onwards, shocks became significantly more frequent and shock magnitudes significantly higher. Up to 1967 over 100 epicentres had been located in the reservoir area. Magnitudes were generally below 4.0; but on 13 September 1967 two magnitude 5.0–5.5 earthquakes caused minor damage. The largest shock (the so-called Koyna earthquake, magnitude 6.4) occurred on 10 December 1967 and was followed by three other large shocks on 12 December

1967 (magnitude 5.4), 24 December 1967 (5.5) and 29 October 1968 (5.4). Minor seismicity continued until the spring of 1970. As Figure 4.5.4 shows, epicentres were clustered around the lake.

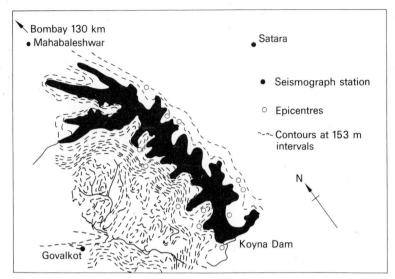

Figure 4.5.4   The distribution of major epicentres in the Koyna Dam area. *Source:* Balakrishna and Gowd (1970).

Figure 4.5.5 illustrates the relationship between the reservoir water level and the weekly frequency of earthquakes from June 1963–December 1967. There are peaks in the water level and peaks in the earthquake frequency; but the two sets of peaks do not correspond directly. However, it should be noted that such a lack of correspondence does not necessarily disprove a causal connection because there could easily be a time lag between peak water load and the resulting shocks.

Features of particular interest in Figure 4.5.5 are (i) water was retained above 642 m for a long time during August 1965–October 1965 and high seismic activity occurred during November 1965, and (ii) the highest water level was retained for the longest time between August 1967 and December 1967 and coincided with the period of greatest seismic activity. Whenever the water level has risen above 642 m and has been retained for a longish time, seismic activity has significantly increased but with a time lag. As with Lake Mead, the evidence for a causal connection between water load and earthquake frequency is again circumstantial and a comparison of seismic activity before and after reservoir filling is not possible. Again, however, the Koyna reservoir is widely believed to have caused the earthquake

208

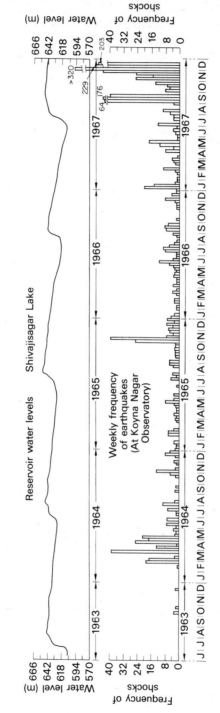

Figure 4.5.5 The relationship between the reservoir water level in Lake Shivajisagar and the weekly frequency of earthquakes in the Koyna region, 1963–1967.
Source: Guka, Gosavi, Varma, Agarwal, Padale and Marwadi (1968).

series. On the other hand, this supposed connection is disputed by
some scientists, partly because the Koyna reservoir is relatively small
and the region is geologically similar to that of the Grand Coulee Dam
site (U.S.A.) where no earthquakes have been recorded (however, the
geological structure below the surface may not be the same), partly
because several other dams in similar geological settings fairly near
Koyna have apparently not led to seismicity, and partly for a reason
relating to possible mechanisms, which we will discuss later.

For different reasons, Lake Mead and Koyna are perhaps the two
best known examples of suspected reservoir-related earthquakes but
are by no means the only ones. Others are:

Lake Kariba: This lake, along the Rhodesia–Zambia border, was
filled from 1958 onwards. Prior to this the region was regarded as
aseismic, no earthquakes being reported; but three permanent seismological observations in Rhodesia, Zambia and Malawi were not
established until 1959. Earthquakes were first recorded near the lake
in 1961. Seismic activity then increased; and a strong earthquake

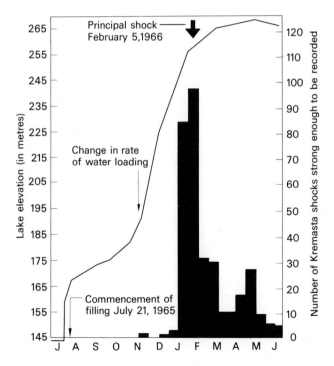

Figure 4.5.6 Local seismic activity in the Lake Kremasta region during the filling of the
lake, 1965–1966. *Source:* Galanopoulos (1967).

sequence began on 14 August 1963, a few days after the maximum water load had been reached. Between 14 August and 8 November 1963 nine shocks with magnitudes in the range 5.1–6.1 were felt. Earthquake activity has continued since then but at a reduced rate; only one large shock (magnitude 5.5, April 1967) has been felt since 1963. All major epicentres were concentrated in an area roughly 0.4° square, close to the deepest part of the reservoir.

Lake Kremasta: Filling of this Greek lake began in July 1965; and earthquake shocks were first felt, but not recorded instrumentally, in August 1965. The rate of water loading increased rapidly from November 1965 to January 1966 (see Figure 4.5.6). Seismic activity also increased rapidly during this period, culminating in a magnitude 6.3 shock in February 1966, just before the water level reached its maximum. This earthquake killed one person, injured sixty, produced landslides and slumps and damaged 1680 houses. Many smaller earthquakes followed up to November 1966, at least six of which had magnitudes higher than 5.0. No reports are available for the subsequent period. Prior to these events, the only two seismic stations in Greece were located at Athens and Patara; but four additional seismographs were installed soon afterwards, the closest being 115 km from the lake. However, Lake Kremasta is known to be located in the seismically active arc extending from the Mediterranean north along the Adriatic coast. Nevertheless, shock epicentres in this region between 1951 and 1965 were concentrated 40 km away from the dam site whereas since the filling of the lake most shocks have occurred close by.

Lake Marathon: Filling of this lake, also in Greece, began in 1929 and earthquakes were first felt in 1931. Earthquakes have continued since then, the most important being two shocks of magnitude greater than 5.0 in 1938. All but two of the many shocks occurred during periods of rapid water level rise; and all epicentres lie within 15 km of the lake. Historically, this was the first suspected correlation between reservoir filling and earthquakes but remained largely unknown until such correlations became an important issue during the 1960s.

Lake Monteynard: Filling of this lake, in France, began in 1962 and was completed on 20 April 1963. A magnitude 4.9 shock was recorded on 25 April 1963 and a magnitude 4.4 shock two days later. A new earthquake swarm began in 1966, soon after the lake had again reached its maximum level, the largest shock in the series having magnitude 4.3. All epicentres were close to the lake. A seismograph was not installed in Monteynard until August 1963, prior to which the nearest was 110 km away.

Lake Vogorno: The filling of this lake, which is impounded behind the Contra Dam in Switzerland, started in August 1964. Earthquakes began in May 1965, the most severe occurring in October and November 1965, several weeks after the maximum water level had been reached. The lake was later emptied and refilled, resulting in a decrease in seismic activity and apparently a complete cessation in April 1968.

Lake Grandval: Filling of this lake, in France, was commenced in 1959 and completed in 1960. Minor earthquakes began in 1961. In 1962 the reservoir was emptied and refilled; but when the water level again reached maximum (in 1963) a violent shock occurred beneath the lake. Many shocks subsequently occurred, the two strongest coming at times when the water level was at its highest.

Oued Fodda Reservoir: This is another old example (in Algeria) which remained largely forgotten until recently. Filling of the reservoir began in 1932 and frequent shocks occurred near the dam from January 1933 to May 1933. But no earthquakes have occurred since then.

Taking the evidence altogether, it now seems certain that reservoirs can give rise to earthquakes, although it must be said that there are many reservoirs which have apparently not led to seismicity. In considering the case for reservoir-related earthquakes, the following points should be borne in mind:

(i) There is no well-documented example for which seismic records taken before and after the loading of the reservoir are available. The evidence which is most likely to prove the case one way or the other is thus entirely absent. Nevertheless, there is a strong circumstantial case for saying that the construction of some reservoirs has led to stronger and more frequent earthquakes.

(ii) This case is strengthened by the fact that the epicentres of the shocks occurring during and after the loading of a reservoir are usually closely associated geographically with the reservoir in question. By contrast pre-existing seismicity, if any, in the area usually fails to exhibit this association.

(iii) The increased seismicity associated with the filling and early years of a reservoir often decreases over a period of several years and in many cases ceases altogether ultimately.

(iv) There is seldom a direct correlation in time between maxima in the water load and maxima in the earthquake frequency. Where correlations are suspected the increased seismicity appears to lag in time behind the increased water load. However, the time lag varies and in a few cases is zero.

(v) Most reservoir-induced earthquakes are of small magnitude, usually 3.0–4.0 or lower. However, some quite large individual shocks have been produced, at least two of which have caused death.

(vi) There is a strong implication that water loads do not lead directly to earthquakes but, rather, trigger the release of pre-existing tectonic forces. In this case, the ability of a reservoir to produce earthquakes will depend critically on the local subsurface geology; and this would explain why all reservoirs do not lead to earthquakes.

Nuclear explosions

The evidence for earthquakes induced by underground nuclear explosions is far less equivocal than that for reservoir-induced shocks. For one thing, nuclear explosions (United States ones, that is) usually take place at known times and locations, so that seismic monitoring can be carried out both before and after the blast. As a result, the existence of nuclear-induced earthquakes, or explosion aftershocks, is not in doubt. All explosions with a yield equivalent to an earthquake of magnitude 5.0 or greater are followed by seismic activity for at least a day. (A 1 megaton explosion is roughly equivalent to an earthquake of magnitude 6.5.) Most of the aftershocks have much smaller magnitudes than that of the initiating explosion; but explosion aftershock magnitudes up to 4.0+ have been measured. Such aftershocks can take place up to several tens of kilometres from ground zero.*

One of the most spectacular explosion aftershock sequences came from the nuclear test BENHAM, a 1.1 megaton explosion detonated 1.4 km beneath Nevada in December 1968. During the first day following the blast, earthquakes over 1.3 in magnitude were occurring at the rate of about 1000 a day (see Figure 4.5.7). During the next three days this rate decreased exponentially to about 10 events a day. It then increased to over 100 shocks a day during the fourth week before continuing its decline to less than 5 events a day after six weeks. All

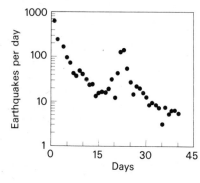

Figure 4.5.7 The number of earthquakes a day with magnitude greater than 1.3 following the underground nuclear explosion BENHAM. *Source:* Hamilton and Healy (1969).

the aftershocks were within 13 km of ground zero and most were within 5 km.

The Denver earthquakes

The event which, more than any other, brought home the force of the possibility that man might modify the earthquake-tectonic environment was the discovery around 1965 that man-made earthquakes were occurring in the Denver, Colorado, area of the United States as a result of the injection of fluid into the ground. The fluid in question was contaminated water produced as a by-product in the manufacture of chemical warfare materials. Such materials have been produced by the U.S. Army at the Rocky Mountain Arsenal (Colorado) since 1942; but up to 1961 the waste water was disposed of by evaporation from dirt reservoirs. At this time, however, the water was found to be contaminating the local ground-water supply and endangering crops. Evaporation from watertight reservoirs was tried but proved unsuccessful, whereupon the U.S. Army hit upon the idea of drilling an injection disposal well. The well was completed to a depth of 3671 m on 11 September 1961.

The location of the Rocky Mountain Arsenal well, about 19 km to the northeast of Denver and just to the east of the structural axis of the Denver Basin, is shown in Figure 4.5.8. The position of the well with respect to the subsurface geology of the region is shown in Figure 4.5.9. The base of the well lies in Precambrian granite gneiss, the upper boundary of which lies about 3900 m below the surface of the outcrop of similar rock to the west of Denver.

Figure 4.5.10 (b) illustrates the history of injection of contaminated waste water into the well up to September 1965. Injection under pressure began on 8 March 1962 and continued to 30 September 1963 at an average rate of about 5.5 million U.S. gallons a month (1 U.S. gallon = 3.8×10^{-3} m^3). For technical reasons, the well was shut down from the end of September 1963 to 17 September 1964 when injection recommenced by gravity discharge (that is, with no pressure at the well head) at an average rate of about 2.0 million U.S. gallons a month. However, from 6 April 1965 injection under pressure was resumed at an average rate of about 4.0 million U.S. gallons a month, the pressure being about fifty percent up on the initial phase; and in June 1965 the rate and pressure of injection were further increased. On 20 February 1966 (not shown in Figure 4.5.10) injection was stopped in response to public pressure.

Up to April 1962, the Denver area was noted for its lack of seismicity. There was, to be sure, an earthquake of intensity VII on the Modified Mercalli Scale in the Denver region on 7 November 1882; but from that time until 1962 no earthquake epicentres were recorded either by

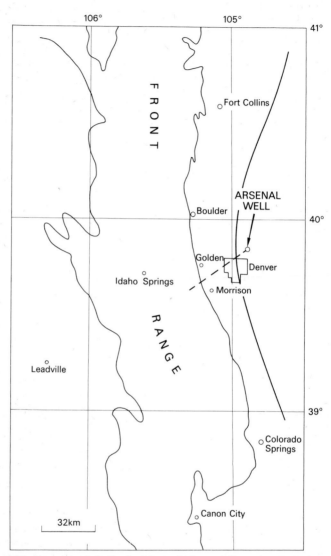

Figure 4.5.8 Location of the Rocky Mountain Arsenal disposal well. The heavy line passing through Denver represents the structural axis of the Denver Basin. The dashed line marks the approximate position of the geological cross-section in Figure 4.5.9.

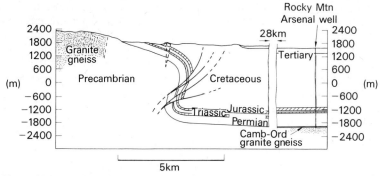

Figure 4.5.9 Geological cross-section from the Rocky Mountain Arsenal well to the outcrop of Precambrian granite gneiss west of Denver. The approximate position of the section is indicated by the dashed line in Figure 4.5.8. *Source:* Boos and Boos (1957).

the U.S. Coast and Geodetic Survey or by the Regis College Seismological Observatory located 16 km southeast of the Rocky Mountain Arsenal. However, during the period April 1962–September 1965, no less than 710 epicentres were recorded in the vicinity of the well, mostly within 8 km. Magnitudes were in the range 0.7–4.3.

Pressure injection into the well began in March 1962 and the first

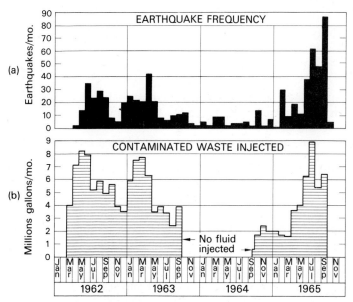

Figure 4.5.10 Comparison of the monthly number of earthquakes in the Denver area (a) with the monthly volume of contaminated waste water injected into the Rocky Mountain Arsenal well (b), March 1962–September 1965. *Source:* Evans (1966).

earthquakes ever recorded in the Rocky Mountain Arsenal area occurred the following month. That in itself was a suspicious circumstance; but a comparison of the subsequent earthquake frequency shown in Figure 4.5.10 (a) with the rate of water injection shown in Figure 4.5.10 (b) gives an even more convincing correlation. Between March 1962 and September 1963, injection was frequently stopped for technical reasons. During this period there is no direct month-to-month correlation, although the high injection months of April, May and June 1962 appear to correspond with the high earthquake frequency months of June, July and August. Similarly, the high injection months of February and March 1963 may correlate with the high earthquake month of April. The no-injection period of September 1963–September 1964 coincides with a period of minimum earthquake frequency; and the period of low volume gravity injection (September 1964–April 1965) is characterized by two months (October 1964 and February 1965) of earthquake frequency greater than that of the previous year. During the period of very high pressure injection (June–September 1965) the correlation between injection rate and earthquake frequency is more direct.

In practice, the overall correlation is brought out best not by looking at the month-by-month pattern but by dividing the whole period into its five characteristic subperiods:

A: April 1962–April 1963—high injection at medium pressure
B: May 1963–September 1963—medium injection
C: October 1963–September 1964—no injection
D: September 1964–March 1965—low injection at zero pressure
E: April 1965–September 1965—high injection at high pressure

The earthquake frequency–fluid injection relationship for these five periods are shown in Figure 4.5.11. The correlation is so clear that further comment is unnecessary.

The above correlations are due to David Evans, a consulting geologist in Denver, who, in November 1965 was first to suggest publicly a link between the earthquakes and the well. It is for this reason that Figures 4.5.10 and 4.5.11 end with September 1965; but seismic monitoring was, of course, continued. Figure 4.5.12 shows how the monthly earthquake frequency varied with the monthly average well head pressure right from the first injection in March 1962 through to 1968. The general correlation for the period 1962–1965 is confirmed and extends into 1966. From the latter end of 1966, however, the pattern of activity changed.

Injection of fluid into the well was terminated in February 1966; but earthquakes continued at a rate varying from four to seventy-one a month. At first, as the well head pressure decreased the number of earthquakes followed suit. But from about the middle of 1966 some-

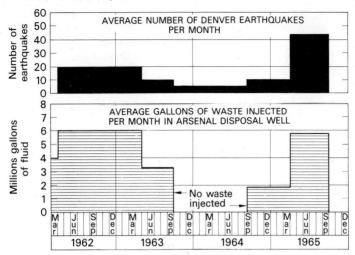

Figure 4.5.11   Comparison of the earthquake frequency and the volume of waste injected during five characteristic periods. *Source:* Evans (1966).

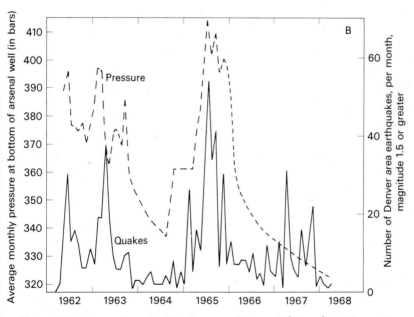

Figure 4.5.12   Comparison of well head pressure (1 bar $= 10^5$ N m^{-2}) and the number of earthquakes in the Denver area on a monthly basis. Note that only earthquakes of magnitude 1.5 or greater are included in this diagram. *Source:* Healy, Rubey, Griggs and Raleigh (1968).

thing unexpected began to happen—the earthquake frequency started to rise again even as the well head pressure dropped. Moreover, on 10 April 1967—14 months after injection had ceased—the largest earthquake yet felt (magnitude 5.0) hit the Denver area. Nor was this all. On 9 August 1967 there was a second large shock of magnitude about 5.2 and on 26 November there was a third, of magnitude 5.1. It thus appears that there is no simple direct relationship between pressure and earthquakes.

Causes of man-made earthquakes

From the evidence presented above, it is clear that underground nuclear explosions produce earthquakes and near certain that some reservoirs and injection of fluid into the Denver well do too. But how do they? How is it that man-made forces, which on the face of it appear relatively feeble in comparison with the tectonic forces at nature's command, are yet able to activate those natural forces?

When the apparent connection between reservoir load and earthquakes at Lake Mead was discovered, a suggestion was made that the water load was causing movement along pre-existing subsurface faults in the area—faults which in the very recent past had been inactive. The idea here is that the weight of the water depresses the underlying crustal blocks, producing motion along the faults in the block, and that this fault movement gives rise to earthquakes. Later, calculations were made to show that the energy of the earthquakes at Lake Mead could be accounted for by as little as thirty percent of the energy involved in the depression of the crust. But whereas this hypothesis appeared adequate to explain the Lake Mead shocks, it is now clear that it cannot apply to all reservoirs where earthquakes have been produced because in some the water loads are far too small. For these cases, some other explanation must be sought; and this naturally leads to the suspicion that, whatever this explanation is, it may well apply to Lake Mead too.

Although it is unlikely that the original explanation for reservoir-produced earthquakes is correct, it did, nevertheless, introduce two important ideas which have carried through to the present day. The first is that a reservoir—and, by extension, the injection of fluid into a deep well—can only usually lead to earthquakes in regions where faults already exist. Such faults may have been inactive immediately prior to the construction of the reservoir, and such inactivity may have obtained for millions of years; but, in general, the presence of *potentially* active faults appears to be necessary. Conversely, the absence of such faults would account for the lack of seismicity in such areas as that of the Grand Coulee Dam.

The second idea follows naturally from this; that the water load *triggers* a series of events, the potential for which was there in the first place. (We have already had a suggestion of this when discussing Figure 4.5.1.) In the original explanation for reservoir-produced earthquakes, the pre-existing situation was simply a fault, or series of faults, which, though stationary, have an obvious potential for movement; and this movement was supposedly triggered by an applied (water) load. But the modern hypothesis goes further than this by saying not only that there are pre-existing faults but also that such faults are in a state of tectonic strain.

We have already seen in section 4.2 ('causes') that if a state of strain continues to build up along a fault, the fault will slip (producing an earthquake) when the shearing stress overcomes the frictional resistance. The modern hypothesis of reservoir-induced or injection-induced earthquakes suggests that under normal circumstances this condition for an earthquake to occur has not yet been reached in the areas concerned but *is* reached when sufficient fluid is added. In other words, the fluid does something to trigger off the release of the natural tectonic strain earlier than would otherwise have been the case. This may be called the straw-that-broke-the-donkey's-back hypothesis— obviously a straw cannot break a donkey's back by itself, but when added to the load already there it can act as, well, the last straw.

So what is the nature of this last straw? It seems that the fluid does not increase the shearing stress along the faults (as in the original theory) until the frictional resistance is overcome and slippage occurs, but that it reduces the effective frictional resistance. In other words, the fluid quite simply lubricates the faults and thus allows them to slip at a lower shearing stress (induced tectonically) than that at which they would have slipped (if at all) in the absence of fluid.

As an analogy, consider two blocks, A and B, which have flat surfaces pressed together (see Figure 4.5.13). Suppose that each block is pressing against the other with a pressure $S/2$; the total pressure across the boundary between blocks is then S. Pressure = force per unit area

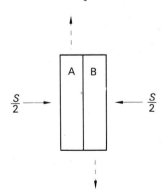

Figure 4.5.13 Diagram to illustrate the theory of man-made earthquakes.

(units: $N\,m^{-2} = Pa$), which is a stress. S is thus the *normal stress* across the boundary—the stress at right angles to the boundary.

What we would like to know is the stress required to cause the blocks to slide against each other in the directions shown by the dashed arrows. This stress is, of course, a *shearing stress* (along the boundary); and the value of the shearing stress required to set the blocks moving is known as the *shearing strength* of the material in question. Empirically, the shearing strength, τ, is found to be:

$$\tau = \text{frictional resistance} = \mu S \qquad (4.5.1)$$

where μ is a constant for the material concerned, known as the *static coefficient of friction*.

If a fluid is now introduced between the blocks, the effect is to reduce the frictional resistance between them. This is equivalent to saying that μ is effectively reduced. However, so far we have implicitly assumed that the material forming the blocks is impermeable, whereas crustal blocks in nature are not. In fact, crustal material contains pores within which fluid can reside. Thus although the introduction of fluid into the region between crustal blocks effectively reduces the frictional resistance, it is actually more reasonable physically to regard this as a reduction in S rather than in μ. It has been established both theoretically and experimentally that if p is the pressure of the fluid in the pores, the effective normal stress across the boundary is $S-p$; and so in general the shearing strength τ is given by:

$$\tau = \mu(S-p) \qquad (4.5.2)$$

What this means is that if the pore fluid pressure (p) in the vicinity of a fault is increased, the shearing strength (τ = the shearing stress required to produce slippage) is reduced. Thus the introduction of a fluid into a fault or fracture zone will reduce the shearing strength.

The envisaged sequence of events in the filling of a reservoir or in the injection of fluid into a well is thus this: Prior to the introduction of the fluid the natural tectonic stress (τ') along the subsurface faults is less than, but fairly close to, τ. Thus no slippage occurs because τ has not been reached. However, this does not necessarily mean that $p = 0$ because there may already be some 'natural' fluid present. All that is necessary is that $\mu(S-p)$—that is, τ—should be greater than the natural tectonic shearing stress. Or mathematically:

$$\tau' < \tau = \mu(S-p) \qquad (4.5.3)$$

As 'artificial', or extra, fluid is introduced, p increases and so $\mu(S-p)$ and τ decrease. As soon as τ decreases to the value of τ', slippage will occur and an earthquake is produced. At this point:

$$\tau' = \tau = \mu(S-p) \qquad (4.5.4)$$

Actually, the above model has made one further simplifying assumption which is not valid in the natural situation—and that is that the boundary between the blocks is flat. In practice, a natural fault surface is much more likely to be jagged and irregular; and this will have the effect of increasing the shearing strength. In other words, the value of τ given by equation (4.5.2) will be an underestimate. Mathematically, this may be accommodated by introducing an extra term on the right hand side of equation (4.5.2), which then becomes:

$$\tau = \tau_0 + \mu(S - p) \tag{4.5.5}$$

τ_0 is known as the *cohesive strength* or *intrinsic strength*. Obviously, when $S - p = 0$, $\tau = \tau_0$; and so τ_0 is the shearing strength when the effective normal stress across the fault is zero. What equation (4.5.5) shows is that slippage (and hence an earthquake) cannot be expected to occur simply when the pore fluid pressure is increased to S, so that $S = p$ and $S - p = 0$. To obtain slippage, p must be increased to above S, so that at slippage:

$$\tau' = \tau = \tau_0 + \mu(S - p) \tag{4.5.6}$$

Equation (4.5.6) is equation (4.5.4) revised to take account of the cohesive strength.

Finally, it may well be asked at this stage how the above model could possibly apply to underground nuclear explosions. After all, nuclear explosions introduce no extra fluid but produce earthquakes nevertheless. The answer probably is that, although explosions introduce no extra fluid, they temporarily redistribute the natural pore fluids already present so that at certain points the pore fluid pressure is locally raised to the value necessary to cause slippage and produce an earthquake.

The Rangely experiment

The fact that the introduction of fluid into fault zones appears to lead to the release of tectonic strain in certain cases has led some scientists to suggest that this phenomenon may possibly be used to modify the tectonic environment in such a way as to prevent large shallow earthquakes. The idea behind such a scheme is particularly well illustrated by the example of the San Andreas fault. As we saw in section 4.4, some segments of the San Andreas fault are now active—that is, fault creep is occurring along these segments, accompanied by comparatively small earthquakes which tend to prevent the accumulation of extremely high strain. On the other hand, some sections of the San Andreas are 'locked'. The strain here is building up to high values; and the expectation is that this strain will ultimately be released suddenly in the form of one or more extremely large shock. Is it possible, then, that by carefully introducing fluid into these locked sections, the strain energy could be released in a series of relatively small shocks causing little damage, rather than in large devastating shocks which will otherwise certainly occur at some time? In view of the large population in the San Andreas fault zone, this is clearly an idea which can hardly be tested directly in the present state of knowledge. What is obviously required is some situation in which controlled experiments may be carried out to gain a better understanding of what is involved, rather than relying on the evidence of the uncontrolled experience of reservoirs and the Denver well.

Controlled experiments as envisaged here are currently being carried out by the U.S. Geological Survey at the Rangely oil field in Colorado —another site, incidentally, at which earthquakes were first produced accidentally by fluid injection. In this field, the oil is trapped in an anticlinal structure at a depth of about 2 km, the actual reservoir rock being sandstone. In 1958 the oil company concerned began to inject

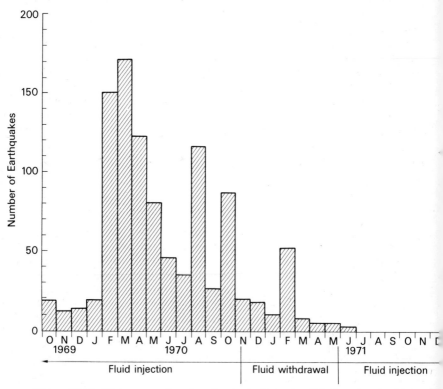

Figure 4.5.14 The pattern of earthquakes in the Rangely oil field, Colorado, from October 1969 to December 1971. *Source:* Healy, Lee, Pakiser, Raleigh and Wood (1971).

water into the sandstone in order to raise the pressure in the field and thus increase the recovery of the oil. A seismic array was installed 50 km to the northwest of Rangely in 1962 and immediately began to record earthquakes. Thus there has been seismic activity in the region since at least 1962; but this is yet another situation where the seismicity prior to the introduction of fluid is unknown.

In October 1969, during a period of normal fluid injection by the oil company, the U.S. Geological Survey installed a dense array of seismic stations close to the oil field. The epicentres of the many shocks which took place over the following year were found to be closely related to the field geographically and were located along the southwesterly prolongation of a fault already known to pass through the field. In November 1970 the injection was stopped. At first, the wells concerned were allowed to flow under their own pressure; but as the flow decreased, pumps were used to reduce the pressure even further. During the pumping the seismic activity decreased considerably. By April 1971 the number of earthquakes per month had decreased to less than ten, compared with a peak of over 170 in March 1970, and the number within 1 km of the bottom of the injection wells had decreased to zero. The pattern of earthquake activity from October 1969 onwards is shown in Figure 4.5.14.

In May 1971 injection was started up again. Much now hinges upon whether or not the strong seismicity can be induced to return.

Further reading

R. L. Kovach (1971), Earthquake prediction and modification, in I. G. Gass, P. J. Smith and R. C. L. Wilson (Eds.), *Understanding the Earth*. Sussex, Artemis Press and Cambridge, Mass., M.I.T. Press.
R. H. Tucker, A. H. Cook, H. M. Iyer and F. D. Stacey (1970), *Global Geophysics*. London, English Universities Press.

APPENDIX ONE

The Seismic Reflection Method

At sea, seismic reflection profiling is usually carried out by transmitting elastic waves vertically downwards from a moving ship, and timing their return to the ship following reflection of the waves at subsurface discontinuities. On land, however, it is much easier to arrange a separation between source and detector. The theory of the method used is shown in Figure A1.1.

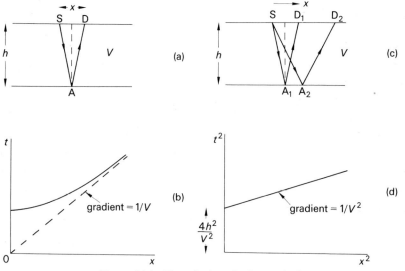

Figure A1.1 The seismic reflection method.

Consider a single layer of thickness h (both boundaries being horizontal) and in which the velocity, V, is constant. For the reflected wave SAD in (a):

224

$$\text{travel time, } t = \frac{\text{distance SAD}}{V} = \frac{2\sqrt{h^2 + x^2/4}}{V} \tag{A1.1}$$

$$\text{whence:} \qquad h = \frac{\sqrt{V^2 t^2 - x^2}}{2} \tag{A1.2}$$

x and t are measured, and if, in addition, V is known, the thickness of the layer may be determined.

Equation (A1.1) shows that the time–distance curve is a hyperbola as shown in (b). The straight line through the origin and asymptotic to the hyperbola has gradient $1/V$ from which, in principle, V may be calculated. Unfortunately, the only part of the hyperbola usually obtained in practice is the near-horizontal part around $x = 0$, which is not sufficient to enable the straight line to be constructed accurately. So V must be obtained by other means.

There are several different ways of determining V, one of which is to measure the arrival times of reflections at two different detectors as shown in (c). There are thus two different arrival times, t_1 and t_2, and two different distances, x_1 and x_2, corresponding to D_1 and D_2 (waves SA_1D_1 and SA_2D_2), respectively.

By squaring both sides of equation (A1.1):

$$t^2 = \frac{4(h^2 + x^2/4)}{V^2} = \frac{4h^2 + x^2}{V^2} \tag{A1.3}$$

If t^2 is now plotted against x^2, a straight line of gradient $1/V^2$ will result as shown in (d). V may thus be determined. However, this method is poor where the topographic relief of the reflecting horizon is high or where the horizon is not horizontal.

APPENDIX TWO

The Earth's Density

Determination of the density distribution in the Earth involves numerous assumptions. The traditional method begins with the assumption that the Earth is in hydrostatic equilibrium,* which is probably nearly true below the crust. The variation of pressure (p) with depth is then given by:

$$\frac{dp}{dr} = -\rho g \tag{A2.1}$$

where ρ is the density and r is the distance measured from the Earth's centre. The negative sign arises because p increases with depth; that is, p increases as r decreases.

At a point distance r from the centre of the Earth, the gravity results only from the attraction of the mass (m) within the sphere of radius r. (For example, if g is measured in a coal mine, it will depend only on that part of the Earth's mass below the point of measurement and not that part of the Earth's crust above.) We may thus rewrite equation (2.5.4) in this context as:

$$g = \frac{Gm}{r^2} \tag{A2.2}$$

Then combining equations (A2.1) and (A2.2):

$$\frac{dp}{dr} = \frac{-\rho Gm}{r^2} \tag{A2.3}$$

Now, the bulk modulus (k) is defined by the equation:

$$\frac{d\rho}{dp} = \frac{\rho}{k} \tag{A2.4}$$

and so equations (A2.3) and (A2.4) combine to give us the quantity we wish to determine, namely, the rate of change of density with depth ($d\rho/dr$), for:

$$\frac{d\rho}{dr} = \frac{d\rho}{dp} \cdot \frac{dp}{dr}$$

$$= \frac{\rho}{k}\left(\frac{-\rho Gm}{r^2}\right) = \frac{-\rho^2 Gm}{kr^2} \tag{A2.5}$$

But according to equations (2.1.1):

$$\mu = \sqrt{\frac{k+4\mu/3}{\rho}} \quad \text{and} \quad w = \sqrt{\frac{\mu}{\rho}}$$

and combining these by eliminating μ:

$$\frac{k}{\rho} = u^2 - \frac{4w^2}{3} \tag{A2.6}$$

Then putting (A2.6) into (A2.5):

$$\frac{d\rho}{dr} = \frac{-\rho Gm}{r^2(u^2 - 4w^2/3)} \tag{A2.7}$$

Equation (A2.7) is known as the *Adams–Williamson equation* after its originators.

The Adams–Williamson equation applies only in regions with uniform composition and physical properties; and in applying it to the Earth it is thus necessary to assume that each of the Earth's layers possesses this uniformity. Even so, because the equation gives the variation of ρ with depth in terms of ρ itself, it cannot be solved directly. In practice, it is thus applied successively at various depths within the Earth. Starting with an assumed value of ρ at the top of the mantle, the Adams–Williamson equation is applied to calculate ρ deeper in that layer. A new value of $d\rho/dr$ is then calculated for the new density; and the calculations are repeated at greater and greater depths until a discontinuity is reached. A higher density is then assumed for the material just below such a discontinuity and the successive calculations are continued. However, the decision on the magnitude of the density jump across the discontinuity is not completely arbitrary because the complete density distribution must be consistent with the Earth's mass and moment of inertia, both of which may be calculated independently by other methods.

The best known version of the density distribution in the Earth is that determined from the Adams–Williamson equation by Bullen assuming a density of $3320\ \text{kg m}^{-3}$ for the material immediately below the Moho. The Bullen density distribution was shown in Figure 2.10.4 and is shown again in Figure A2.1 (a) where it is compared with distributions by Birch and Anderson (for the mantle) and Anderson (for the core). Birch's distribution is based on an empirical relationship between P wave velocity and density as follows:

$$\rho = a + bu \tag{A2.8}$$

where a is a constant which depends on the mean atomic weight of the medium and b is another constant. Using the limitations imposed by the Earth's mass and moment of inertia,* Birch calculated a and b and hence the density variation. As Figure A2.1 shows, the Birch model gives a higher density than the Bullen model near the top of the mantle but lower density below about 700 km. The Anderson distribution is based on the dispersion of long period surface waves and free oscillations* of the Earth (topics which are beyond the scope of this book) and is strikingly different from the Bullen and Birch models in that it includes regions of very rapid density increase.

A completely fresh approach to the density problem has recently been developed by Press who adopted a statistical procedure, known as the Monte Carlo method,

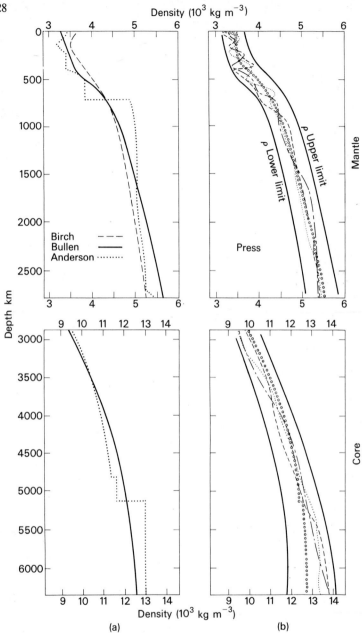

Figure A2.1 Density distributions in the Earth's mantle and core. Models by Bullen, Birch and Anderson are shown in (a). In (b), three plausible models derived by Press are compared with the Bullen model (open circles). *Sources:* Anderson (1967) and Press (1968).

which does not depend on the usual assumptions. About five million random density models were generated by computer. They were then tested against known geophysical quantities such as the Earth's mass, its moment of inertia, and seismic wave velocities. Only six of the models conformed with the known data; and only three were plausible. These three models are compared with the Bullen model in Figure A2.1 (b). Perhaps the most striking characteristic of the Press models is the large fluctuation of density in the upper mantle. Such variations implicitly support the recent discoveries of upper mantle inhomogeneity.

APPENDIX THREE

Notes on Historic Earthquakes

The following notes, intended to accompany Table 4.3.1, are a modified form of the original notes prepared by Båth (1967a). The identifying numbers correspond to the earthquake numbers in the Table.

1: This is usually referred to as the earthquake with the greatest number of killed persons. Although the figure may naturally be uncertain, it is by no means unrealistic considering the 'specific destruction'. Assuming a magnitude of 9, we get $f_0 = 5.8$; a magnitude of 8 would give $f_0 = 7.2$. These values are comparable to those obtained in other destructive earthquakes.

3: This is a striking example of divergent information on the number of people killed. One authority gives 150 000 whereas another gives 5233, based largely on official Japanese sources. The latter figure is probably more correct.

4: This earthquake remains uncertain; and there may be a confusion with (3).

5: This information, which has been found in some earlier lists, could not be confirmed; and the case is uncertain.

6: The Lisbon earthquake is still one of the most well known to the general public. The epicentre was probably located about 100 km west of Lisbon. It had an unusually large macroseismic extent, the radius of perceptibility reaching about 2000 km and the seiche limit about 3500 km, i.e. up to Scandinavia and Finland.

11: This shock was extensively studied by R. Mallet. He investigated especially directions of displacements, but his conclusions were biased by his assumption of a point source with no transverse motion.

13: Most remarkable is that the destruction (of the town Casamicciola) was very local, the area of destruction being not more than 3 km wide, with rapid decrease of intensity outwards. This suggests a very shallow depth of the focus. It has been classified as a volcanic earthquake.

14: Usually referred to as the Mino–Owari earthquake. Large fault displacements were observed, up to 4 m horizontally and 7 m vertically. There was great damage. A second authority reports 25 000 killed persons.

16: This earthquake was extensively studied by Oldham. Two faults were found, the Samim and Chedrang faults, the latter with displacements reaching 11 m.

230

Several secondary effects occurred, such as flooding in the Brahmaputra plain and slides near the Assam hills. Shillong was destroyed, but was rebuilt.

17: Vertical uplifts of 14.5 m were observed on the coast. Remarkable effects on glaciers were found: glaciers which had been retreating began to advance again, but later the general retreat was resumed. There were several major shocks in the area in September 1899, and the next largest occurred on 4 September (magnitude = 8.3).

19: The epicentral area, including Kangra, was on the Tertiary rocks of the foot-hills of the Mimalaya.

22: Investigated in detail by Omori. Strike-slip displacements reached about 2.5 m, but vertical throw not more than half this amount.

23: The San Francisco earthquake has been studied in greater detail, especially macroseismically, than most other earthquakes. It is clearly related to the San Andreas fault: right hand strike-slip block faulting extending over 300–430 km, i.e. more than for any other known earthquake. The isoseismals were corres-pondingly elongated along the fault. Maximum horizontal displacements amounted to about 6 m, on soft ground even more, whereas the maximum vertical displacements did not quite reach 1 m. The fires which broke out caused far more damage than the earthquake itself (compare Tokyo 1923).

28: Extensive ground displacements were reported.

31: Vertical displacements of 3–4 m were found. Buildings in Pleasant Valley were damaged, but there is no report of any person killed.

32: The macroseismic area included the whole of China. The largest destruction occurred around Tsinning. There were major fractures of the ground, landslides, etc.

34: This is one of the most well known earthquakes, usually called the Kwanto earthquake from the name of the province. Maximum displacements of 4.5 m were found. Bottom soundings in the Sagami Bay after the earthquake seem to indicate vertical displacements of the ocean bottom of 100–400 m in some places. However, these measurements have to be taken with caution. The earthquake was followed by destructive fires in Tokyo and Yokohama.

35: Talifu in northwest Yunnan province was almost completely destroyed.

36: Usually referred to as the Tango earthquake, from the province name, another case of a very well-investigated earthquake.

37: Large fractures were formed. The damage was greatest at Nan-Shan, and the vibrations were felt as far as Peking.

39: Vertical displacements of about 5 m were found, related to the White Creek fault (South Island), also considerable landslides. Severe damage to buildings in Buller and Murchinson counties.

41: Usually referred to as the Hawke's Bay earthquake. This was the first great earthquake disaster in New Zealand, especially strong at Napier and Hastings. Displacements of 1–2 m were found at many places. The isoseismals were elon-gated in the direction of the islands and the shock was felt over the whole of New Zealand. The fires and landslides which followed the earthquake added to the damage.

43: Large fissures were opened in alluvium, of which one, 5 m deep, 10 m wide and nearly 300 m long, remained open, while others were filled. Almost all houses were either tilting or sinking into the ground, the sinking amounting to about 1 m. The effects are typical for great thicknesses of sediments and alluvium.

45: Quetta was almost completely destroyed, but was rebuilt.

47: The macroseismic area was roughly elliptical with axes of 1300 km (east–west) and 600 km in length. Clear evidence of strike-slip, amounting to 3.7 m, and smaller vertical displacements were found. The tectonics of the area has great similarities to the San Andreas fault in California. High activity continued for several years with notably large shocks in 1942, 1943, 1944.

51: This is outstanding among South American earthquakes, partly because of its destructive power (to a large extent due to landslides), partly because it was the first for which faulting was clearly demonstrated. Purely vertical displacements reaching a maximum of 3.5 m were observed along a 5 km fault scarp trending northwest with the eastern block moving up relative to the western block.

53: Intensities were much larger on alluvium (where large fissures opened) than on surrounding bedrock.

54: Considerable damage was caused in a district which had not been affected by strong earthquakes for several centuries.

55: The town of Ambato was most damaged. There were considerable landslides and topographic changes in the Andes (according to newspaper reports).

56: This earthquake was more damaging in Assam than the one of 1897 (16) and the effects were exhibited as shaking, floods and topographical changes (mainly from slides). The macroseismic area was very large, the radius of perceptibility reaching 1400 km. There were numerous aftershocks covering an extensive area, more than 700 km in east–west extension.

57: According to newspaper reports, several hundred people were killed, twenty-eight on Hokkaido. There was considerable damage and a tsunami. Significant variations of the Earth's magnetic field were found after the earthquake.

58: This was the largest earthquake in California since 1906 (23). It caused considerable damage to buildings, oil wells, refineries, dams, roads, bridges, etc. The main shock, which occurred on the White Wolf fault, exhibited mainly dip-slip (vertical displacements over 1 m), whereas the aftershocks were dominantly of strike-slip type. Because of their occurrence in an area which is well covered by seismograph stations, this earthquake and its aftershocks are among those best known so far.

59: This was the strongest shock felt in North Africa for over 100 years. Vertical soil displacements of 0.6–1.0 m extended over more than 20 km in length. In Algeria, the coast ranges are the most active seismically, and the present shock belongs to the Dahra range, one of the most active along the coast. From macroseismic evidence the focal depth is calculated as being only 8–9 km. A 'relay shock' of magnitude 6.2 occurred on 10 September 1954, about 40 km north of this epicentre.

61: Newspapers give various numbers of people killed: 224 or 600, including some guesses of 10 000. Usually, the lowest numbers are most reliable.

62: The earthquake was felt most strongly on the Santorin Island in the Aegean Sea. It was accompanied by a tsunami and volcanic eruptions, according to newspaper reports.

63: Anomalies found in the intensity distribution were closely related to local geology and soil conditions. Damage at greater distance from the epicentre is often due to predominantly longer periods, which cause resonance with some structures.

64: Newspapers reported severe effects in an area extending from the Altai mountains to the Gobi desert with great topographical changes, landslides, etc. In the mountains a rift 20 m wide and 250 km long was found. One mountain range is reported to have increased 6 m in height.

65: Newspapers reported 1780 killed.

66: Felt over an area 200 km in extension along the Fairweather fault. Observed displacements amounted to 7 m horizontally and 1 m vertically, especially at Lituya Bay and Yakutat Bay, with southwest side moving relatively northwest and up, in conformity with motions along the San Andreas fault in California. In addition, landslides, sand blows, fissures and extensive minor faulting were observed.

67: The maximum observed intensity was 11. There was no real tsunami, contrary to some reports. Two minor shocks were noticed before the main shock.

68: The destruction was largest to constructions on the alluvial plain, where most of the city of Lar is located, but much less to buildings on the surrounding rock. The damage was almost total along a very narrow band right through Lar.

69: According to one authority the number of deaths amounted to only 500; in addition about 1000 were killed by the tsunami. The active area had a width of some 160 km and a length of almost 1600 km. The fault movement began in the north and progressed southward. As a consequence, periods of surface waves recorded in Peru were much greater for waves arriving by the short arc than in the opposite direction (Doppler effect). Surface wave data demonstrate dextral strike-slip, especially near the ends of the aftershock zone, with vertical movement in the central part. On the other hand, macroseismic data reveal height increases in the north and south of 1–3 m but a decrease in the middle of more than 1 m, with ensuing floods. No clear field evidence of faulting was found. Information on volcanic activity in newspapers was much exaggerated. Only the volcano Puyehue had an eruption 47 hours after the main shock and which continued for several weeks with ash and steam emitting from a fissure on the northwestern flank of the volcano, the ash eruptions being followed by the discharge of viscous lava.

70: This is considered the most devastating earthquake in the history of Iran; and there is at least no indication to suggest that an earthquake as strong as this one has occurred in the area since 1630. It occurred on the Ipak fault and exhibited progressive faulting on the surface with a rupture at least 100 km long. In addition, there were small landslides and rock falls. Although felt over most of northern Iran, the maximum intensity was not rated higher than degree 9. Up to the middle of November 1962, the seismograph stations in Iran had recorded about 1800 aftershocks.

71: This shock has much in common with Agadir (67). Both occurred at night when most people were sleeping; they both had very shallow depth right under the respective cities; and poor building construction increased the disasters tremendously. Because of the shallow depth, the area of high intensity was relatively small in both cases. Of Skopje's population of 200 000, about 170 000 were made homeless. Of 36 000 dwellings, eighty percent were destroyed or had to be pulled down. Some buildings in Skopje with pre-stressed concrete, built to withstand intensity 11, were not damaged. Maximum intensity was rated 10. 295 aftershocks were felt in Skopje up to 15 August 1963. Skopje had earlier been destroyed by earthquakes in the years 518 and 1555.

72: This was the most destructive earthquake of the west coast of North America this century; and we have to go back to 1899 (17) to find a larger shock in this area. There was severe damage at Anchorage, Seward, Cordova, Valdez and Homer, mainly because of fires and tsunamis. Two fissures were observed in the centre of anchorage, up to 10 m deep and 15 m wide. Tsunamis were observed on Kodiak Island (3 m high), Yakutat Bay (reported as 8 m high), west coast of North America (Washington, Oregon, California, especially Crescent City), Hawaii, Japan, Chile and on Easter Island (0.3 m high). Effects on boats at the American coast of the Mexican Gulf are rather to be interpreted as a seiche phenomenon. Minor volcanic activity (Mount Redoubt, Shishaldin, St. Augustine) is reported to have preceded in the earthquake. There were numerous aftershocks.

APPENDIX FOUR

Glossary

Most of the terms in *Topics in Geophysics* are defined or described in the text; and these are not repeated here. The Glossary is limited to those few terms for which detailed explanation in the text was inappropriate or which are on the borderline between science and common knowledge. The explanations given here are not necessarily rigid definitions but are intended to convey the basic ideas. Words defined in the Glossary are marked with an asterisk (*) in the text where they first appear.

AXIAL MODULUS: If a body is stressed longitudinally (for example, a wire with a weight attached at the bottom), the resulting ratio of stress to strain is known as *Young's modulus*. In such a situation, as the wire is stretched its radius will decrease. However, if two perpendicular stresses are applied to prevent the change in radius, the new longitudinal stress required to produce the same amount of stretching as before will be different. The axial modulus is the ratio of the new longitudinal stress to the new strain. In other words:

$$\text{axial modulus} = \frac{\text{longitudinal load/cross-sectional area}}{\text{increase in length/original length}}$$

for the case where the lateral dimensions of the body are not allowed to change.

BATHOLITH: A stock-shaped mass of igneous rock, originally intruded, which maintains its diameter or grows broader with depth.

BULK MODULUS: The ratio of stress to strain when the volume of a body is compressed or dilated. In other words:

$$\text{bulk modulus} = \frac{\text{compressive (tensile) force per unit area}}{\text{change in volume/original volume}}$$

Because the compressive force per unit area is, of course, the pressure (p), the bulk modulus (k) is given by:

$$k = \frac{p}{\Delta V/V}$$

235

where V is the original volume and ΔV the change in volume. Moreover, because the mass of the body remains constant, $\Delta V / V = \Delta\rho/\rho$, where ρ is the density. So:

$$k = \frac{p\rho}{\Delta\rho}$$

CHONDRITE:
: Stony meteorite containing chondrules (small round bodies comprising mainly olivine or enstatite) embedded in a fine-grained matrix of pyroxene, olivine and nickel–iron with or without glass.

CONDUCTION:
: The transmission of heat from places of higher temperature to places of lower temperature in a substance by the interaction of atoms or molecules (in the case of a fluid) or electrons (in the case of a solid) having greater kinetic energy with those having less.

CONVECTION:
: The transmission of heat through a fluid by the actual movement of the fluid.

FREE
OSCILLATIONS:
: The oscillations of the Earth when allowed to vibrate freely as a whole (analogy: the ringing of a bell). Free oscillations are excited by large earthquakes but die away in, at most, a few days.

GROUND ZERO:
: The 'epicentre' of an underground nuclear explosion.

HYDROSTATIC
EQUILIBRIUM:
: The equilibrium form of a mass of fluid—in the case of the Earth, a rotating mass of fluid.

MOMENT OF
INERTIA:
: The moment of inertia (I) of a body about any axis is the sum of the products of the mass (Δm) of each element of the body and the square of its distance (r) from the axis—$I = \Sigma r^2 \Delta m$.

RADIATION:
: In the context of this book, the transmission of heat in the form of rays or waves.

RIGIDITY
MODULUS:
: The ratio of stress to strain when the stress is a shear. In other words:

$$\text{rigidity modulus} = \frac{\text{tangential force per unit area}}{\text{angular deformation}}$$

THERMISTOR:
: A semiconductor device used to measure temperature. The electrical resistance of the semiconductor decreases rapidly with increasing temperature. To measure temperature, the resistance is first measured and converted to the corresponding temperature using a calibration.

APPENDIX FIVE

List of Sources

This list brings together, in alphabetical order, all the references to specific authors throughout the book. *Topics in Geophysics* is intended as a teaching book; and so, wherever possible, the use of references in the text has been avoided. However, there are several reasons why the names of scientists have not been eliminated completely, especially from Figures and Tables. For one thing, geophysics (unlike, say, basic physics) is a relatively young subject in which much of the knowledge is of recent origin and thus clearly attributable to specific scientists, most of whom are still living and working. Secondly, in common with the other Earth sciences, geophysics contains a large component of intelligent speculation which often gives rise to conflicting theories for the same phenomenon. To some extent, this is a feature of all science, of course; but in the Earth sciences the critical data to resolve such conflicts are usually more difficult, if not impossible, to obtain because of the basic problem of the Earth's inaccessibility. Thus rival theories tend to be current for a long time, during which it is convenient to distinguish between interpretations using the names of their originators. And finally, names are useful likewise in differentiating between rival empirical relationships between parameters representing the same phenomenon.

In the list which follows, where a reference is to a scientific journal the usual convention has been adopted in which the name of the journal in italics is followed by the volume number in bold type, then the page numbers in roman type, and finally the year of origin. Thus *Geophysical Journal*, **9**, 69–83, 1964 means that the scientific paper concerned forms pages 69–83 of Volume 9 of Geophysical Journal which was published in 1964. Where books and reports are concerned the publisher and date (in parenthesis) is preceded by the names of the Editors of the book, if appropriate.

Agger, H. E. and Carpenter, E. W., A crustal study in the vicinity of the Eskdale-muir seismological array station, *Geophysical Journal*, **9**, 69–83, 1964.

Allen, C. R., in *Proceedings, Conference on the Geologic Problems of the San Andreas Fault System* (Stanford University, 1968).

Anderson, D. L., Latest information from seismic observations, in *The Earth's Mantle*, Ed. T. F. Gaskell (Academic Press, 1967).

Balakrishna, S. and Gowd, T. N., Role of fluid pressure in the mechanics of transcurrent faulting at Koyna (India), *Tectonophysics*, **9**, 301–321, 1970.

Barazangi, M. and Dorman, J., World seismicity maps compiled from ESSA, Coast and Geodetic Survey, epicenter data, 1961–1967, *Bulletin Seismological Society America*, **59**, 369–380, 1969.

Båth, M., Earthquakes, large, destructive, in *International Dictionary of Geophysics*, Ed. S. K. Runcorn (Pergamon Press, 1967a), pp. 417–424.

Båth, M., Earthquakes, magnitude and intensity scales of, in *International Dictionary of Geophysics*, Ed. S. K. Runcorn (Pergamon Press, 1967b), pp. 424–426.

Benioff, H., Seismic evidence for crustal structure and tectonic activity, *Special Paper, Geological Society America*, **62**, 61–74, 1955.

Boos, C. M. and Boos, M. F., Tectonics of eastern flank and foothills of the Front Range, Colorado, *American Association Petroleum Geologists Bulletin*, **41**, 2603–2676, 1957.

Bott, M. H. P., Terrestrial heat flow and the mantle convection hypothesis, *Geophysical Journal*, **14**, 413–428, 1967.

Bott, M. H. P., *The Interior of the Earth* (Arnold, 1971).

Bott, M. H. P., Holder, A. P., Long, R. E. and Lucus, A. L., Crustal structure beneath the granites of south-west England, in *Mechanism of Igneous Intrusion*, Eds. G. Newall and N. Rast, *Geological Journal Special Issue No. 2*, pp. 93–102, 1970.

Bott, M. H. P. and Scott, P., Recent geophysical studies in south-west England, in *Present Views of some Aspects of the Geology of Cornwall and Devon*, Eds. K. F. G. Hosking and G. J. Shrimpton (Royal Geological Society of Cornwall, 1964).

Breiner, S., *The Piezomagnetic Effect in Seismically Active Areas*, Thesis, Stanford University, 1967.

Bullard, E. C., Everett, J. E. and Smith, A. G., The fit of the continents around the Atlantic, in *A Symposium on Continental Drift, Philosophical Transactions Royal Society*, **258A**, 41–51, 1965.

Bullen, K. E., *An Introduction to the Theory of Seismology* (Cambridge University Press, 1963).

Carder, D. S., Reservoir loading and local earthquakes, in *Engineering Geology Case Histories Number 8*, Ed. W. M. Adams (Geological Society of America, 1970), pp. 51–61.

Clark, S. P., *Handbook of Physical Constants, Memoir, Geological Society America*, 1966.

Cook, A. H., *Gravity and the Earth* (Wykeham Publications, 1969).

Cox, A., Geomagnetic reversals, *Science*, **163**, 237–245, 1969.

Crain, I. K., The glacial effect and the significance of continental terrestrial heat flow measurements, *Earth and Planetary Science Letters*, **4**, 69–72, 1968.

Davies, D., A comprehensive test ban, *Science Journal*, 78–84, November 1968.

Drake, C. L. and Nafe, J. E., The transition from ocean to continent from seismic refraction data, in *The Crust and Upper Mantle of the Pacific Area*, Eds. L. Knopoff, C. L. Drake and P. J. Hart (American Geophysical Union, 1968), pp. 174–186.

Eaton, J. P., Crustal structure from San Francisco, California, to Eureka, Nevada, from seismic-refraction measurements, *Journal Geophysical Research*, **68**, 5789–5806, 1963.

Espinosa, A. F., Engdahl, E. R., Tarr, A. C. and Brockman, S., A preliminary report of near-field seismic monitoring of the San Fernando earthquake aftershock series, in *The San Fernando, California, Earthquake of February 9, 1971* (United States Government Printing Office, 1971), pp. 135–141.

Evans, D. M., The Denver area earthquakes and the Rocky Mountain Arsenal disposal well, *Mountain Geologist*, **3**, 23–36, 1966.

Ewing, M., The sediments of the Argentine basin, *Quarterly Journal Royal Astronomical Society*, **6**, 10–27, 1965.

Galanopoulos, A. G., The influence of the fluctuation of Marathon Lake elevation on local earthquake activity in the Attica Basin, *Annales Géologie des pays Helleniques*, **18**, 281–306, 1967.

Gaposchkin, E. M., Tesseral harmonic coefficients and station coordinates from the dynamic method, in *Smithsonian Astrophysical Observatory Special Report 200*, Eds. C. A. Lundquist and C. Veis, 1966.

Garland, G. D., *The Earth's Shape and Gravity* (Pergamon Press, 1965).

Garland, G. D., *Introduction to Geophysics* (Saunders, 1971).

Guha, S. K., Gosavi, P. D., Varma, M. M., Agarwal, S. P., Padale, J. G. and Marwadi, S. C., *Recent Seismic Disturbances in the Koyna Hydroelectric Project, Maharashtra, India* (Central Water and Power Research Station, India, 1968).

Gutenberg, B., *Physics of the Earth's Interior* (Academic Press, 1959).

Gutenberg, B. and Richter, C. F., *Seismicity of the Earth and Associated Phenomena* (Princeton University Press, 1954).

Hagiwara, T. and Rikitake, T., Japanese program on earthquake prediction, *Science*, **157**, 761–768, 1967.

Hales, A. L. and Sacks, I. S., Evidence for an intermediate layer from crustal structure studies in the eastern Transvaal, *Geophysical Journal*, **2**, 15–33, 1959.

Hamilton, R. M. and Healy, J. H., Aftershocks of the Benham nuclear explosion, *Bulletin Seismological Society America*, **59**, 2271–2281, 1969.

Hammer, S., Terrain corrections for gravimeter stations, *Geophysics*, **4**, 184–194, 1939.

Hayes, D. E., A geophysical investigation of the Peru–Chile trench, *Marine Geology*, **4**, 309–351, 1966.

Healy, J. H., Lee, W. H. K., Pakiser, L. C., Raleigh, C. B. and Wood, M. D., Prospects for earthquake prediction and control, *Tectonophysics*, **14**, 319–332, 1972.

Healy, J. H., Rubey, W. W., Griggs, D. T. and Raleigh, C. B., The Denver earthquakes, *Science*, **161**, 1301–1310, 1968.

Heezen, B. C., The deep-sea floor, in *Continental Drift*, Ed. S. K. Runcorn (Academic Press, 1962), pp. 235–288.

Heiskanen, W. A. and Vening Meinesz, F. A., *The Earth and its Gravity Field* (McGraw-Hill, 1958).

Herrin, E., Regional variation of *P* wave velocity in the upper mantle beneath North America, in *The Earth's Crust and Upper Mantle*, Ed. P. J. Hart (American Geophysical Union, 1969), pp. 242–246.

Hill, D. P. and Pakiser, L. C., Crustal structure between the Nevada test site and Boise, Idaho, from seismic refraction measurements, in *The Earth Beneath the Continents*, Eds. J. S. Steinhart and T. J. Smith (American Geophysical Union, 1966), pp. 391–419.

Holmes, A., *Principles of Physical Geology* (Nelson, 1965).

Horai, K. and Simmons, G., Spherical harmonic analysis of terrestrial heat flow, *Earth and Planetary Science Letters*, **6**, 386–394, 1969.

Howell, B. F., *Introduction to Geophysics* (McGraw-Hill, 1959).

Isacks, B., Oliver, J. and Sykes, L. R., Seismology and the new global tectonics, *Journal Geophysical Research*, **73**, 5855–5899, 1968.

Iyer, H. M., Seismology, in *Global Geophysics*, Ed. G. Sutton (English Universities Press, 1970), pp. 67–144.

Jones, A. E., Earthquake magnitudes, efficiency of stations, and perceptibility of local earthquakes in the Lake Mead area, *Bulletin Seismological Society America*, **34**, 161–173, 1944.

Julian, B. R. and Anderson, D. L., Travel times, apparent velocities and amplitudes of body waves, *Bulletin Seismological Society America*, **58**, 339–366, 1968.

Kosminskaya, I. P., Belyaevsky, N. A. and Volvosky, I. S., Explosion seismology in the USSR, in *The Earth's Crust and Upper Mantle*, Ed. P. J. Hart (American Geophysical Union, 1969), pp. 195–208.

Kosminskaya, I. P. and Zverev, S. M., Deep seismic soundings in the transition zones from continents to oceans, in *The Crust and Upper Mantle of the Pacific Area*, Eds. L. Knopoff, C. L. Drake and P. J. Hart (American Geophysical Union, 1968), pp. 122–130.

Langseth, M. G., Techniques of measuring heat flow through the ocean floor, in *Terrestrial Heat Flow*, Ed. W. H. K. Lee (American Geophysical Union, 1965), pp. 58–77.

Langseth, M. G. and Von Herzen, R. P., Heat flow through the floor of the world oceans, in *The Sea*, Volume 4, Ed. A. E. Maxwell (Wiley–Interscience, 1970), pp. 299–352.

Lawson, A. C., *The California Earthquake of April 18, 1906* (Carnegie Institution Washington, 1908).

Lee, W. H. K. and Uyeda, S., Review of heat flow data, in *Terrestrial Heat Flow*, Ed. W. H. K. Lee (American Geophysical Union, 1965), pp. 87–190.

MacDonald, G. J. F., Geophysical deductions from observations of heat flow, in *Terrestrial Heat Flow*, Ed. W. H. K. Lee (American Geophysical Union, 1965), pp. 191–210.

McConnell, R. K. and McTaggart-Cowan, G. H., Crustal seismic refraction profiles, a comparison, *Scientific Report 8*, University of Toronto, Institute of Earth Sciences, 1963.

Menard, H. W., Geology of the Pacific sea floor, *Experientia*, **15**, 205–213, 1959.

Menard, H. W., *Marine Geology of the Pacific* (McGraw-Hill, 1964).

Mescherikov, J. A., Recent crustal movements in seismic regions: geodetic and geomorphic data, *Tectonophysics*, **6**, 29–39, 1968.

Morgan, W. J., Rises, trenches, great faults, and crustal blocks, *Journal Geophysical Research*, **73**, 1959–1982, 1968.

Nafe, J. E. and Drake, C. L., Physical properties of marine sediments, in *The Sea*, Volume 3, Ed. M. N. Hill (Interscience, 1963), pp. 794–815.

Pakiser, L. C., Structure of the crust and upper mantle in the western United States, *Journal Geophysical Research*, **68**, 5747–5756, 1963.

Pakiser, L. C., Eaton, J. P., Healy, J. H. and Raleigh, C. B., Earthquake prediction and control, *Science*, **166**, 1467–1474, 1969.

Press, F., Density distribution in the Earth, *Science*, **160**, 1218–1221, 1968.

Rikitake, T., Earthquake prediction, *Earth-Science Reviews*, **4**, 245–282, 1968.

Sass, J. H., The Earth's heat and internal temperatures, in *Understanding the Earth*, Eds. I. G. Gass, P. J. Smith and R. C. L. Wilson (Artemis Press, 1971), pp. 81–87.

Scott, N. H., Preliminary report on felt area and intensity, in *The San Fernando, California, Earthquake of February 9, 1971* (United States Government Printing Office, 1971), pp. 153–154.

Sheridan, R. E., Houtz, R. E., Drake, C. L. and Ewing, M., Structure of continental margin off Sierra Leone, West Africa, *Journal Geophysical Research*, **74**, 2512–2530, 1969.

Simmons, G. and Roy, R. F., Heat flow in North America, in *The Earth's Crust and Upper Mantle*, Ed. P. J. Hart (American Geophysical Union, 1969), pp. 78–81.

Smith, A. G. and Hallam, A., The fit of the southern continents, *Nature*, **225**, 139–144, 1970.

Smith, T. J., Steinhart, J. S. and Aldrich, L. T., Crustal structure under Lake Superior, in *The Earth Beneath the Continents*, Eds. J. S. Steinhart and T. J. Smith (American Geophysical Union, 1966), pp. 181–197.

Sykes, L. R., The seismicity and deep structure of island arcs, *Journal Geophysical Research*, **71**, 2981–3006, 1966.

Talwani, M., A review of marine geophysics, *Marine Geology*, **2** 29–80, 1964.

Talwani, M., Le Pichon, X. and Ewing, M., Crustal structure of the mid-ocean ridges 2. Computed model from gravity and seismic refraction data, *Journal Geographical Research*, **70** 341–352, 1965.

Talwani, M., Sutton, G. H. and Worzel, J. L., A crustal section across the Puerto Rico trench, *Journal Geophysical Research*, **64**, 1545–1555, 1959.

Thompson, G. and Talwani, M., Crustal structure from Pacific Basin to central Nevada, *Journal Geophysical Research*, **69**, 4813, 1964.

Toksöz, M. N., Chinnery, M. A. and Anderson, D. L., Inhomogeneities in the Earth's mantle, *Geophysical Journal*, **13**, 31–59, 1967.

Tsubokawa, I., Ogawa, Y. and Hayashi, T., Crustal movements before and after the Niigata earthquake, *Journal Geodetic Society Japan*, **10**, 165–171, 1964.

Vening Meinesz, F. A. Plastic buckling of the Earth's crust: The origin of geosynclines, *Geological Society America Special Paper*, **62**, 319, 1955.

Vine, F. J., Sea-floor spreading—new evidence, *Journal Geological Education*, **17**, 6–16, 1969.

Von Herzen, R. P., Maxwell, A. E. and Snodgrass, J. M., Measurement of heat flow through the ocean floor, in *Symposium Temperature, 4th* (Reinhold, 1962), pp. 769–777.

Wadati, K., Earthquake, depth of (Deep-focus earthquake), in *International Dictionary of Geophysics*, Ed. S. K. Runcorn (Pergamon Press, 1967), pp. 389–392.

Woollard, G. P., The interrelationship of the crust, the upper mantle, and isostatic gravity anomalies in the United States, in *The Crust and Upper Mantle of the Pacific Area*, Eds. L. Knopoff, C. L. Drake and P. J. Hart (American Geophysical Union, 1968), pp. 312–341.

Wyllie, P. J., *The Dynamic Earth: Textbook in Geosciences* (Wiley, 1971).

Index